– Passages –

Passages

– Journeys in Polynesia –

GRAEME LAY

First published 1993
Tandem Press
2 Rugby Road
Birkenhead
Auckland 10
New Zealand

© 1993 Graeme Lay

ISBN 0 908884 20 6

'Daughters for the Return Home' and 'Tahiti, Moorea' were first
published in *Metro* magazine; 'Constitution Week on Rarotonga'
was first published in *Jetaway* magazine, and some episodes set
in the Society Islands, the Cook Islands and Western Samoa
were broadcast by Radio New Zealand as part of the
series,'Island Fling'. 'A Gulf Log' won the PEN Lilian Ida Smith
Award for non-fiction in 1988, but has
not been published previously.

Designed and produced by Linda Cassells and Associates

Printed in New Zealand by GP Print

For my father, Donald Luigi Lay

Contents

Many people contributed to the compilation of this book.
Without their hospitality, inspiration and support,
I could not have gone nearly so far.
I thank them all, most sincerely. They are:
in Apia, Repeka and Laloifi LeLaulu;
on Aitutaki, Papa Tunui;
in Auckland, Richard Hall and Erich Oettli;
on Moorea, the Mahe family;
on Niue, Faama Viliamu;
in Papeete, the staff of Opatti,
the Tahiti Tourist Promotion Board;
on Rarotonga, as always, Mike Mitchell;
and Gilly, who was able to share
only some of these journeys with me.

*   *   *

This is a work of non-fiction, the first such book
I have written. If, from established habits, fiction has
infiltrated the writing, then so be it. After
all, there is usually fact in fiction, so why
not fiction in fact? It is the writer's art to make
the two indistinguishable. All that really matters
is that the reader believes.

In most cases names are real, but in others they have been
changed, in order to protect the guilty.

Introduction

I WAS NEARLY THIRTY YEARS OLD when I first travelled to a Pacific Island, and yet some of the first words I learned to speak, as a toddler in Foxton, New Zealand, were in a Pacific language. My father was an army telephonist during World War II, in Fiji, where he learned to transcribe Japanese into Morse code. This was not a skill which would have wide peacetime application, but when he was demobilised my father brought home phrases which he used often when I was learning to speak. 'Ni sa bula vinaka,' and 'Ni sa moce,' he would say, and at the dinner table, 'Solia mada mai na sucu, yalovinaka.'

My father kept his war souvenirs — sergeant's stripes, regimental badges, ration books, photographs — in a chocolate box in his chest of drawers, and from time to time I would take these mementos out, handling them as carefully as birds' eggs. Best were the photographs, black and white, wide-bordered, showing a platoon of Kiwi men in tropical uniform, sitting under tall palm trees or on white sand beaches. Few signs of battle fatigue showed on their faces, which was hardly surprising, given that the savage battles of the Coral Sea were taking place many miles to the north. For these soldiers Fiji must have been only slightly more rigorous than a Viti Levu Club Med. I knew that my father hadn't been in the real war, and this was disappointing to me, but the photos compensated.

Along with the photos of the soldiers were those showing the Fijians: big, cheerful looking men in grass skirts, their splayed feet planted firmly but apparently painlessly on what I could see were white-hot rocks; and others of grinning, frizzy-haired women with smooth, dark, naked breasts. These in particular

– 9 –

drew my attention. What a nice place, I thought, where women could walk around like that so openly. They were my first Pacific images, my father's war photos, and they are pressed into my memory like leaves between tissue paper.

Some of the first books I read were adventure stories set in the Pacific. My father had handed on to me a copy of R.M. Ballantyne's *Coral Island*, which he had been given as a boy. I read it in bed one day when I was at home from school, sick. It enthralled me, that story of a trio of boys learning how to survive alone on an uninhabited island, with its attendant perils of sharks, savages, coral, water spouts, tidal waves and storms. Many years later I read Bill Pearson's conscientious analysis of nineteenth century Pacific literature, *Rifled Sanctuaries*, and his condemnation of Ballantyne's and others' racist arrogance towards what the Victorians viewed as savage heathens. The Pearson hypothesis intrigued me. I felt no guilt about taking pleasure from *Coral Island*, even though as a young white boy I had readily identified with the English lads and their struggle for survival. Perhaps even at an early age I was capable of distinguishing fact from fiction, of knowing *Coral Island* was, above all, a story, and one which exhilarated me. If it did me harm, it was not lasting, and along with my father's photos, *Coral Island* remains for me unforgettable.

Yet when I planned my first travel from New Zealand, the Pacific was furthest from my thoughts. The longer the journey, I thought, the more exciting the destination. And that meant, by my crude reckoning, New Zealand's Antipodes, Europe. That long-settled, composite continent proved to be every bit as entrancing up close as it was from the other side of the world. On my return to the country of my birth after three years in Europe, I missed and pined for its history, its architecture, its antiquities, its cuisine, its wine, its complexities. But all that I could afford was the Pacific.

The island I first saw was New Caledonia. Although it is not the most beautiful of islands, its appeal for me was instantaneous. I loved its exoticness, its melange of peoples, Asian, Melanesian, European. I loved the feeling of being perpetually warm. Europe lost a little of its allure. It was my first realisation that to experience history, cultural diversity and beauty, it was not necessary to fly across the world.

Since then I have travelled much in that realm of blue, the Pacific, returning to favourite islands, or encountering new ones. The region has never disappointed me. And during my travels I have observed an interesting change in the type of people who travel through the Islands. Everywhere now, even on remote islands, there are young, well-educated Europeans — Italians, Swedes, Germans, British — who have discovered that the Pacific offers an environment still largely uncontaminated by rampant industrialism and urban growth.

Why do the Islands draw me back? For many reasons. Like most writers, I react strongly to beauty, and the Pacific, in spite of isolated despoliation and militarisation, is indisputably one of the most beautiful regions on earth. There are the intoxicating scents of the Islands' flowers, the grandeur of their mountains, the colours of their lagoons. Such beauty is in itself a literary aphrodisiac. There is poetry in this beauty, as artists like Melville, Maugham, Michener, Brooke, Stevenson and Gauguin found, and recorded.

The inhabitants of the Islands are also a rich source of inspiration: the locals, the Europeans and the products of their union. Outsiders who have made the Islands their home are a diverse and often bizarre bunch. They're nearly all men who consciously or subconsciously play out the role of exiles. They nearly all take Island wives, continuing a tradition going back centuries, and by them have large numbers of beautiful children who almost always grow up embracing their mother's culture, mainly because their fathers don't have one. Miscegenation has produced people of startling beauty throughout the Pacific, the 'new race' as the New Zealand writer Sylvia Ashton-Warner called them. Wherever you look in the Islands you see these beautiful young people with their acorn-brown skin, burnished black hair and green or brown eyes.

And back at the waterfront bar, Dad is entertaining and being entertained by his mates. They are a rich seam of raw material for a writer, these papa'a, popa'a, palagi men: sardonic, philandering, generous, comic, restless, watchful; playing out their lives in their chosen Eden, forever tormented by the thought that in coming to this island they may have taken the wrong option.

For the Islands are beautiful, yes, paradise, no. I am well aware that to visit the Islands is by no means the same as living in them. The emigration which has affected almost all the Islands is the most obvious indication that to be surrounded by sea, sand and tropical vegetation is not in itself enough. The cargo cult still holds, but the people of the Pacific now go to where the cargo is. And who can blame them? Only a writer can romanticise life on a remote atoll, where medical facilities are minimal and drought and cyclones hover just over the glorious horizon. So many have left for expanded opportunities in Auckland, Sydney or Los Angeles, yet there are few Pacific emigrants who do not still hold to a dream of what they left behind: islands where their line and language go back a thousand years, a place where their culture and their true identity was shaped, where they are not known just by the pejorative, Islander.

And a small but significant reverse movement has begun, as work and wage rates decline in the industrialised countries of the Pacific rim. Some of the migrants are coming back, to start businesses, or retire, to see out their last years in the sun. The Islands must be good retirement territory, when you've toiled for years in the factories of South Auckland and struggled to bring up your kids and give them the education you missed out on yourself.

There is also a trend to send 'back' some offending Kiwi street kids to the islands of their parents' birth. It is a rehabilitation policy not universally welcomed in the recipient islands, particularly when imported petty thieves ply their trade in the Cook Islands, or remitted kids spray graffiti on the beautiful stalactites of Niue, making their mark in the only way they know how. Even when adolescents return to their parents' islands with purer intentions, cultural misunderstandings arise. One sixteen-year-old, New Zealand-born Samoan boy staying on Savai'i in his family's village was told to go up to the plantation for the morning. He went, with his camera, his baseball cap and his Nikes, and returned half an hour later.

'Why are you back already?' his uncle demanded.

The boy tapped his camera. 'I've got my photographs.'

The camera was confiscated, replaced with a machete, and the lad was instructed 'not to come back until lunchtime'.

For those who stay behind, and for the Europeans who have adopted the Islands as a home, there is an awareness that their environment is increasingly fragile. Mass tourism threatens to inundate the region with hedonistic, careless transients. Some popular islands already have visitor numbers greatly in excess of their permanent populations, and the numbers show no sign of decreasing.

The greatest perceived threat from all this is AIDS. At every airport and in many public places in Polynesia you see the signs, usually crude, always dire, incorporating deadly symbolism. 'AIDS Means Death' and that type of thing. In this respect the Islands today are rather like those isolated villages in medieval Europe, where people went to flee the Black Death. Polynesians are aware that they're relatively free from this modern scourge, and they want to keep it that way. One island even had a proposal to AIDS-test every visitor, leading to jokes about renaming one part of the local luxury hotel the HIV-wing. It was misguided, but, from their point of view, understandable. Those aforementioned Euro-Greenies haven't got just the environment on their mind. Here are these hordes of palagi visitors, mostly young, horny, fresh from the metropolitan centres of Europe and North America, flying in, yearning to experience a cultural (that is sexual) Pacific encounter or two or three. Who knows where they've been, and what viruses are coursing merrily through their veins?

After all, Europe has brought many plagues in the past, and not too distant, either. The influenza epidemic which struck Western Samoa in 1918 killed twenty percent of the population, and was the result of blatant negligence by New Zealand officials.

AIDS awareness is one thing, but in the meantime the tobacco companies continue to push their noxious product throughout the Pacific, where smoking is rife. When I was in Tonga one company had a campaign as simple as it was lethal: smoke three packs and get a fourth, 'free'. In comparison with this, AIDS is still a relatively remote threat.

No writing is ever easy, but there are particular linguistic perils awaiting anyone who makes the Islands of the Pacific their literary subject. One of Ernest Hemingway's maxims was, 'beware of adjectives', and it is salutary advice when writing about the Islands, where platitudes lurk like stonefish in the lagoon.

The natural loveliness of the tropical Pacific is insistent, however, and must be recorded. Gauguin placed his Tahitian subjects in their setting and captured its flamboyant hues, but his colours have few useful equivalents in words. How can a writer adequately describe the elegance of a line of waving palm trees, the blinding blues of a lagoon, the greenness of volcanic peaks or the clarity and scale of a star-pricked Pacific sky? The Islands are often almost too beautiful for words. That doesn't prevent the tourist-brochure writer from trying, however.

According to the brochures, Pacific gardens are always 'lush', the lagoons 'opalescent', the resorts 'nestle in a tranquil, idyllic setting' by a 'sparkling, white sand' beach. All clichéd, but still true, for the coastal and botanical attractions of the Islands are ubiquitous. For the writer who seeks to go deeper, though, the adjective 'alert' must be maintained.

Passages is about people and places, not scenery. It confines itself to the south-western region of Polynesia, if 'confined' is the right word for an area covering eight million square kilometres. The book includes the account of a voyage off the coast of northern New Zealand, as it is sometimes forgotten that New Zealand is an integral part of Polynesia, forming as it does the south-western apex of the vast triangle which extends east to Easter Island and north to the Hawaiian Islands, encompassing one of the largest cultural entities on earth. *Passages* concludes somewhere over the islets of Ha'apai, in the Tongan group.

It was never my intention to include in this book all the islands of south-west Polynesia, indeed it would be folly to try to do so. Just in the region known as French Polynesia there are over one thousand islands. The book concentrates instead on places which are relatively accessible, and which are of particular cultural significance, such as Raiatea, or of geographical distinction, like Niue, the world's largest coral rock.

I have no Pacific war mementos for my children to wonder at, as I did with my father's Fijian souvenirs. Far better, my children have seen several of the Polynesian islands for themselves. There in a week they learn more than in a term in a classroom. They, like my generation, have thankfully been spared a global conflict, for if there is a third world war there will be few souvenirs of it, and certainly none that could be contained in a chocolate box. I hope my daughter and two sons will see Europe, too, but having travelled to the Pacific first, I think they, unlike me, will have done things the right way round.

Passages is neither anthropology nor travel guide. The region has an oversupply of those. Rather, it is an account of some of my journeys through the maritime galaxy called Polynesia, and some of the people encountered there. It is intended as a kind of journal whose entries record one writer's impressions of a world which he came to late, but gratefully.

The Kingdom of Tonga

E VEN NOW, AS I STAND IN THE DARK outside Fua'amotu Airport waiting for a taxi, I'm not entirely sure why I came to Tonga. I'm on my way to Western and American Samoa to undertake some research for a book of short stories, saw that the plane went via Tonga, and on a whim decided to stop over. All places are interesting in some way, I reasoned, so why not Tonga, the only monarchy in the Pacific? The onward flight doesn't go for another five days, so I'm here until next Wednesday evening.

A taxi draws up out of the still warm night and I hail it. I don't have any Tongan money, I don't know anyone here, and the single piece of useful information I've got is the name of a Nuku'alofa guest-house, given to me by the Canadian engineer I sat next to on the plane, and which I supply to the driver of the ageing Toyota taxi as we move off.

All I can see of Tongatapu Island is that it's flat and it has many palm trees. We move along long, straight roads containing many cavities. The driver and I make desultory conversation, then his car radio begins to crackle. Voices come on, then are replaced by other voices. Many of the callers — it's obviously some kind of talkback show — are highly excited. One word is repeated by every caller. Pa'anga.

'What's the programme about?' I ask the driver.

'The mini-games. These people, they call the radio, they say how much money they give for the mini-games.'

Mini-games? A contest for small people? Or possibly small games — table tennis, arm wrestling, marbles — for ordinary-sized people.

'What are the mini-games?'

'Games for people all over the Pacific. Guam, Tahiti, Vanuatu, Cook Islands, Pup-pu New Ginny. Every four years we have South Pacific Games, every two years we have mini-games.'

'For all Pacific countries?'

'Yes. But not for New Zealand and Australia.' He laughs. 'They too big, too much people.'

'What sort of games will you be having?'

'Ten-nis, golf, athol-letics, volley-ball, netball. Lots of games, hundreds of people.' Voices are still coming through the radio static. 'That's why people ring up and give money. Mini-games costs a lot of money.'

So, my arrival in Tonga has coincided with a major international sporting event, but I have not read one newspaper item in New Zealand referring to this tournament. Apparently as far as the New Zealand press is concerned, the South Pacific mini-games is a non-event.

The guest-house, located in a leafy street somewhere in darkest Nuku'alofa, supplies me with a room with many louvre windows, a concrete floor, a large bed and a private bathroom. The room is in the centre of the courtyard of a large, rambling house with numerous semi-detached units, set amid banana palms and hibiscus bushes. Weary from an excess of in-flight food and drink, I go directly to bed. To bed, but not to sleep. Dogs bay and bark all night and in the unit next door a group of cheerful evangelical Christians from the States sing songs to the Lord until three in the morning. When the dogs and the Christians are at last laid to rest, the roosters take over. One crows continuously for two hours, just outside my window. I get approximately an hour's sleep. At eight o'clock I get up, shower, check out and call a taxi to take me to Keleti Beach.

The Canadian mentioned Keleti Beach. 'It's outa town but it's quiet, and the beach is kinda nice.' Quietness is a high priority at the moment. Writers need quietness the way fish need water. Writers immerse themselves in quietness, breathe it in, convert it into books. The photosynthesis of silence. The only book I could have written in that guest-house is one entitled 'How to murder a Cock/Dog/Evangelical Christian'.

Still in this splenetic mood, I'm driven out of town and along more straight, flat roads lined with long grass and coconut palms. Then we come to what is clearly an arterial road, and turn on to it. We pass a large stadium. This driver, who so far has not spoken, says, 'That is National Stadium. New. French give us money for it. Mini-games start here tomorrow.'

It certainly looks impressive, the high grandstand, the big track, the line of flag-poles, surrounded by stands of palm trees. I think idly that I might go and have a look at the athletics, if there is time. The taxi turns off the main road and along an unsealed one, then off the unsealed road and along a dirt track which runs between unfenced verges of rank grass. At the end I see a hand-painted sign. Keleti Beach Resort.

Just inside the entrance to the one-level, breeze-block, louvre-windowed building is a reception desk and a small lounge area containing a round table and chairs. A series of shells on strings comprises a kind of curtain between reception and a large, rectangular, concrete-floored courtyard behind it. The wings of the buildings lining the courtyard have wide eaves sheltering rows of metal tables and chairs. Lines of coloured light bulbs are strung across the yard. The yard and enclosing buildings put me in mind of an army barracks, except that through the far, open end of the courtyard I can see the horizon, a line of streaky cloud, and the brilliant blue sea.

Behind the L-shaped reception desk is a woman of about fifty. She has brown hair tied back in a bun, a skin as pale as putty and spectacles with very thick lenses. A fold of white skin under her chin, and a wide, tight mouth, give her a froggy appearance. Her upper arms are very wide, with bags of flesh hanging from them. She has a paperback novel in one hand, a cigarette in the other. She looks up, arranges her face into a tight smile. She has light blue eyes. Very calculating, light blue eyes. 'Good morning.' Her accent is American.

'Hello. Do you have a vacancy?'

'We sure do.' She sets the cigarette down on a clamshell ashtray. 'We can do you a whole fally fer thirty puh-ungas a night, haff a fally fer twenny-five puh-ungas, or a dorm-it-tory for ten.'

Dormitory has a boarding school ring to it, but this is neutralised by the ten pa'anga aspect. I'm a budget traveller, so I ask to see a dormitory room. The woman leans back, calls imperiously at the shell curtain. 'Ladu!'

A Tongan boy of about sixteen, curly-headed, handsome, well built, with high, prominent cheek bones, appears. He is wearing a yellow T-shirt, blue lavalava and jandals. The woman passes him over a key.

'Take this gennnel-man down to the dorm-it-tory block and show'im Room One.'

I follow the lad down a descending concrete path lined with red and yellow crotons. At the bottom of the path is a custard-coloured, rough-cast concrete, two-storeyed building with a flat, sloping roof and a concrete terrace along its frontage. Behind the building is a cluster of tall coconut palms, and in front of it is a sweep of lawn from which sprout small palms and hibiscus bushes. Latu unlocks the first door of the building and I walk in.

The room is narrow but contains two beds — one on either side of the room — made up with blue linen. The floor is bare concrete but there are louvre windows at the front and rear. Under the window by the door is a small table and a chair, behind the door is an open rail from which hangs a number of wire coat hangers. The room is cool, it has everything I need, and I can hear no dogs, roosters or evangelists. There is a power point by the door. I can put my electric typewriter on the little table, plug it in, and look straight out across the garden while I work. And all for ten pa'anga.

'Bathroom is along there,' says Latu, wide-eyed with enthusiasm.

'This'll be fine, thanks. I'll come up and sign the register when I've unpacked.'

I walk out onto the narrow concrete terrace. The sky has become grey, but it's very warm. Below me the grass slopes away to an area planted thickly in banana palms and aloes. To my right I can see the thick concrete path undulating between the dark red, green and yellow crotons and up to a number of well-spaced, oval fales which are yellow-walled and roofed with corrugated iron painted red. The office-block and dining area up on the rise to my right is ramshackle, but the profusion of plants and palms draws attention away from its unsightliness. Above all, although I can see a harem of scratching, pecking chickens being guarded by a ginger-plumed rooster down on the grass, I can hear no noise except for the sea. And thinking of the sea, I set off down the sloping lawn to inspect it.

A sandy track passes between boulders of black basalt on the far side of the lawn. I pass along the track, the powdery sand squeaking under my feet. Tiny, mercurial skinks dart left and right out of my way. The track opens out on to a small beach at the foot of a basalt escarpment about five metres high. The sand is still damp on the surface from the dew, but underneath it is deep and soft. I sink down onto it and stare at the sea.

The lagoon is narrow, and floored with coral twisted into myriad shapes. Clear, sandy-bottomed pools separate the ridges of coral, which ascend in a series of steps to the reef itself. On the top the reef is level, but on the landward side it is terraced, so that it resembles a line of ziggurats. In front of the terraces is a pool of calm, clear water, and from the milk-white sand protrude skeletons of dead coral, jagged and brown.

But it is the terraced reef that my eyes are drawn to. Over and through the reef the sea is surging, foaming, exploding upwards in a series of continuously performing blowholes. The spectacle captivates me. It is like watching a long line of fountains, programmed to play at slightly varying intervals, forever. The water looks irresistible, but my togs are not yet unpacked. Later I'll swim, after I've signed in and set my room up properly. But still I make no move, and it is not until half an hour later that I tear myself away from the hypnotic scene.

It's Saturday. Tomorrow, being the Pacific Sabbath, the shops will be closed and nothing will happen, so if I want to see the town properly, I'd better do it today. There is a resort mini-bus that goes to Nuku'alofa, but I've missed it, the woman at the desk tells me. Her name is Joyce, and when she sees that I've written 'writer' on the registration card, she's suddenly very friendly. 'Did yuh bring yuh books with yuh? There's just no damn books in this country. I read everything, always have, but here? Just fucking Bibles.'

I offer to lend her some novels, then ask how I can get into town. She suggests a taxi, but then I notice an old bike in the yard. Could I borrow that? Sure . . .

On a decent bike, Tongatapu would be ideal terrain for a cyclist. There are few hills and little motorised traffic. This bike is way past its best, though. It has no brakes, and it's long been a stranger to an oil can. I don't think it's been ridden this far since Queen Salote was on the throne. Still, it gets me along a lot faster than walking.

The greyness has gone from the sky, replaced by a deep blue and traces of white cloud. Following Joyce's directions, I cycle along narrow, straight, dusty white roads between long grass and stands of scruffy coconut palms until I join the main road. Big, crammed buses overtake me, their dark-faced passengers peering at me curiously through the open windows. Little children stop and stare at me as if I've got two heads. Cycling cannot be a common mode of transport in Tonga, I conject as I push on towards the town.

Nuku'alofa is a dusty, old-fashioned town with narrow streets and crooked, two-storeyed buildings. Everything looks old: the wooden buildings, the vehicles, the merchandise in the shadowy shops. There are lots of people standing about looking as if they have nothing much to do and all the time in the world to do it. But I like the town, there is something so sleepy and unhurried about it that it appeals. It could be the inertia capital of the Pacific, or the perfect location for a movie set in nineteenth century Mexico. I prop the bike up on a fence and have a Coke at a rough wooden table beside a food stall.

Watching the people standing about or strolling past is an absorbing activity, and as I'm doing so I realise that there is an influx of visitors to Nuku'alofa. They are young men and women who stand out in their bright tracksuit uniforms of many colours, they stroll among the locals with upright bearing and proud faces. They are, I realise, the athletes, here for the mini-games. Their tracksuits proclaim their nationalities and their sports. There are netballers from the Cook Islands and sprinters from Vanuatu; weight-lifters from Nauru and tennis players from Tahiti; boxers from Papua New Guinea and golfers from Guam. They walk along the street with the easy litheness of natural athletes, and all are resplendent in their uniforms, bursting with vitality. They look as if they just can't wait to run, jump, hit a ball, press a weight or pin an opponent to the mat.

Watching them gives me a new appreciation of Pacific solidarity. They are here not just because they are athletes, but because they are people who inhabit a particular region and who feel part of it. Some, I can see, are Melanesian, some Polynesian, some palagi, some of mixed race. What unifies them is the ocean which surrounds them. Again I feel a twinge of resentment that this big gathering is going unnoticed by the New Zealand media.

The bike has become an encumbrance in town. I can't leave it anywhere, because it doesn't have a lock and chain, and lacking brakes, it can't be ridden in the traffic, so I walk and push it down Taufa'ahau Road, across the intersection of Wellington Road to the waterfront and the Royal Palace.

The traditional rulers of Tonga — the Tu'i Tonga — went back a thousand years; the present monarchy goes back to Tonga's constitution of 1875. Written by an ambitious Methodist missionary called Shirley Baker (a man), the constitution en-shrines absolute power in the monarch, his appointees and thirty-three noble families. All land is owned by the monarch, and about one hundred thousand commoners vote for just nine of the thirty parliamentarians. (So grateful was King George I to his friend for securing the throne for the house of Tupou that he made Shirley Baker Minister of Foreign Affairs, Comptroller of the Revenue, and Premier. This did not endear Shirley to all Tongans, and in 1887 he only just survived an assassination attempt.)

Now, near the end of the twentieth century, Tonga retains its feudal system, being currently ruled by Taufa'ahau Tupou IV, who succeeded his mother, Queen Salote, in 1965. A feudal monarchy, modelled on the English system, in the south-west Pacific Ocean.

The palace is not a large building as palaces go, but it's stylishly colonial, with white walls, red roof, attractive fretwork around the verandahs, finials and pretty bargeboards on the gables. The building is set on a velvet lawn. Palace guards in immaculate white jackets, dark, red-striped trousers and smart hats eye me with more than passing interest as I lean the bike on a concrete gate-post and peer at His Majesty's pad. One guard has a fixed, very bright bayonet on his rifle. There have been brave stirrings of democracy in the kingdom lately, and these chaps look as though they're very keen to enforce the status quo.

Later on this trip I hear many comic stories about the king. Monarchies in the modern world are never far from being absurd, and Tupou's is not helped by the fact that he is an extremely large fellow. Most King of Tonga stories have an avoirdupois theme. My favourite is the one told to me by a nun in Samoa. She said that some nuns in Tonga asked His Majesty to lunch. Being solicitous hostesses, they then asked the convent carpenter (was his name Jesus? I was tempted to ask but didn't) to join two big chairs together, to comfortably accommodate the regal bum. The special chair did the job very well until His Majesty stood to leave. The chair came with him, and it took the combined efforts of several nuns to separate the monarch from his improvised throne. There's definitely something very Gilbertian about the whole set-up, I think, as I mount my brakeless bike and ride off down Vaha'akolo Road on the first stage of my return to Keleti Beach.

I set my typewriter up on the table under the dormitory window and plug it into the power point by the door. I've purloined a table of the right height from the dining room. The bottom of the louvre window is level with my chest, so that I can see out over the lawn, the palms and the basalt boulders. There is a peep of the sea and a sweep of sky. It's tranquil and beautiful, and soon I'm typing conscientiously, glancing up at the scenery periodically for refreshment, like a swimmer taking breath. Hunt and peck, hunt and peck. I'm writing a story about a Cook Islands dancer who works in central Auckland, and as many writers have found, detaching myself from the setting of the story by a couple of thousand kilometres, rather than being an impediment, seems to be assisting the story. Distance lends clarity as well as enchantment. Hunt and peck, hunt and peck. She's an interesting character, this dancer. I like her a lot. She's a plucky girl, too, the way she turns her art into a profession.

After my fifteen-hundred-word quota has been filled, I get up and stretch. The palms are casting long shadows across the lawn as the sun sinks. It's been a gruelling day, what with biking and writing, and I decide to lie down on the bed for an early evening nap. In three minutes I'm asleep.

'Aaaa . . . aaah . . . aaah . . . aaah . . .'

The appalling sounds of human suffering which have shattered my sleep are coming from the other side of the concrete block wall, just to my right. I sit bolt upright. The choking is replaced by a low moaning and groaning.

'Uuuuh . . . uuuuh . . . uuuh . . .'

Good God, what's happening in there? Is one person slaying another, or is it suicide? I get up and put my ear to the wall. There's a crash, followed by a snapping of wood, as if furniture is being broken, then a groan. A period of silence, then snoring. The snoring increases in volume, and my concern for whoever is next door is replaced by resentment. It's just what I don't need, a vomiting, snoring drunk for a neighbour. As I get ready for my evening meal I think, I'll move further down the dormitory if necessary to get away from the swine who's disturbing my peace. After locking my door, I pause and peer in through the louvres of Room 2. I can only see, amid the darkness, a broken bed on which there is a shadowy, huddled human which I think is male.

The resort dining room is long and rectangular, lined with louvre windows, tapa-patterned curtains and with real tapa cloth stuck to its walls. Latu, dressed in a white, long-sleeved shirt, is a very attentive waiter — as well he might be, for apart from myself there are only two other diners.

He is a big man in his late forties, with slicked-back hair and a large, slumped stomach. He smokes continuously, even as he eats. He looks like a Doug. She is plump and brown-haired, dressed in a plain blue, short-sleeved cotton frock. She can be no older than seventeen. She looks down all the time and barely utters a word when he speaks to her. Doug looks at her in quite a kindly way, but she persists in looking down bleakly at the tablecloth. She looks like a Rochelle. There is a melancholy air about the couple. Are they father and daughter? I don't think so. Even though there is a certain similarity about them, the way Doug looks at her is not the way a father looks at his daughter. Lovers then? Probably. The presence of the odd couple spurs my imagination. Where did they meet? In a factory? In an office? What did he say to her, to get her to come away with him, a man three times her age? '*I'll tell you what, Rochelle, if you ah . . . come back to my flat . . . after work . . . I'll shout you a holiday. An overseas holiday. On a tropical island. The whole works, sun, sea, sand, palm trees. Won't cost you a cent. Tonga, how about Tonga? A holiday in Tonga, just the two of us. We could leave at night. No one else will ever know. What do you say? Rochelle? Rochelle?*'

I leave the dining room and walk across the courtyard to the lounge. It too is a long narrow room lined with louvre windows. It contains a few worn vinyl sofas and chairs, and french doors which open out on to a broad verandah. I can see a table tennis table and weight-lifting equipment on the verandah. The bar is at one end of the lounge. It has a small, horseshoe-shaped counter, above which is a sheet of steel reinforcing mesh, painted cream, in which a head-sized hole has been cut. Behind the mesh is a man of about sixty, and in front of it, sitting on a stool, is a much younger man. Facing each other, with the steel grid between them, the scene resembles a central American prison on visiting day. As I approach the bar the older man looks up, says in a drawl, 'How yer doin?' Joyce's husband, I surmise.

He is scrawny, slack-shouldered, balding, with folds of skin hanging from his turkey neck. A cigarette droops from a corner of his mouth. Why does everyone in Tonga smoke, I wonder. I ask for a Royal beer, posters for which I have noticed in town, and the American ambles off down a passage and opens a fridge. The man on the stool looks at me crookedly. He is about thirty, with cropped brown hair, a fleshy, flushed face and brown eyes. He wears a tight white T-shirt and jeans. His eyes seem to be having difficulty focusing. He blinks, shakes his head as if trying to dislodge water from his ear, then peers at me.

'Ow's ut goin' thun?'

'Not so bad, thanks.'

'Jost arrived, 'av yer?'

'Last night. From Auckland.'

'Me too, just arrived. I'm frum Brimming'im. Ing-land.'

'That's a long way from Tonga.'

'Bit of a boos ride, yus. Me name's Rob.'

'Graeme.'

As we shake hands the barman returns with a bottle of Royal beer and pours it into a plastic cup. I try it. It's dry, well chilled and has a pleasantly bitter aftertaste. I observe from the label that it's brewed in Tonga, with Swedish assistance. Then I say to the Englishman, 'That's good beer, don't you think?'

'It's all right, yus. I've ud worse, like.'

'Do you live here, Rob?'

'Me? Shit no, oim just vistin'. Oi luv in Feegee.'

'What's that like?'

'Fosters. All Fosters in Feegee. Same again thanks Bill.'

Not quite understanding him, I ask, 'Have you seen much of the Pacific?'

'Seen it awl. Bin everywhere.'

'I'm on my way to Samoa. What's that like?'

'Vailima. Not a bud brew neither. Gerries do thut wan.' He puts one hand flat down on the bar for a moment, to steady himself. His face has gone a terracotta shade. 'Least ut's Vailima un Western Sa-mower. In Pago Pago ut's Budweiser. American there, y'see.' He rolls his eyes ceilingward, recites. 'Niue, Steinlager. Tahiti, Hinano. Raro-tong-ga, Cooks lager.' He belches gently, interrupting the litany of lager. 'Bot doan't go ter fookin' New Cally-doanya, yer cunt get a decent beer there. All wine. Too many Froggies, y'see.' Looking perplexed, he peers through the mesh at Bill, who's pouring him another Royal. 'Bot Tahiti's got froggies, and they've got beer there. Hinano. Foony thut is. Why is thut, Bill? Why cunt yer get a decent beer in New Callydoanya?'

'That is something,' the barman drawls back wearily, 'that I just can't tell you. Only place I ever bin in the Pacific is right here in Taang-ga.'

With extreme lethargy, and much sighing, Bill tells me his background. He and Joyce had run what he calls 'a sanitorial maintenance operation' (could he mean 'cleaning', I wonder?) in Chicago, but the winters had got just too cold for them. They read books on the Pacific, decided on Tonga, wrote to the government and were offered a two-year work and residence permit if they would run the Keleti Beach Resort. They sold everything and came here six months ago.

'So how do you like it?' I ask.

Bill sucks at his gums, swallows, pulls at the crêpey skin on his neck.

'Wal, it is warmer than Chicago, no question 'bout that . . . I mean the john hasn't frozen over here yet . . . But as far as the tourist trade is concerned . . .' For the third time he leaves his sentence unfinished, and instead looks out over the lounge, leaving its emptiness to speak for itself. I feel very sorry for him, and as an expression of this sorrow, order another two beers for Rob and myself. Bill brings them, and I say to the brummer, 'Are you staying in one of the fales here, Rob?'

'Fook no, oim in the dorm-i-tory block down the path.'

'Oh? What number?'

'Noomber two.'

I pause, look at him closely.

'Did you arrive late this afternoon, by any chance?'

He grins inanely. 'Thut's right.' He blinks with the effort of recalling even his recent past. 'I was a bit pissed, uctually. Ud a few too many beers on the plane. Thun I had a ruff taxi ride 'ere, and chooked oop in me room.' He brings the lager up to his mouth, sips gratefully. 'Oim all right now, though. Now I've ud a few beers . . .'

I like the Keleti Beach Resort. It doesn't bother me that it has Albanian architecture, or that it's way out of town; it's quiet working in my dormitory room — Rob hasn't vomited or collapsed again since I arrived — the food is tolerable, the beer cold, and any time the words don't flow I simply stroll down to the little cove and watch the sea playing through the blowholes. After a time staring at the reef the characters who have taken leave from my imagination come back again, ready for the fictional fray. I've also been on a half-day tour of Tongatapu, and was amazed to find some marvellous prehistoric, stone constructions including something called the Ha'amonga-'a-Maui Trilithon, which is like a smaller version of Stonehenge. I've discovered an excellent Tongan-French restaurant in Nuku'alofa — Chez Alice and André — which has a menu as good as anything I've seen in French Polynesia, and an equally impressive Chinese restaurant in the basement of the Catholic Basilica.

What is strange about Keleti Beach though, is that there are so few other guests. They can now be counted on the toes on one and a half feet, because Doug and Rochelle have stolen away in the night, presumably to pursue their sad relationship in other parts. They have been replaced by a trio of beautiful young Italians — two men and a girl, all in their early twenties — who look as if they may be making a Gucci advertisement somewhere on the island.

The Italians breakfast early, radiating a style and sophistication which looks very out of place in the concrete and formica dining room, then vanish for the day in a taxi, returning, still radiant and voluble as the sun goes down. Apart from this stunning ménage à trois there is Rob, myself, and a sweet, darkly tanned Danish couple who are so wrinkled and ancient that they look as if they've been dug from a peat bog in Jutland. They totter to the beach in the morning, sleep in the afternoon and watch old videos in a corner of the lounge each evening.

Rob is a drunk, a no-hoper and a layabout of the first order. I like him a lot. I like his melanistic sense of humour, his carelessness and his total dedication to booze. There's always something appealing about a thorough and amusing drunk, the way they live for the moment and so obviously relish getting totally intoxicated at every opportunity. But the presence of this happy dipsomaniac is doubly fortuitous for me, because I'm now writing a story about a youthful alcoholic, an ex-rugby star who has taken to the bottle. Rob is clearly not a rugby player, but in all other respects he is the perfect model: his brick-red face, rolling eyes, disjointed conversation and anarchic sense of humour — these disconnected mannerisms are just what I have in mind, and whenever I lose the image of Victor Donovan, my alcoholic, all I have to do is trot along to the bar any time after breakfast and there he is, sitting, swaying on the stool in front of the steel reinforcing mesh, waving his glass extravagantly, as if he is conducting the Birmingham Symphony Orchestra. Rob even speaks at dictation speed.

'Oi loov Feegee, y'gnaw? Oi live inna village, a little village, wiv the chief — the rut-toos's daughter. She . . . what the fook's 'er name again? Hahahahahahaha . . . She's all right, y'gnaw? I still cunt think of 'er name, boot it'll coom, it'll coom . . . Anyway oim a sparky, a nelectrician, so oim a bit oova magic mun like, t'the Feegeeans, oi fix their videos and thut, und when oi do they giv me presents, like a case of Fosters . . . hahahahaha . . .'

It wasn't hard to picture Rob in 'his' village, lurching about among the empty Fosters cans, mending the occasional fuse or broken toaster to demonstrate his magic: reprehensible behaviour in one sense, but in another just part of an old English colonial tradition of the white man who is a failure at home but an outrageous success in the outermost islands of the Empire. I find it impossible to dislike Rob; his devotion to the bottle is shameless and absolute, he will eventually drown in a lake of lager, and it will be the most pleasurable experience of a short, confused life which has overflowed with self-indulgence.

But for Joyce and Bill, I get the impression that life has been long and luckless, and that one of their unluckier decisions was the one to leave the USA and move to Tonga. For Joyce this realisation manifests itself in a rejection of all things Taan-gun (after a year in the country, she can't even pronounce the name of the place correctly). At every opportunity she rails against the people, the climate, the politics, the economy, the king, the church, the food. ('Do you know that last year the Taan-guns had to import coconuts from the Cook Islands? *Coconuts!*') I am bewildered by the intensity and breadth of her attack: it is all-encompassing, passionate, and most depressing, totally sincere.

Bill, in contrast, is only afflicted with a tiredness which is exhausting just to witness. Everything he does is done slowly and to the accompaniment of sighs and groans; even when he sits out by reception and reads a paperback novel I lent him, he groans every time he turns a page, not over the progress of the plot (it is a Maurice Gee novel), but with the extreme effort it requires to move on to the next page. It is not Tonga that has done this to him, I conject. Bill looks like the sort of guy who was born exhausted.

Then, on my fourth morning at the resort, as I walk past reception on my way to breakfast, I am startled to see that Joyce is transformed. She is vibrant, goggle-eyed with joy. 'Guess what, Graeme? Guess what . . . ?' *You found a Tongan you like?* I feel like suggesting, but instead I say lamely, 'I've no idea, Joyce.' She makes little clapping movements with her hands, like a gleeful toddler.

'The whole fucking Pap-oo Noo Gin-yin mini-games team is comin' here tonight fer a party! A hunnert-and twenny of the mother-fuckers!'

She pours out the details, her frog eyes almost bounding from their sockets. The Papua New Guinean team will be here at seven tonight, for a meal, followed by a dance. Why the Keleti Beach Resort? I cannot resist asking. Unoffended, Joyce explains that no other place on the island would take such a large group at such short notice.

'Wow,' I reply, impressed but still doubtful. 'Can you cope with as many as that without warning?'

Joyce's eyes retract, the lids narrow. 'At twenty puh-ung-ga a head, we'll fucking well cope all right . . .' She leans across the desk and calls out to where Bill is readying the van for a trip into Nuku'alofa for supplies. 'Bill! *Bill!* Soy sarce! Don't ferget the soy sarce! Twenny bottles!'

As I enter the bar after a long day at my Olivetti, Rob raises his glass. 'Bula vanaka, my son.'

'And malo ei leilei to you. Had a good day?'

'Aw, yeah, not so bud. Few beers after breakfast, bit oova kip after loonch, game o table tunnis wiv Latu, few more beers after thut. Now oim all ready for the party. Uv you seen whot's happening outside?'

Rob leads me to the windows of the lounge. At the far end of the concrete quadrangle, above the cliff that faces the sea, a number of Melanesian men are busying themselves with microphones, amplifiers, drums and a big switchboard. Flex entrails cover the floor, and big speakers have been set up on either side of the thatched shelter.

'Who are they?'

'Pup-oo New Gin-yins. Boogers uv brought their own bund.'

They arrive in three coaches, and enter the resort tentatively, self-consciously, groups of men and women dressed in vivid red and yellow tracksuit tops and black bottoms with red, patterned stripes up the sides. On the breast and back of their tops are outlines of a bird of paradise. On their feet they wear dark sneakers. Their faces are as black as basalt, their hair frizzy, their teeth almost luminously white, their foreheads are wide. Many of the men are shorter than the women, but they're perfectly proportioned, muscular and neat, while the female team members are slender and lithe. Latu, in bright white T-shirt bearing a Keleti Beach Resort emblem, tracksuit pants and white sneakers, shows the guests to the metal tables around the quadrangle. He is assisted by a small palagi boy in a lavalava and roman sandals. They both carry woven trays.

Soon the tables are full, men on one side of the quadrangle, women on the other. It's dark now, and the coloured lights are switched on. There are no festivities yet though, the team just sits, sipping Coca-cola or cream soda from the can, occasionally standing up to photograph one another. Each flash of the camera is followed by a burst of mirth from the subjects, and the exposure of teeth as dazzling as the flash which precipitates it.

Rob and I take a seat at a table near the reception area. Rob is growing very agitated. He nudges me excitedly as the women continue to crowd into the courtyard. 'Hey, look ut thut wun over there, look ut the boom on 'er. I never seen so mooch bluk velvet t'gether in wun place . . .'

A tall Melanesian man in a green blazer steps up to the microphone, and the team quietens in a moment. He speaks first in pidgin, then in English. He calls for impeccable behaviour, self-discipline, good sportsmanship, total commitment. Then he steps back a little.

'I now have much pleasure in calling upon our Minister for Sport, Culture and Youthful Affairs, the Right Honourable George Banuba!'

Sustained applause greets the movement to the microphone of a tall, heavily built man in white dinner jacket, grey needlecord trousers and open-necked, floral-patterned shirt. He wears tinted glasses and has a bushy black moustache. On behalf of his government he welcomes the team to the games and also calls sternly for impeccable behaviour, self-discipline, good sportsmanship and total commitment.

'Any team member not behaving in accordance with these rules . . .' he pauses, and his tracksuited audience exchange nervous glances or stare at the floor, 'will, I assure you, be . . . *finished.*' He allows another long pause while he glowers at the crowd, then his big, fleshy face breaks into a broad, white-toothed grin. 'But for now, we can eat, drink our soft drinks, and dance. A good games to you all!'

Joyce and her kitchen girls have worked some sort of miracle. The tables in the dining room sag under the weight of platters of taro, breadfruit, marinated fish, chop suey, fresh vegetables, rice, baked beans and a variety of salads. Latu moves proudly among the visitors, helping with plates, glasses and chairs as the team lines up for their meal. Joyce stands by the kitchen door, scrutinising the table through her thick-lensed spectacles. She wears a long, black, halter-necked dress, and smokes feverishly. Bill is nowhere to be seen. Joyce beckons me over, speaks from the side of her mouth.

'They're quite little, you notice that? They probably woan eat that much. And their manners, I really like their manners. Not like Taan-guns. You ever seen Taan-guns eat?' She spreads her bare arms wide and makes huge sweeping gestures towards her mouth, where the cigarette hangs. 'Taan-guns eat like this.' She makes the sweeping gestures again, removes the cigarette and works her mandibles several times as far as they will go, then shuts them: 'That's how Taan-guns eat . . .'

I queue up too, and take my plate out to where Rob is still sitting and casting giddy looks over the crowd. The food is basic fare, but tasty enough. Certainly the Papua New Guineans are showing total commitment to the meal. And in one respect, Joyce is right: they are an extraordinarily polite and well-behaved group. They laugh, and chat, but there is no rowdiness of any kind. Whenever I've heard mention of Papua New Guinea, it's usually been in association with the rascals, and their brutal raping and bashing activities around Port Moresby, even though in my experience of the Pacific, the biggest rascals originate outside the region. Anyway, these people constitute the most courteous and self-disciplined sports team I've ever seen. They're also very happy; it shows all over their beaming faces and in their open laughter. The Papua New Guinean mini-games team is having the time of their lives.

At the far end of the courtyard the band launches into a reggae number, and several of the Papua New Guineans leap up and begin to boogie. In some cases men cross the yard and choose a partner, in other groups women get up and dance in a line without male assistance. The dancing snowballs, and in minutes the courtyard is jumping.

The Right Honourable George Banuba is sitting at a table beside mine and Rob's, just below the reception area. Sharing his table are three strapping, unsmiling young men in pale safari suits. The Minister seems in semi-jocular mood, tapping one foot to the beat, but from time to time frowning and sweeping the dance-floor with his gaze, searching the team for any breach of conduct. Rob returns from the bar with four bottles of Royal and lines them up carefully on our table. He slops some lager into his glass.

'Well, uv you enjoyed Tong-ga thun, me old Kiwi mate?'

'I have, Rob, I have.'

He holds an imaginary microphone up in front of my face.

'And what do you think of Tong-ga, Sir?'

I clear my throat. 'There is nothing wrong with Tonga that a good revolution couldn't fix.'

'Hahahahaha . . . thank you, end of interview. You uv bin shot und your 'ead stook on the froont of 'is Mujesty's suff-fari wuggon.'

Crimson-faced, Rob rocks back on his chair, attempting at the same time to focus on the people on the now-crowded dance floor in front of us. He tips his seat back too far, rocks forward, regains his balance and his glass but in the process slops a gout of beer over its rim and onto the designer trousers of the Right Honourable Minister at the next table.

As Rob's chair legs crash back to the floor, the Minister rises, very slowly, very deliberately, at the same time making broad sweeping strokes with one hand, to remove the lager from his thigh. Having done so, he then stands over the Englishman, glares down at him from what seems an enormous height and says in a tone of palpable menace, 'I think . . . that you . . . have had . . . too much to drink.'

Rob swivels in his chair and looks up at the burly politician. He stares at him for some moments, getting him into focus, then says in a tone of total nonchalance, 'Und I think . . . thut you . . . ought to go und get fooked.'

As one, the three minders at the next table rise from their seats and advance on us. The Minister's right hand reaches for the back of Rob's shirt. I jump up and slip between the Papua New Guineans and the Englishman, who has calmly turned back to attend to the balance of his drink. I hold both my hands up to the Minister, who looms as large and menacing as a grizzly bear.

'It's okay, it's okay, he didn't mean it, really . . .'

The hostility in the Minister's eyes diminishes, and his hand drops to his side. As it does so, the other three men halt their advance. I go on. 'I'm sorry about your trousers, but let's not let it spoil the party, okay?'

The Minister stands glaring at Rob for a little longer. His large jowls are covered in black stubble and his eyes are shaded by an untrimmed hedge of eyebrow. His big chest is rising and falling steadily. Suddenly his face breaks into a gap-toothed grin, although his brown eyes remain unamused.

'A good party, yes, with civilised behaviour from everyone.' He looks past me to Rob, who seems oblivious to everything except his drink. The Minister's grin fades. 'And they always say . . . ' he concludes coldly, 'that it's we *natives* who can't hold our liquor.'

The band gets louder, the dancing more joyful. The whole courtyard is a seething mass of grinning, jigging, twisting, shouting, tracksuit-clad figures. Flash-bulbs pop as the team members put the party on record. Rob grins.

'Not a bud mob, are they? Hey look ut her . . .' He points admiringly to a petite, shapely girl of about eighteen, dancing at the end of a line of swaying women athletes. She is dark, vivacious, surpassingly pretty. Rob's eyes bulge. 'Oi wouldn't mind playing hide the sausage with her.' He waves at the girl, who looks away in embarrassment. Rob subsides into deep thought.

'Do you know, I've never fooked a white woman. Never.'

I clap him on the shoulder. 'That's all right Rob, I've never fucked a black one.'

Suddenly the band stops playing. They step back a little, making room for their jovial, rotund leader, who bends his head to the microphone.

'Ladies, gentlemen, team members, it gives me very great pleasure to invite a special guest to sing for us tonight. This person is already a star in his own right, and as such is known to many of you. To others he will be strange. But he has agreed to sing for us, and it is my honour, not to mention my privilege, to welcome him to the microphone. Ladies and gentlemen, I give you . . . ' there is a drum roll from behind him '. . . our Minister for Sport, Culture and Youthful Affairs, Mis-ter George Ban-u-ba!'

Rob and I spin around. Sure enough the Minister is on his feet and beaming. He walks down through the applauding crowd and up to the microphone. He detaches it deftly from its stand, comes forward.

'Fellow countrymen, women, I would like to sing a bracket of songs for you, starting with a personal favourite.' He turns to the guitarist, makes counting down movements with his head, swings back to the audience. 'Aha la Bamba la Bamba . . .'

The audience explodes like fireworks, jumping, squealing, grabbing partners, clapping, singing, dancing, snapping their fingers. And when la Bamba is finished, had there been a roof over the resort dance floor the applause would have lifted it. Even Rob is yelling and clapping, even Joyce is jumping. The audience will not let the Minister go. He sings Elvis, Abba, the Beatles, Harry Belafonte, Stevie Wonder — nothing seems beyond his repertoire — while his team rocks and rolls and boogies and sings. I think, as I watch the happy throng, that if the Papua New Guineans show this amount of commitment on the sports field, they will be unbeatable.

Bill takes me to the airport in the resort van. It is a night flight, and we drive to the airport along unlit roads with only the silhouettes of the palms visible against the purple sky.

'Do you think you'll stay in Tonga?' I ask him. He pauses.

'Maybe. I don't mind it myself, but Joyce . . . Wal, she's not that keen on the place, y'know?'

'I got that impression myself.'

We drive up to the nearly deserted terminal building and I get my case out of the van. Bill walks with me over to the check-in counter. His shoulders sag low, a cigarette still hangs from his lower lip. I thank him, shake his hand, tell him how much I've enjoyed my stay. He smiles wearily, sceptically. He looks like an old basset hound, but he summons up a forlorn smile.

'Good luck with yer short stories,' he says.

'Thanks. Oh, the fare for bringing me out here? How much?'

He waves his hand carelessly, then stops, frowns. 'Joyce didn't ask you fer the fare?'

'No.'

'She'll be expecting me to get it, then.' He heaves a great sigh that makes his frame deflate further, looks up at me apologetically. 'That'll be . . . ten puh-unga.'

When I get back to New Zealand a fortnight later, one of the first things I do is search past newpapers for the results of the mini-games, to see how the Papua New Guinean team performed. My search is in vain: the games have gone unreported.

A Gulf Log

1 JANUARY, 9.30 A.M.

Tending a slight hangover from a New Year's Eve session with Devonport friends, I drive my teenage sons Matthew and Benjamin to the Hobbs Bay marina, on the Whangaparaoa peninsula. The car is laden to the gunwales with sleeping bags, snorkels and flippers, surfboards, beer, Vegemite and other items indispensable for a gulf cruise. On the way north the high East Coast Bays Road gives us glimpses of the gulf waters. They are flecked with white by a wind which appears to be from an easterly quarter.

THE MARINA, 10 A.M.

The thirteen-year-old motor launch *Wanderer* lies tranquilly at her berth beside the new walk-on, walk-off jetty. She is 33', powered by a Ford 115 diesel motor. She has attractive lines, is game rigged, with a flying bridge. We liaise with friend and skipper Erich, a Swiss-Kiwi dairy farmer from Kaukapakapa and his children Glenn and Emma. Below decks *Wanderer* is comfortable and well equipped. The children will sleep up for'ard, Erich and I in the main cabin. We stow food, clothing, diving, fishing and surfing gear. I know Erich well enough to appreciate that he is a man of diverse talents, but we have not been to sea together before. We are hoping to make Great Barrier Island to-day, but from the marina the sky is unseasonably grey, the wind cool. Erich squints at the sky as we prepare to cast off.

'We'll go for Kawau,' he says, 'make for the Barrier when the wind drops.'

Returning the gear trolley to the end of the jetty, I pass a weatherbeaten, bow-legged mariner with ears like anchor-flukes. He wears shorts, a grubby singlet and bare feet. The old man gives me an odd, curious look. 'Going to give it a go, eh?' he says. I nod matter-of-factly by way of reply, but the question puzzles me. What can he mean, *give it a go*? We're off to Great Barrier, via Kawau, at the height of summer, to see for ourselves that mysterious, tantalising island which has for years inflamed my curiosity, which on a map of the gulf lies like a piece of giant jig-saw, and which on a clear day can be glimpsed, apparently floating and endless, a ragged line across the north-eastern horizon. It is only about six hours away, I have been informed by nautical friends. *Give it a go.* What can the ancient mariner have meant?

Tier upon tier of waves, whipped into a series of mobile mountains by the thirty-knot easterly, rush towards us. *Wanderer* rises, pitches, drops, rolls, spray cascades over the flying bridge, three metres above the surface of the sea. Erich wrestles with the wheel, nods into the distance. 'Bit lumpy!' he shouts, and his voice is whipped away by the wind. We are apparently the only vessel on the sea, and the easterly is out to demonstrate the folly of our venture. As *Wanderer* drives into the face of another white-capped cliff, my nerve fails. 'I'm going below, boys, coming?' They grip the rails, exchange glances, shake their heads. 'For Christ's sake then, hang on!' I pause to stare at one more wave which has reared before us, its crest ripped into shreds of spray, then back down the companionway, clinging to the rail like a rodeo cowboy to a heaving steer. And as I take a last look at my boys, I wonder, where do they get their physical courage from? I step down onto the convulsing cockpit. Certainly not from their father.

Standing, staring sternward, bracing myself against the cabin door frame, I reach for one of the guidebooks I have brought. It begins, 'The waters of the Hauraki Gulf offer some of the finest sheltered cruising waters in the world.' I toss the book away bitterly, look instead at the end of the nearby peninsula, where giant waves are exploding on the rocks at the foot of the cliffs, which we are moving past with appalling slowness.

Tiri passage, and *Wanderer* is now broadside to the waves. We wallow and roll through what seems like 180 degrees. A brute of a wave strikes us, a locker door is flung open, and the Vegemite jar becomes a missile. In our wake the dinghy slews, lurches, takes water aboard. I scramble about in the cabin on all fours, eyes averted from the sea, stuffing jars and cans back in lockers, hearing the glasses rattling in their holders like a cheap chandelier.

When at last I look up I see through the cabin window that the land has become a blue smudge which is there one second, and plummets out of sight the next. There appears to be no sky, just streaming spindrift and a frenzied sea which has come all the way from South America to take out its fury on us. It is a nightmare from which I cannot awaken. What kind of fool, I think, would take his children to sea under a Swiss skipper, from a country which has no coastline? Writers should not go to sea at all, they have too much imagination. But what about Conrad, Hemingway? Yes, but Conrad sailed on proper ships, not launches, and Hem had a professional skipper for *Pilar*, a Cuban who did all the real work while the writer drank scotch and bragged. But you, you mustn't hate the sea like this, after all, you have lived within its scent all your life. No writer worth his salt can do without the sea, it is the writer's balm and inspiration. No writers in Bolivia, or Botswana, or Hamilton. Or Switzerland. *Wanderer* lurches again, and a pile of plastic plates become frisbees in the cabin. Is it my cursed imagination, or is the throbbing motor starting to falter? What if we drift, founder? I can see water slopping up over the transom. Should I start bailing? I close my eyes, grip a post, brace myself once more against the insane rolling, wait for the inevitable Mayday, or oblivion. Hours pass.

'Graeme! Kawau!'

My gulf stream of consciousness has been interrupted by Erich's call from the flying bridge. I open my eyes. The rolling is not so great, the sea now merely scuffed. Minutes later it turns to green silk as we glide into the lee of the island. Oh Kawau, blessed island, oh island in the sun! For the sun has broken through the cloud, is illuminating the pine plantation on its southern headland, and the vile wind is thwarted by the hump of ginger, bush-covered land.

I join the others on the upper deck. They are soaked but otherwise unharmed, exclaiming at what they have just been through. Around us, yachts slide through the bay towards Bon Accord harbour, Governor Grey's mansion comes into view through a bay filled with a foliage-free forest of masts. To *Wanderer*'s stern, the white horses continue their wild canter shoreward, but for the time being we are beyond their reach.

NORTH COVE, KAWAU, 5 P.M.
I stand on the bow and release the anchor, which slips into the still, clear water. The flukes gleam as the anchor zig-zags to the bottom. I am filled with respect for the skipper, with admiration for the children. And as the sun throws a glow over Kawau Bay and *Wanderer* rolls gently at anchor in the cove, I think, the sea is a bitch, a beautiful bitch.

2 JANUARY
Kawau is New Zealand's Isle of Wight, without the roads. While the other islands of the gulf are caught between the vehicle and the deep blue sea, Kawau has solved its roading problems simply by not having any. Here everything and everyone goes by water. The houses — not just baches — perch jauntily on the hillsides, surrounded by thick manuka. Many have pretty, wallaby-proofed gardens. One in Bon Accord harbour has a section bright with red and mauve hydrangeas which stand out against the green tea-tree like gems on a brooch. The jetties poke out into the bays to intercept the ferries which bring bread, milk and mail over from Sandspit. We cruise past one jetty which bulges in the middle. It's a helipad, complete with a

cherry-red chopper. The house above this jetty flies the Confederate flag. There are few beaches on Kawau, and no pasture, only manuka, kanuka, puriri, pine, some young kauri and the grey-green pohutukawa, clinging to the marmalade-coloured cliffs and headlands.

As we motor slowly to Mansion House Bay, the children swarm over *Wanderer* as if they have been at sea all their lives. Already she has become their floating home. We anchor in the bay and row ashore in the dinghy. Dozens of brightly coloured inflatables — tenders for the yacht fleet anchored in the bay — lie on the gravel beach like a school of stranded tropical fish. Mansion House has been superbly restored, its north frontage decorated with latticework, verandah brackets and teardrops, and enclosed by a fence of white pickets. It looks, in its elegant setting, rather like an old Southern mansion, as if it too ought to be flying the Confederate flag. It's surrounded by palm and pine, peacocks shriek in the subtropical garden at the rear, wekas peck among the shrubs. There are ponds, paths, a sweep of lawn, a tastefully designed kiosk. Everything here is an attractive blend of native and exotic, both a reflection and a legacy of Governor Grey himself.

We stroll through the garden, where backpackers mingle with geriatric Americans and anoraked yachties, and come to the broad track which leads to Coppermine Head. The track climbs through a pine plantation, follows a cliff, descends to Dispute Cove. Around the rocks, on a rocky point, stands the old Coppermine, a weather-blasted ruin which is a poignant memorial to the Cornish miners who came across the world to tunnel here for the copper ore which still stains the headland luminous blue. The sandstone walls and tapering brick chimney are a striking landmark, but my thoughts are with the miners who came here when Auckland was little more than a tent town. Why did they come? How did they live? What did they do for food, shelter, sex? And what became of them? There could be a novel in their story.

We picnic in Dispute Cove, on Vegemite sandwiches and hard-boiled eggs, beneath a karaka tree filled with fat tuis. But out in the bay the cold wind, now from the south-east, still whips the open water. Back on the jetty in Mansion House Bay the Sandspit ferries are crammed with returning day-trippers, but it is the big ferry — the *Supercat* — berthed on the other side which captures the children's attention. *Wanderer* could pass between its twin hulls with room above to spare. The cabin windows are smoky glass, which makes them irresistible. Matthew and Ben put their noses to the windows. Elderly, lugubrious faces glare back from their luncheon tables.

3 JANUARY

'Auckland Radio Auckland Radio Auckland Radio, this is ZMB 5049 *Wanderer*, do you copy? Over.'

We are beginning to accept as normal this curiously old-fashioned piece of communications foreplay, and to appreciate the superb service which follows. ZLD Auckland Radio transmits vital information from its station on Musick Point all over the Gulf, twenty-four hours a day. Marine weather forecasting, search and rescue, radio-telephone connections with home — a marvellously reassuring service for those on the water. A call to them connects us to our wives for a chat, then provides the latest weather forecast. '. . . south-easterly winds, twenty-five knots gusting to forty knots . . . a wind warning applies to the gulf . . .'

'Damn the wind! Never mind, it's hiking again today kids. Vegemite or jam in the sandwiches?'

Deep inside the kanuka forest it's very cool, very still. There is no undergrowth, and the track is wide and smooth. To our left is a stream bed filled with lilies, from somewhere to our right we can hear a tui's electronic song. The track narrows and steepens as we approach the spine of the island. Suddenly, up ahead, there is a grey flash. Matthew points excitedly. 'Look . . .'

Two furry creatures bound at amazing speed between the kanuka trunks. Officially, the descendants of Grey's menagerie are noxious pests, unofficially the wallabies are comical, cute, outlandish. We encounter a dozen before we reach the top of the hill.

From the sixty-metre cliff the Hauraki Gulf is a living map spread open before us. The dark blue water is stippled with white, and huge swells crash on the rocks far below. There is only one vessel — a yacht, tiny in the distance — within sight. The wind warning was real. We sit and scan the gulf, ticking off the islands from Bream Head to Cape Colville. Taranga and her Chickens, the Mokohinaus, Colville Rock, Little Barrier. And spreading itself across the horizon, the long, serrated, indigo island that Cook named Great Barrier.

In the evening we dine on fresh scallops plucked from the bottom of the bay by Erich and cooked in white wine, and kahawai caught from the launch and smoked. It seems that we have been aboard *Wanderer* for weeks, not days, and that there is no other way of life. We all sleep easy, sedated by the sea. I wake at seven in the morning, turn over in my sleeping bag and listen for the now-familiar moan of the sou-westerly above Kawau's hills. The howling has ceased.

4 JANUARY

'. . . the marine weather forecast for the next twenty-four hours. Fair weather, winds fifteen knots, freshening to twenty knots by afternoon. Seas moderate. There are no wind warnings . . .'

We refuel at the Kawau Yacht Club, buy another packet of Honey Puffs, fresh bread, milk. There is a queue at the wharf for water and diesel. A plastic gin palace three storeys high cruises up, a pale, fat, ageing man jumps out onto the wharf, followed by a knock-kneed, straw-haired blonde. The fat man strides down the wharf, sets his hands on his hips, glares around. 'Who's in charge here?' he demands. No one takes the slightest bit of notice of him, and he slides away, scowling, to the back of the line.

Erich turns *Wanderer*'s prow eastward, into the gentle swell. The forecast is confirmed by the clearing sky and the soft following wind. None of us bother to suppress our excitement. Kawau was fun, but an island with helipads which gets its *Herald* by eight in the morning can scarcely be classified as frontier material.

In half an hour we are passing Tokatu Point, part of a steady stream of yachts and launches heading Barrierward in the fairest weather in a week. The remaining cloud is melting in the climbing sun, the sea is the deepest of blues, the wind a sou-wester of no more than ten knots.

Erich hands the wheel to Glenn, goes to the tackle box and takes out a garish green, plastic lure. 'Bought it in Singapore,' he declares proudly. The lure resembles a Hawaiian hula dancer, with the head of a squid and hooks for legs. It seems obvious that no fish will be brainless enough to be duped by it, but I don't voice these thoughts as Erich attaches the lure to a game rod and line and trails it in *Wanderer*'s wake, where it bobs and tumbles near the surface.

We are on course for the northern end of Little Barrier, cruising at nine knots. Gradually the land at our stern recedes, turns to a blue shadow. By mid-morning the heat is fierce, searing our sun-blocked legs and faces, turning the swells to flashing mirrors. *Wanderer* rolls on, and dead ahead is Little Barrier, its face still in shadow but growing larger, emerging from the water high and jagged, like Neptune's crown.

Birds, birds, birds. They are everywhere. Gulls, petrels, gannets, shearwaters, penguins, providing us with an unending sideshow. The yellow-necked gannets plummet like Olympic divers, the little blue penguins flop gamely in the swells, then dive just as we overtake them. Best of all is the tiny, white-faced storm petrel, nick-named the J.C. bird, which walks, or more precisely steps across the water, setting its feet down daintily in mid-flight, then stepping off again. It is a brilliant display of natural beauty which entrances us all. The children begin to count the little blue penguins, then give up. There are just too many bobbing on the swells.

Gradually the shadows which veil the western face of Little Barrier, and the cap of cloud which sits on the summit, are lifting, and the sun is revealing bush and jagged peaks, cliffs and ravines. A suitable sanctuary for the native birds — kakapo, stitchbird and saddleback — which rats, stoats, cats have hunted to the edge of extinction on the mainland. The illegality of landing on Little Barrier makes it tempting to do so. The view from the summit of Hauturu, the volcanic crag, which at 722 metres is the highest point in the whole gulf, must be incomparable. Here too is one of the only nesting places of

Cook's petrel. As we cruise around to the northern side of the island, we wonder at the extraordinary efforts of the wildlife people, who have rid its peaks and ravines of feral cats. Tarzan himself would be grounded by Hauturu's terrain.

We chug to the northern end of Little Barrier, to where the wind and water-scoured cliffs soar hundreds of metres above boulder beaches, and anchor in Te Ananuiarau Bay. Almost at the very moment that Erich dons his scuba gear and drops overboard into the depths, the wind freshens from the west. *Wanderer* begins to strain at her leash, then to pitch. I scan the water with some anxiety. What the hell do I do if he doesn't come up again? I can't even work the capstan, let alone call up Auckland Radio. The anxiety spreads as the time passes. Emma frowns at the heaving water. 'Dad's been down there a long time,' she says. 'But he's got a whole tank of air,' says Glenn, doing his best to keep up morale.

To take our minds off the infinite number of calamities which could result from Erich not resurfacing, we fish over the stern. Up they come in minutes, a lucky dip of leatherjacket, maomao, snapper, yellowtail and parrotfish. This is an angler's fantasy, to bait two hooks and haul up the line a minute later with a full house. But Erich is still down, and my eyes keep straying from that rocky shore to the now choppy sea. Is it merely my imagination again, or is the distance between us and the rocks really diminishing? I stare at the pitted cliffs above us. They are a geologic layer cake. Red whorls of ancient lava are capped with thick layers of sandstone, caves stare from the rock like eye sockets from skulls. And the wind is still freshening, and *Wanderer* is now rolling wildly, and the waves are crashing on the boulders, which seem only metres away. 'Where is Dad?' says Emma, speaking for us all.

I go below to try to start the motor. We have to get out of here. Just as I'm about to press the starter I see through the cabin window a gloved hand, bursting from the water beside the boat.

I lug Erich and his catch aboard. Ten good-sized, squirming crays. They join the fish in the sea-water locker in the stern. Ben chuckles. 'Like Kelly Tarlton's,' he says.

Around Ngatamahine Point there are more cliffs, and head-lands chewed by the sea. We glimpse the peak of Hauturu, sticking up like a gunsight at the top of a ravine. We feel minute in the face of such grandeur. If Cook had come closer he would surely not have attached the word 'little' to this place. The island is colossal. One writer has likened it to a molar, but in view of its role in conservation one could extend the metaphor and call it the gulf's wisdom tooth.

The fish have, with their usual fickleness, stopped biting as suddenly as they began. We weigh anchor again and set course eastward, for Great Barrier. The following wind is now twenty knots, and *Wanderer* wallows its way across the water. Again Erich tosses out his ludicrous lure and sets his rod firmly in its holder on the top deck. Once again the lure bounces in our wake. After a time I offer to reel it in. 'No, no, leave it there, you never know,' he replies, but by now the Singaporean bauble is the object of general derision, spurned by every fish in the gulf.

Glenn takes the wheel and Erich and I drink cans of cold beer. The late afternoon sun is casting a fiery glow over the sea between the Barriers. Ahead, the mass of land occupies the entire horizon, and is looming larger by the minute. Erich points to a massive block of bare rock, rising sheer from the water to our right. 'Wellington Head!'

We stare at the huge headland, a monument to the Iron Duke, which rises 110 metres straight from the sea. Wellington Head is split from top to bottom by an enormous crevice, and the setting sun has given the rock a golden hue. As we chug past the outcrop I wonder how many times Wellington, Hobson — Mount Hobson, the summit of Great Barrier, is now in sight, too — how often their names have been perpetuated by place? No doubt the old warrior would have approved heartily of this headstone. From its top it must be possible to scan the gulf from here to Cape Brett, perhaps even see the Mercury Islands. We pass around Wellington Head and into the still waters of a long passage which I see on the chart leads to Port Fitzroy. I reach into the fridge for another can of beer.

As I do so, above me I hear the scream of a reel ratchet, followed by a yell from above.

'Strike!' Erich tumbles down the companionway, bringing the rod with him. 'Slow her down, Glenn,' he shouts, and *Wanderer*'s engine is reduced to a low throb. The line is as tight as a violin string, and looks just as frail. Erich strains, gives the fish more line. The rod curves into a question mark. Whatever it is that's down there is big and powerful. The upper deck of the *Wanderer* has become a balcony as the children crowd the rail, peer down and speculate excitedly. Erich reels in more line, pauses, reels again. I bend over the stern, gaff in hand, staring at the milky-green water. Erich, rod butt rammed into his groin, heaves and grunts. 'Big bastard,' he pants, reeling it in a little more. The line zig-zags, moves closer to the boat. I grip the gaff.

A flash of silver and it is here, surfacing. I lunge with the gaff, hook it cleanly through the brain, haul it aboard.

It is a kingfish, a fish of exquisite beauty, more than a metre long, sleek, white-bellied, with silver-green flanks like shot silk. It lies in the stern, dying, its yellow fins aquiver, its huge eyes losing their lustre, the lure dangling from its streamlined, toothless mouth. Seconds later it is still, a creature of courage, strength, nobility, a fish well named.

An hour later we are at anchorage at the head of the passage, near Port Fitzroy. We all swim in the cool, deep waters of the sound, exhilarated by the events of the day, by the new land all around us. Later we dine on snapper and crayfish, the children fall asleep, and Erich and I drink wine in the moonlight. As we sit on deck and listen to the lapping of the water on our gunwales, from somewhere in the hills behind us comes the skirl of bagpipes. A wailing note is held, echoing around the sound. Who is this lonely piper who is calling to us and the moon? Could it be a lament for our noble catch? No matter, it is an eerie but affecting way to end our day. I take another draught of wine. All days should be like this one.

Constitution Week on Rarotonga

I RAN INTO MRS TARUIA IN THE Newton Post Office. Hadn't seen her for ages. She grinned, gave me a hug.

'What are you doing now?' I asked her.

'Still cleaning, up at the hospital. Hanging on to my job.'

'How are the girls?'

Tereapii was in Brisbane, Kathy was married and living in Rarotonga, Mareta was doing her nursing training at ATI. 'How about yourself? What are you doing?'

'I'm working at home. Writing. I'm going to Rarotonga this year, too.'

'Yeah? When?'

'In the winter sometime. August, September maybe.'

'You should go for Constitution Week.'

'What's that?'

'Our independence celebrations. Dancing competitions, singing, sports. I went last year, with my sister. Hadn't been back for five years. Great time.'

'When is it?'

'First week in August.'

'Every year?'

'Every year. You should go. It's fun.'

It begins, like most other things in the Cook Islands, with a prayer. It is the afternoon of the last Friday in July, in Avarua, the only town on the island of Rarotonga. I'm standing on the low wall outside the Banana Court bar, near the roundabout. Crowds line the one street, most of Rarotonga's nine thousand people must be here.

On my way here, half a kilometre or so back along the waterfront at Avatiu, I passed floats being assembled for the parade. Now I look up at the sky. High above the town, the jagged, green, bush-covered peaks are gathered about with dark clouds. Will the showers come now or later?

The Prime Minister steps forward and ignites the celebrations flame by the traffic roundabout in the centre of Avarua, the compere comes forward to the microphone, the parade begins to move. Constitution Week has begun.

The floats move erratically but happily into Avarua from my left, led by a troupe of marching girls in blue costume. They swing their arms, step highly and giggle self-consciously as they go, as aware as the crowd is of their imperfections. But no one minds, I've already found out that the Cook Islanders, as well as being a relaxed and affable people, have a great sense of the ridiculous.

Yesterday at the Rarotongan Hotel, where I'm staying, an English woman and her husband came to my room for drinks. My room has a high ceiling, and the fan in the centre of it was churning away effectively. The woman looked up at it.

'How come your room's got a fan?' she demanded.

'Haven't they all?' I replied.

'Ours hasn't, has it Robert?' she said to her husband accusingly.

He shook his head sadly.

She continued to eye the fan reproachfully, then when we went to dinner in the dining room, she went up to the assistant manager, a young Rarotongan man, and said belligerently, 'How come our room hasn't got a fan and his has?'

The assistant manager, normally a cheerful, obliging fellow, frowned.

'Which one is your room?'

'Number thirty-two.'

'Thirty-two . . .' Still frowning, he nodded, slowly. 'No fan in your room because you have a low ceiling.' He was speaking very slowly, very deliberately. 'If we have a fan in your room, and you sit up in bed . . .' He thrust his face towards the woman and made a sharp sideways movement across his neck with his hand. '. . . fan will cut your head right off!' There was no more mention of fans.

More floats move into my view. On one whose banner exhorts in large lettering, 'Clean Water And Good Sanitation For All' a participant picks up one of the new plastic lavatory pans on display, waves it around, places it over his head and squats suggestively, just as the float approaches the official party by the roundabout. Another float consists of a Toyota jeep towing a large branch on a trailer. In the foliage of the branch hang one flying fox and one dead pig. This enigmatic exhibit causes helpless and infectious hilarity all around me. One lady falls off the wall, she is laughing so much, and when her friends help her back up they are all laughing so hard that they fall off too.

All Rarotonga's government departments are represented in the parade. The Department of Labour and Works float features a big crane, a compressor, and a truck with a group of overall-clad workers on its tray. One worker demonstrates his pneumatic drill on a heap of rocks. The drill splits the rocks in seconds, strikes the steel tray underneath, bounces about loudly and uncontrollably. There is more hilarity all round, and I nearly come off the wall myself. The driller stops, grins with delight at the crowd reaction and drills the truck tray again.

The Education Department float bears a troupe of infant dancers on its top. They sway their hips and move their arms in perfect, miniature representation of their parents, and the performance draws loud applause. A temperance advocate on the Christian Youth float brandishes an empty beer bottle meaningfully at the crowd of customers watching the procession from behind me, on the verandah of the Banana Court, then makes what is clearly a speech on the Evils of the Demon Drink. The patrons laugh, and toast him with their full glasses.

Firms from the island's private sector are represented. A resort hotel carries a live band which strums out hot numbers on its electric guitars under a canopy of palm leaves, while a pig roasts on the trailer behind it.

Some of the Te Avi Maori dance troupe ride past on horses, dressed in real Royal Canadian Mounted Police uniforms. They have recently returned from a cultural trip to Canada, the man next to me says, reminding me that the Cook Islanders' dancing prowess is a valuable export commodity.

The parade passes through the town centre: past the little market, past the Banana Court, past the roundabout where the judges sit making notes. As it passes the roundabout the Ministry of Works crane pauses, swings its gantry, deftly uplifts a derelict dinghy handily placed beside the road, then rumbles on, the dinghy swinging in the air.

The last float passes, and the winners in each section — Most Artistic, Best Advertising, Most Humorous — are announced to cheers, then the crowd disperses. Soon afterwards the rain comes, in a teeming, windless deluge which I witness comfortably from the venerable premises of the Banana Court. It is still raining when I drive back around the island to the hotel, and it continues to for twenty-four hours. The rain is welcomed locally as there has been a drought on Rarotonga for many weeks.

Constitution Park is the setting for the festival of song, dance and legend which opens on the Saturday following the parade and continues every night for a week. Located just outside Avarua, the park contains an open-sided pavilion and a large stage decorated with palm fronds and hibiscus flowers. Outside the pavilion are small booths selling drinks, ice cream and candy-floss. For each evening's programme the festival items are divided into five: legend, action song, ute, drum dance and guest artist performance, while on Sunday night in this devout nation there is imene tuki, hymn singing, from various of the Cook Islands.

It's Monday night, and there are teams from the islands of

Mauke, Atiu and Aitutaki, among others from the different districts of Rarotonga. I watch the performance from the side of the pavilion. Overhead the night sky is indeed wide and starry, and the fronds of the huge palms in the park move gently, gracefully, in the faint breeze. Many spectators wear garlands in their hair, and the warm air is thick with the fragance of pandanus and frangipani. Infants doze in the arms of aunts or grandmothers. A thin dog trots across the front of the stage. Then the lights around it flash on and off twice, warning the capacity crowd that the performance is about to begin. There is a prayer, a blessing, and the first of the legends begins.

An announcer explains the meaning of the legends, for the benefit of papa'a visitors like myself, as the dialogue is in Cook Islands Maori. But if details of plot and character sometimes remain unclear to me, the dramatic impact is still formidable. The legends are melodramatic, crammed with conflict, passion and humour, and the audience follows each story keenly, dissolving into mirth at what is unmistakably a ribald line, or when an actor searches the stage ceiling silently, imploringly, searching for a forgotten phrase.

The legends over, the songs and dances begin. The stage lights flash on, revealing the dancers. Their art is something of which I could never tire. The women are graceful, sensuous, seductive, the men muscular, vigorous, exuberant. All smile radiantly as they sway or leap, singing in perfect harmony to the amazingly rapid, rythmic tattoo of the wooden slit drums beaten by the men at the side of the stage.

The crowd is shamelessly partisan. When the island of Atiu performs, Atiuans in the audience clap and shout for more; when it is Aitutaki's turn, the Atiuans listen in tolerant silence, swamped by the yells and applause of the Aitutakians.

Most joyous of the audience are the short, massive mamas, some who look over seventy, who leap up during their island's item, running barefoot to the area in front of the stage, then breaking into dance themselves, fat arms raised high, huge hips swaying, faces alight with youthful memories, their smiles surpassed only by those of their children and their grandchildren performing on the stage above them. And when each item is over, the money bowl at the front of the stage overflows with notes.

As I watch, captivated by the rhythms and the costumes, I'm conscious of the fact that apart from the visual pleasure in the dancing, there is satisfaction too in the knowledge that what I'm witnessing is pure Polynesia, not some ersatz cabaret act put together to pull in the tourist dollar. When I walk back across the darkened park to my car, the tattoo of the drums follows me through the tropical night.

August 4 is Constitution Day, a public holiday. This year has seen one election and a current political crisis which may precipitate another, I learned upon my arrival in Rarotonga. Now, at eight o'clock in the morning in central Avarua, the traffic has been closed off again, but the crowd is nothing like the size of the one which watched the parade, and I'm able to get quite close to the heart of the ceremony.

The Girls' and Boys' Brigades, Girl Guides and Boy Scouts assemble in front of the Courthouse, where three flags hang from three poles, and where on a red mat the chairs are set out under a canopy, awaiting the arrival of the dignitaries. The seating is clearly hierarchical: angled wooden forms beyond the canopy for the public, vinyl padded chairs with arms and a single squab for cabinet ministers, and in the centre of the front row, four two-squabbed chairs for the Chief Justice, the Queen's Representative and their wives.

Today, a lawyer friend explains to me, there is no chair for the Prime Minister. Because of the political upheaval he has had to resign just thirty-three hours before the ceremony. Until a new leader is elected by a majority in the House of Representatives, leadership of the island nation, under the terms of the very constitution we have come here to honour, is vested in the Queen's Representative.

The seats are quietly filled until only four at the front remain vacant. Then the Chief Justice, bewigged, bemedalled and robed in scarlet, is shown to his seat, along with his wife. At precisely nine o'clock the Queen's Representative arrives, and as he does, the band breaks into 'God Save the Queen'. He inspects the Girls' Brigade, then, this demanding duty to the nation discharged, takes his place in the centre of the front row. The anthem of the Cook Islands is played, and only a light shower which falls during its playing dulls the performance, something of a reminder perhaps of the crisis through which the Cook Islands is passing. The politicians are undoubtedly scheming, but as I study their expressions during the speeches I can see no signs of ambition in their faces. In fact, as the speeches end, and the dancing begins — again, each island is represented — there is decorum, courtesy and pride all round. Mostly pride, and I think, yes, rightly so. For in spite of the crisis, order and stability have been maintained.

In the middle of Constitution Week in this nation of fifteen scattered islands and atolls whose population totals only eighteen thousand, something special has happened: the constitution, the statutory hoop of iron holding the islands together, has been seen by its people to work. And I can't help wondering how New Zealand, the colonial ruler of the Cook Islands for sixty-four years, would react in a similar crisis. New Zealand does not have a written constitution.

The celebrations are not over yet. There is sport (cricket, rugby, golf, bowls, netball, karate, a road race and women's rugby), a choir competition at the park, the announcements of the festival winners, the presentation of trophies. Then, at the week's end, the singing subsides, the last speech and prayer are said. The dancers and the sports team leave their hostels beside the park to return to Penrhyn, to Mitiaro, to Mangaia, to Atiu, to Aitutaki, to Manihiki. The politicians return to Parliament to resolve their differences passionately, but democratically.

Constitution celebrations in the Cook Islands are over until the last Friday before August, next year. Mrs Taruia was right. It's great fun.

Niue: Rock of Ages

Sunk are thy bowers, in shapeless ruin all,
And the long grass o'ertops the mouldering wall,
And trembling, shrinking from the spoiler's hand,
Far, far away thy children leave the land.
— *Oliver Goldsmith*, The Deserted Village, *1770*

Aeons ago a crustal convulsion beneath the Pacific heaved a huge coral atoll and its lagoon up sixty metres above the sea. In time the coral fossilised into limestone and its surface weathered into a veneer of soil which supported tropical bush and rainforest. About one thousand eight hundred years ago people from Tonga and Samoa discovered the big uplifted rock, named it, settled it, adapting skilfully to its topography, living by fishing and farming.

James Cook and his crew sighted Niue's rugged shores on 20 June 1774. Cook took possession of the island for Britain the next day, somewhat unconvincingly, for on the three occasions he tried to land on the west coast, coral rocks and small arms fire were exchanged, obliging the Englishmen to sail away without making satisfactory landfall, although the explorer fixed its position nicely. Cook had his revenge on the locals by naming Niue 'Savage Island', a name which to this day Niueans find offensive.

As he sailed away west, Cook noted of the island with felicitous imagery, 'To judge the whole garment by the skirts it cannot produce much, for so much as we saw of it consisted wholy (sic) of coral rocks all overrun with trees shrubs etc and not a bit of soil was to be seen.'

The Yorkshireman then speculated on how the coral rocks, first formed in the sea, came to be thrown up to such a height, a pertinent question which had to await the following century and the new science of geology for a definitive response.

In the 1840s the English missionaries came, and with the assistance of a Niuean convert, Peniamina, Christianised the island. Niue chiefs gained British protection in 1900, and in 1901 Niue was annexed to New Zealand. In 1974 the island achieved self-government in free association with New Zealand, the most significant implication of this being that Niueans had open access to that country.

Niue is like a big dish, 258 square kilometres in size, diamond-shaped, raised above the Pacific Ocean in the centre of a triangle formed by Samoa, Tonga and Rarotonga. It is a rough diamond, its cliffs battered and undercut by the sea, its ancient coral pinnacles scalpel-sharp, its coastline and skirting reef offering no still-water anchorage. There is no surface water: no streams, rivers or lakes, and droughts are not uncommon. The island absorbs the tropical rainfall like a giant sponge, so that the main water supply must be extracted through artesian bores.

For years on Niue they tried to earn an export income from their traditional occupation, agriculture — copra, coconuts, kumara, passionfruit, limes. Nothing worked. One local entrepreneur even tried freezing and exporting the very good, dry-grown Niuean taro to New Zealand, but the scheme came to grief for the usual reasons — poor distribution and marketing. The skeletal soil, periodic storms and droughts, fickle shipping and prohibitive air freight costs meant that agricultural schemes on Niue, as elsewhere on isolated Pacific islands, usually ended in backbreak and heartbreak.

Emigration began in the fifties and sixties and reached a peak in the following decade. Niueans, drawn by relatively high wages and overtime in the factories of Auckland, turned their backs on their bush gardens, left their villages and took the plane to New Zealand. The main export of Niue became Niueans. Whole families flew away, wrote back and encouraged the rest to uproot themselves. The contemporary population figures stand out as starkly as the coral pinnacles which surround Niue: 2,200 still live on the island, 2,000 live in Sydney, 12,000 in New Zealand.

And as the people flew away, remittances and New Zealand aid money became the primary source of income for Niue, the aid going mainly towards maintaining a bloated government bureaucracy. By 1988–89 New Zealand 'Development Assistance' money, as it was decorously termed, totalled NZ $9.2 million, or $4,180 per capita for the 2,200 people left on the island. This was the second in total (to the Cook Islands) in absolute terms, but by far the highest per capita figure from New Zealand to a Pacific nation.

While some on Niue stretched the point by claiming that such financial help to people who are in law New Zealand citizens could not be strictly considered 'aid', the machete-wielding aid-cutters in the New Zealand government were not moved by semantic distinctions. In 1991 financial aid was cut by half a million dollars, and the Niueans were urged to get on and develop their private sector. The first of the lay-offs of public servants began.

So how can the remaining 2,200 people on the world's largest coral rock survive today? How can they earn the cash to pay for expensive but essential imports like machinery, fuel, aluminium boats and freezers? To finance their hospital and pay for their children's education when the New Zealand government is cutting financial aid? What future can there be for an island which is separated from its nearest neighbour by five hundred kilometres of open ocean, an island where the soil is so thin that a compressor and a pneumatic drill are needed to dig a decent grave to bury its dead? They opt, inevitably, for tourism.

But then there were the airline woes. A scheduled air link with the world beyond is a remote island's life-support system, but in the late eighties a pilots' strike and a dispute with the New Zealand Civil Aviation Authority caused the suspension of

Niue's main air service. For two years the only regular way in or out of the island was the once-a-week flight by small plane via American Samoa, a circuitous and uncomfortable access route which impeded all but the most resolute and resourceful travellers. Gradually and not without difficulty, a major air service was re-established. The island's hotel was repaired following a cruelly destructive cyclone. Niue became poised to try to make itself pay in the only way possible.

Friday, 28 August 1992 is the most significant day yet in the island's attempts to create a tourist industry. A Boeing 737, leased to the Niue government from Polynesian Airlines, lands at Hanan Airport, Niue Island, in the early evening, with a full load of passengers. Nearly all are New Zealanders who have responded to an expensive promotion campaign, a vile local winter and a cheap package deal offering a week on Niue Island. Hardly any of them have been here before, including myself.

As I emerge from the airport it's immediately obvious that the arrival of the once-a-week flight is a big event on the island. There are hundreds of excited people outside, laughing, calling, taking bags, draping fern garlands around necks. The plane is going on to Rarotonga, and I have time to greet my friend and writing colleague Dick Scott, who's been on Niue researching his book on the 1953 murder of the New Zealand resident commissioner. Dick's now onward-bound for Rarotonga, in pursuit of others who still remember the traumatic affair.

Our bags are piled aboard a truck and we are taken by bus to the Niue Hotel, a few minutes' drive from Alofi. This was the building that was blitzed by Cyclone Ofa on 4 February, 1990, despite being on a cliff-top twenty-five metres above the sea. A mounted series of photos on the bar wall shows the devastation. The hotel looks like a Sarajevo suburb, bombarded not by mortars but by coral boulders hurled at point blank range by a frenzied sea.

Today the rebuilding of Niue's only hotel is complete. Although it lacks a true Pacific atmosphere — there are no fales, few mature trees or gardens, and the architecture is Kiwi provincial — it is clean, airy and modern. The rooms are comfortable and there is a swimming pool on the lawn which also gives grandstand views of Alofi Bay and the schools of tuna and whales which from time to time cavort their way along the coast.

Niue lacks the spectacular peaks of the high volcanic islands, and its few beaches are concealed, enfolded by coral rock, but I soon appreciate that this island has an undeniable beauty all its own. The ubiquitous coconut palms lend grace to any landscape, the occasional banyan, aerial roots streaming groundward, stands majestic amid the bush, and the many acacia trees with their feathery foliage and outsize pods give an African aspect to the island.

Although the highest point on Niue is sixty-eight metres, the elevation is fairly uniform, giving views of the sea from any point on its perimeter, which was in pre-uplift times the rim of the atoll. The centre of the island is bush-covered, but even here the old coral protrudes like harrows through the vegetation or farmed plots. And all around the island, where the rim dips or plunges to the sea, the landforms are a wonder.

Rainfall soaks into Niue, permeating the coral rock, forming a lens of fresh water metres underground. Around the edges of the island, at sea level, the water leaks out, sometimes forcefully, eroding the limestone and sculpting the rock into a karst landscape. At Avaiki, on the west coast, the track from the plateau to the sea descends through a sloping cavern, emerging onto the reef.

The cave is festooned with stalagmites and stalactites, pale brown in colour, their ends dripping like the dicks of old men. On the walls and ceiling the rock is smooth and tactile, shaped into fantastic patterns, like globs of candle-wax. In places the stalagmites and stalactites have met, forming fluted columns of stone, like petrified tree trunks, and at the base of the caverns are blue-green pools, part-fresh, part-saline, where tiny fluorescent fish and sea urchins make their home.

In several places around Niue's coast the emerging fresh water has cut gashes in the rock, creating chasms with walls fifty metres high.

Togo chasm is reached after a level walk through a virgin rainforest of mahogany, Tahitian chestnut, pandanus and banyans. The forest ends abruptly, giving way to a steeply sloping zone of coral pinnacles from which there are huge views of an ocean so blue it is almost purple. I pick my way through the pinnacles, which can lacerate at a touch. The track plunges further, swings right, and I am at the chasm lip. Then a sturdy ladder takes me down a further nine metres to the floor of the Togo chasm.

It is covered with coral sand of the purest white, hurled there during tropical tempests through a cave at the ocean end. The sand is as soft as powder, and provides a nursery for a number of coconut palms which have taken root on the canyon floor. The surrounding rock walls are dark grey and perfectly perpendicular, over thirty metres high on the landward side, only a little less on the seaward, and the chasm itself is only a few metres across.

Togo is like a secret chamber, soundless, utterly windless, pure, a unique wonder of the Pacific. I wander up to the end, scramble over a heap of boulders. At this the landward end the floor of the chasm is covered with moss, and the palms are more profuse. I go a few more metres until the way is blocked by a pool of murky green water. The canyon tapers, and there is no way in without special equipment. I return to the soft, white sand, stand and gaze up again at the sheer rock walls, think perversely, what a magnificent place for a candlelit dinner party. This impure notion is replaced by the refrain of an old song which springs to mind: 'Rock of Ages, Cleft for Me'.

A few weeks later, back in Auckland, I attend the launching of the first Niuean novel, *The Shark that Ate the Sun* by John Puhiatau Pule. The launch is held in conjunction with an exhibition of paintings, Liku, by Pacific artist Mark Cross. Almost magically, the Cross paintings of Niue's coastline capture its beauty. They are imbued with the island's light, filtered through its caves and chasms. The paintings are spellbinding in their blend of the natural and the mystical.

John Pule's novel, the story of an emigrant family who exchange life on the Rock for one of degradation and violence in central and south Auckland, is raw, angry, cyclonic in its power.

Together Mark Cross and John Pule have brought the island of Niue to the attention of the world of Art and Letters.

You can't be long on Niue without meeting Russell Kars. If you want anything from a motorbike to a set of golf clubs, from a tour of the island to a bottle of tonic water, Russell will sell it to you.

He's in his fifties, an expatriate Kiwi who came to Niue from Taupo in 1962 after he completed his joinery apprenticeship. He came on a two-year contract and three decades later has no intention of leaving. He married a local girl and they have three daughters and nine grandchildren. Soon his youngest daughter and her doctor husband will be moving back to Niue, where he will be the first New Zealand-qualified Niuean doctor.

Russell is Niue's leading capitalist. He moved into house alterations in 1967, began importing timber and hardware, then taking 'boat-day orders', delivering groceries and frozen foods and supplying the village stores before starting the island's first supermarket. It's called, with a fine disregard for commercial copyright, K- (for Kars) Mart.

Everything about Russell is large: hands, feet, nose, ears. His arms hang loosely at his side, primate-style, half his upper teeth are missing, he has an untidy auburn moustache and a suntanned bald strip down the centre of his head. He wears a loose, tropical shirt, shorts and jandals, the only concession to fashion being the gold chain around his neck. He's involved in car and bike rentals, postcard publishing and island tours, as well as retail food supplies. It was Russell who, a few weeks earlier, drove around the North Island, visiting travel agents and extolling Niue as a holiday destination. It was mainly Russell, in other words, who filled up the 737 I came on. His open nature and fine sense of humour mask a shrewd commercial brain, and, unusually for a businessman in a small community, he's well liked.

As we share a beer I appreciate that Russell has witnessed Niue's evolution from colony to self-government to today's moves to economic independence. In fact his own career has been a precursor of privatisation. He describes the dark times when Niueans were prohibited from buying alcohol.

'They brewed bush-beer, which was made from coconuts, pawpaw, cabin bread, sugar and meths. It was potent, as you might expect. The elders were allowed to buy an allocation of the beer, but they knew that if they took it back to the village everyone else would want some, so they would get their quota and drink it just outside the village, under the mango tree there. Then when the sale of booze was made open, in the late sixties, drunkenness stopped.'

The lesson of prohibition, writ small. Today there is so little crime on Niue that the prison farm has closed down. What few offenders there are are given community work to do.

Later in the week I'm in Russell's rental car office. A well-dressed, middle-aged New Zealand man is returning his hired car, and hasn't been able to top up the petrol tank. He offers to pay cash instead.

'I haven't been far,' he pleads. 'About two dollars worth of gas, I'd say.'

Russell gives him a hooded look. 'Where did you go?'

'Oh . . . up to Avatele, along to Hakupu, back across the island . . .'

I can see Russell mentally tracing this route, calculating kilometreage on roads he must have travelled on a thousand times. The man reaches in his pockets, pulls out a coin.

'As I said, two dollars' worth.'

Russell closes one eye, and declares in a manner brooking no argument, 'Six bucks.'

Every other Saturday on Niue is inter-village cricket day. Matches are played on the village greens, but that's where the resemblance between kilikiti and the English version of cricket begins and ends.

I stand at the end of Alofi's uncut green, the Lords of Niue, trying to make out exactly what's happening. For a start there are more than eleven fieldsman and two batsmen out there — about thirty at a rough count, boys and young men in shorts, gym shoes and T-shirts. Women, girls and very young children watch from palm-frond shelters at either end of the green.

There are wickets, a pitch of sorts, the two batsmen, yes, but their bats are like large, angular war-clubs, and alongside each batsman are a number of other men who carry very long whips. A few fieldsmen stand at the edge of the green, others are on the road, some sit on the wall bordering the green.

A bowler lopes in, hurls down the ball. The batsman swings, connects with it on the full, lofts it high over an acacia tree beyond the edge of the green. Everyone whoops and claps as the chaps with the whips sprint to the other end, turn and run back. The ball is found and thrown to a bowler. It's a very hard ball, the Niue special, unlike the Samoan cricket ball, which is made of bound rubber. This is a lacrosse ball, imported from Canada, and it has the weight and density of iron. But the batsmen have superb hand–eye co-ordination: one smites a full toss across the green, across the road, over the wharf and into the sea, precipitating cheers, shouts and prolonged hilarity. A man in the outfield dons mask and flippers and dives to the bottom to retrieve it.

I can't comprehend the rules, but it's clear that everyone's having a great time. A burst of frenetic belting of the ball and whip-cracking charges between the wickets is followed by long periods of idleness and chat. Perhaps not so different from the flannelled version, after all.

As I watch the Alofi-Hakupu match unfold I see a low, claret-coloured limousine glide up and park across the road from the green. The car has the number plate 1. I immediately recognise the slumped figure, the bald, skull-like head behind the wheel of the limo.

Sir Robert Rex, Premier, took the Rock to self-government in 1974 and has been its first citizen ever since. Now in his eighties and in delicate health, his people are worried about him, not just for his own sake, but because he has no obvious successor. He clearly commands great respect, and it is apparent that nothing, but *nothing,* happens on this island without the Premier knowing or hearing about it. The best story about him I heard concerns his amazing memory.

A lawyer in Alofi told me that he had a client who lived in

Samoa but had Niuean antecedents. The man wished to use this Niuean family connection to claim New Zealand citizenship, but the problem for the lawyer was in obtaining proof that the man's grandfather had indeed been Niuean. The lawyer went to Sir Robert.

'The Premier,' the lawyer told me, 'not only remembered the man, the date his ship sailed from Niue in 1929, the name of the ship which took him, but he told me what clothes my client's grandfather was wearing as he went out to the ship.'*

Shortly afterwards, towards mid-morning, I leave the cricket, but I drive past the green several times that Saturday. The cricket continues, all morning, all afternoon, and concludes only when darkness descends over the island. I ask one of the players — who had to be taken to the hospital to have the webbing in one hand stitched after he stopped a crashing hit — who won. He looks perplexed at the question.

'Uh . . . I think we made about . . . 400 runs. And Hakupu made . . .' he shrugs. 'I don't know what they made. About the same.'

'So who won?'

'I don't know.' He grins. 'It doesn't matter. It was a good game.'

Everywhere in the villages there are empty houses — not derelict, because they were strongly built, with poured concrete walls and roofs of corrugated fibrolite. But now they are windowless and silent, surrounded by incontinent tropical undergrowth. They resemble old-style bus shelters, standing in open reproach of the passengers who have taken one-way tickets to Grey Lynn, Kingsland or Otara.

I have with me a letter from two Auckland Niuean teenagers, Jasmin and April Etuata, to take to their grandmother in the village of Hakupu. I drive into the village in the late morning. There are the usual empty houses, but others which are clearly still inhabited. Washing is spread out on the grass to dry, doors

---

* On 12 December 1992, at the age of eighty-three, Sir Robert Rex died.

are open, but along the dusty limestone road which bisects the village nothing moves. No radios, no children's cries. I knock on a couple of doors before coming upon a house where there is a pareu-clad girl of about nineteen. I show her the name on the envelope. The girl points to a driveway.

'Down there. The old school. She is down there.'

Every village used to have its own school. Another consequence of emigration is that today the primary schools have been rationalised, with the young children all attending one school in the main town of Alofi, leaving a long, empty classroom block in every village.

Empty? Not quite. As I drive across the playing field to the building I see that one room is still occupied — by elderly women, among them Trixie Ikinepule. She is large, dark-faced, welcoming. I give her the letter, which she leaves unopened for the moment. She beckons me into the room.

The women, most in their sixties, sit on the floor around the walls of the room. Mats and pillows in the centre of the room provide a resting place for several pre-school children who look at me inquisitively. The women smile and continue their work, chatting and laughing among themselves.

They are weaving baskets, hats, place-mats and bags, using strips of dried pandanus. Half-completed crafts are everywhere, a white hat with a still-frayed brim, a coiled, catherine-wheel place mat with its palm-frond core protruding, a basket with its handles not yet woven into place.

Niuean crafts are famous, and it's not difficult to see why. The beautiful chequered patterns created by dyeing some of the pandanus black, the intricacy and symmetry of the designs, the care and finish of the weaving: all go to making an item which is at the same time aesthetically pleasing, useful and long lasting. It's clear too that although the work is labour-intensive, it's also sociable, relaxing, and keeps a village tradition alive.

Mrs Ikinepule explains that today her group is finishing a consignment of hats for sending to the women of Rarotonga, who recently sent them boxes of oranges. Hats for oranges. It's not hard to see that the Rarotongan women are getting the best of the exchange.

Niue is a dome of coral rock atop an ancient volcano. It has long been suspected that the volcanic material contains uranium, or gold, or both. For the last few years an Australian drilling team has been boring down into the coral cap. Their deepest hole went down seven hundred metres and still met only coral, another went down five hundred and is rumoured to have come across traces of more interesting material, but nobody's saying just what.

Russell Kars has told me that the Australians want to do more drilling, but they need more money. They won't get any from Russell, he makes it clear; he's already lost capital over the venture.

And the prospect of large-scale mining of this island brings out the rabid greenie in me. Because Niue has no streams to pour sediment into its surrounding sea, and because it has no wide lagoon, it has the clearest, deepest inshore waters of any Pacific island. Mining, particularly strip mining, could turn this place into another Nauru.

When I snorkel off the wharf in Alofi, I can see for nearly forty-five metres. Although I am stuck near the surface like a fly on a ceiling, every detail of the sea bottom far below is visible, every rock, every reef fish, even the outline of a sunken boat. I can see canyons of coral rock and the graceful movements of a small, white-pointed reef shark as it patrols the sea bed like a traffic warden. Then, just one hundred metres from the wharf, there is a sudden fall-off and the deep purple hue of the fathomless ocean abyss. In parts of Niue you can stand on a cliff and cast a line just metres out, and it will land in water over thirty metres deep. And for that reason the island's fishing is uniquely accessible.

Every man here fishes, with a bamboo rod from the rocks, with a net from an aluminium dinghy, or with a prong-like device from a traditional canoe. The Niuean canoe — the vaka — is a small, light outrigger whose hull is hewn from the trunk of a moota tree and whose outrigger is made from a fou sapling. It has to be light to be carried down the cliff on the owner's shoulder. The canoes are kept in the many storm-proof caves which pock the coastal cliffs, and are launched at dusk.

Ernie Walsh is a Kiwi electrician who came to Niue in 1955, married a local girl, returned with her to Christchurch to raise their large family, and came back with her in 1987 to retire. But Ernie has only semi-retired, because he has a five-metre aluminium boat, *Tuaki*, rigged for fishing. He's sharp-eyed, fit, and extremely knowledgeable about local conditions.

The derrick swings *Tuaki* out from the concrete wharf and lowers her into the water. It is nine o'clock on a nearly moonless Niuean night. Ernie starts the 400 hp Mariner outboard, manoeuvres up to the wharf and we climb down into the boat.

There is a light atop a PVC stem on the prow of *Tuaki*, another glows from a stem at the stern. We cruise out through the inky sea, turn east. Conditions are good, with a cuticle moon shining weakly away to the west. My Niuean friend, Faama, stands in the bow, I stand in the stern, braced against a corner railing. The nets we hold have three-metre-long wooden handles which make them cumbersome but give good reach. *Tuaki* rolls gently as we motor along the coast. I peer at the water. What exactly happens next?

Faama shouts from the bow. 'There!'

Looking left, I see a small fish, skittering across the surface of the black water. It darts in one direction, then tacks back in another. Ernie swings the wheel to starboard but the fish has gone.

'Behind you!' Faama calls, and turning, I see the fish zoom like a missile towards the boat. Clumsily I shove the net out, lunge, and hear a whoop of triumph from Faama and a chuckle from Ernie. By extraordinarily good luck for me, and a large amount of ill-fortune for the fish, it has flown straight into my net. I haul the net in, grab the fish and drop it in the bucket, where it flops pathetically, wings beating against the sides of the bucket.

For the next two hours we cruise slowly along the coast, from time to time swiping and scooping at the creatures which leap, flutter and glide at *Tuaki*'s lights. Occasionally the fish leap at the light, land in the water and float inert, wings furled, as if waiting to be scooped up. Others are more assertive. One launches itself from the water like a small rocket and flies straight at Faama's face. He ducks just in time, and it swishes past me and back into the water.

Fly fishing, as it's termed, is a combination of lepidoptery, whitebaiting and small-game hunting. It's also hilarious, at least for those on board, although more than half the fish that come for our light manage to escape the nets. Even those which stun themselves by striking our gunwales usually sink immediately.

Sea snakes, there are also sea snakes everywhere. They lie atop the water, twisted into S-shapes, ribbon-like, unafraid of human intruders. I recall Coleridge.

> *Within the shadow of the ship*
> *I watched their rich attire:*
> *They coiled and swam; and every track . . .*
> *Was a flash of golden fire.*

They are indeed banded, usually yellow and black, and venomous, although their mouths are so small they find it difficult to get a grip on a human. The skin between the fingers is something they can get their mouth around, Faama tells me.

Curious, coming from a snakeless land, I scoop up a couple in the net, but they slip through the mesh. Then Faama nets a bigger one, pulls it aboard and drops it in the bucket. It convulses, writhes its way out, slithers across the bottom of the boat towards me. I have seldom seen anything so repulsive, and am about to leap overboard when I remember that there are many more out there in the water, waiting, so I jump up on the gunwale until Faama, laughing helplessly, snatches the snake up and gives it back its freedom.

At half past eleven, with sixteen flying fish in the bucket, we draw up alongside the wharf. Ernie's wife Hine is there with the tractor, the boat is hooked up to the derrick, Hine drives the tractor off a few metres and *Tuaki* is hoisted from the water and onto her trailer. It's quicker than using a boat ramp, and besides, there is no ramp, even on this the leeward side of the island, because of the persistent swell.

Under the wharf light I examine the catch. Flying fish are

shaped like big herrings, though they have much larger eyes and their skin is slimier, to assist, I assume, their egress from the water. It's their strong tail that they use to break the tension between water and air, the large, delicate, folding wings are used for gliding, and can keep them airborne for fifty metres or so. They're good eating, if a bit bony.

Ernie takes the catch, which will be used as bait for substantially larger prey the day after next. Already I'm of the opinion that if people knew how much fun fly fishing was, they'd be queuing up to do it.

Andrew Hellesoe is twenty-eight. He and his palagi wife, Michelle, live in Beachhaven, Auckland, and have come to Niue for a holiday with their infant son, Luke. Andrew, born in New Zealand to Niuean migrant parents, is tall, athletic, a keen sportsman. He has his own building business, and he and his family have clearly prospered in New Zealand.

This is Andrew's first trip back to Niue as an adult. While here he's been visiting relatives, playing golf, scuba diving. He's enjoying the island, but wouldn't want to live here. His roots may be in Niue, but his branches are in Auckland. He screws his eyes up against the sun, looks pensive.

'It's been great for me, seeing my aunty and other relations. And the scuba diving's terrific. Warm water, so easy to get to. Back at home I go to the Poor Knights. It's good, but it's isolated, and the water's cold.' *Back at home.* He smiles. 'It's good to dive off the Alofi wharf, too, you know? For years my Dad talked about doing that, when he was a kid. Only now I see how important that wharf is to everyone on the island.' He nods. 'I'm a Kiwi, but we'll definitely come back here again.'

Driving through the village of Tuapa, I look again at those abandoned but still habitable houses, and think, why couldn't they be used by budget travellers? It wouldn't take much money to convert them to plain but adequate accommodation. Why doesn't someone do it?

Like the few ideas I ever have for making money, someone's already thought of it. The tourist people and the villagers are considering renting the empty houses for what the industry calls 'long-stay' visitors, people who would like a month or two on the island. European backpackers, who these days swarm all over the Pacific, are the obvious market. Most would relish a few weeks in a Niuean village. I once met a Swedish woman in Samoa who had fallen in love on Niue and with Niue but had to move on because she couldn't find cheap enough accommodation. I could imagine Ingrid in one of those Tuapa houses.

We pull away from the Alofi wharf on *Tuaki* again, this time at dawn. Ernie has her rigged with two rods, one on each gunwale, and two reel lines. Faama attaches lures to the reel lines and bait to the rods. The reels are made, with typical island ingenuity, from old motorbike hubs with handles welded to them, and they trail plastic lures about ten metres behind the boat. The lures are teasers for the main bait, flying fish, which troll much further behind. The two dead fish are attached to traces attached to the rods, and inside the bait are concealed two large, lethal-looking double hooks.

As we roll slowly along the coast the horizon turns an apricot shade and a glowing orange sun rises from the sea. The sky turns bright and clear apart from a trail of small grey clouds just above the horizon. To starboard, Niue is a long, black, level expanse, like the profile of a slumbering whale.

By the time we round the northern end of the island, daybreak is complete and the coastal features are vividly clear. The grey-brown cliffs are about twenty metres high, notched where fresh water has emerged at the lens edge, and neatly undercut by the sea. There is bush on the highest ground, the occasional canoe landing, but no other sign of human settlement. It occurs to me that this, the skirt of the island, must have been Niue just as Cook and his men first viewed it from the *Resolution*, in June 1774.

Now we are adjacent to the eastern coast, the windward side of the island. Although the trade winds are gentle today, the swells are strong and the water occasionally turbulent as current and tide conflict. *Tuaki* rolls on. We can see the lures and baits tumbling in our wake. The sun is hot, the sky almost cloudless, the sea silken. Although we are fishless, it's a sublimely pleasant way to start the day.

And we have company out here, in the form of the little vaka — the outrigger canoes which bob about on the ocean. They're so insubstantial that from a distance it appears that the Niuean fishermen are sitting on the sea, and I wonder how they get on if the weather is less clement.

Faama says, 'Most of those guys can't swim, so if they fall out they're in trouble. But they keep an eye on each other and help out in all kinds of ways. If one hooks into a marlin, for example, the others will see it broach and come over and help get it in. The one who's hooked it wraps the line around his thigh as a brake.'

'A nylon line, around the thigh, with a marlin at the other end?'

'Right. You look at a Niuean man's leg. He'll have line scars across it, if he's a good fisherman. Sometimes they get towed all night by a big fish.'

Could Santiago, Hemingway's old man, have been Niuean? I know there are sharks down there, so maybe 'The Old Man and the Sea' is a very old story.

With the sun climbing the sky and its rays now burning our backs, Ernie turns the boat and we begin the slow journey back. There have been no takers for our trailing morsels. I leave the rod and stand next to the skipper, beside the wheel. Ernie has a gentle, laconic, old-fashioned manner, unmistakeably a Kiwi, but one for whom this island is now part of his lineage.

'I saw an ad in the *Christchurch Press* for an electrician, to install generators on Niue Island. It was 1955, I was a young man, wanted a bit of adventure. I didn't even know where Niue was. But I applied and they flew me up to Wellington for an interview. That impressed me, and when I was offered the job I took it. A day later I was on the boat.' He smiles ruefully. 'Found out later I was the only one who applied.'

'When we reached Niue I saw a big building on the cliff, with a verandah overlooking the sea. I thought, oh the governor or someone must live there, it looked so flash. But it turned out that it was the single men's quarters, where I was going. The bach, we called it. There were a few other Kiwi tradesmen there, a schoolteacher or two. Then I met a local girl and married her, went back to Christchurch and brought our kids up there. Now they've grown up, we decided to retire to Niue.'

'Would they come to live here?'

'No, no. Wages are much too low. The wife and I only get a quarter of the superannuation that we'd get in New Zealand. That's why I'm doing these fishing trips.'

It's after ten o'clock now, the sun too bright for big fish. Ernie points out landmarks on the cliffs as we pass, a church wrecked by Ofa, a canoe landing, a new motel. But he's clearly disconsolate. He squints into the distance.

'I hate taking visitors out and not getting a fish.'

'Well, that's the way it goes. It's good just to get out on the water.'

'Yeah, but I still hate not getting . . .'

'Hey! Hey! Ernie!'

The shout comes from Faama, in the stern. Turning, I see that one rod is bent, its reel shrieking. Ernie shoves the boat into neutral, and as he does so the motorbike hub on the same side as the bent rod begins to spin. A double strike, and no time to get a harness on. I scramble aft, Faama takes the rod from its holder, hands it to me.

'Reel in, reel in! Keep the tension on!'

Braced against the stern rail, rod butt dug into my groin, I obey. What's on the other end is heavy, and fighting hard, but by applying all my energy, I feel it yield. Minutes later I see flashes of electric blue and silver behind the boat, reel harder, and the fish is alongside. Faama gaffs it, hauls the flapping fish aboard, clubs it with a wooden truncheon and goes back to winding in the rodless line.

It's a wahoo, a long, tapering, blue-black fish with a pointed head, large, upright tail and razor teeth. Blood leaks from its gills. Faama winds in the motorbike hub, a relatively simple operation, and hauls a second wahoo aboard. We must have passed through a school of them. There are whoops of glee, and I understand a possible derivation of the fish's name. When you catch one you can't help yelling, 'Wa-hoo!'

Every village on Niue has a church, a big church, sometimes an extremely big church. In Liku, a village whose population has been decimated by emigration, the church is nearly as long as the green adjacent to it, although half the houses surrounding the huge building are empty. The Liku church is built of concrete blocks, it has stainless steel guttering, long-run iron roofing — all imported from New Zealand. The cost must have been staggering. Conscious of the fact that for better or worse Christianity has most of the Pacific islands in an iron grip for a least one day a week, I go along to a Sunday morning service, in the pretty village of Avatele.

The church is large, white, steepled, on a rise above the sloping green. Ladies, all in hats, and men mostly in dark suits are ambling towards the place of worship, which although imposing by virtue of its size, looks a bit run down and in need of a paint job. I'm more used to Samoan churches, whose concrete walls are so clean and white they almost glow.

People greet me at the door, invite me to sit 'anywhere you like'. This is easily done, and although I'm a few minutes late there are only six people inside, scattered about on the wooden pews. I sit on the left-hand side and wait. With its towering ceiling the church is airy and not too hot. The high pulpit is flanked by two lower ones and all are embellished with vases filled with scarlet hibiscus.

A youngish palagi woman comes in, looks around nervously and sits on the pew next to me. She wears a white, floppy sunhat and a dark blue, floral patterned dress. With her very thin, sharp features and stick legs, she looks like a pied stilt.

She tells me that she's from Wellington, and is staying in a village guest-house. What's it like? She looks doubtful.

'I can see the cockroaches, and deal with them. But this morning there were *teethmarks* in my pawpaw.' Then she brightens. 'But after this I'm going back to finish roasting the leg of lamb we brought from New Zealand. We're having roast carrots, potatoes and Surprise peas too. And I'll do gravy. We brought all our food from home, in a suitcase. It makes the holiday much cheaper.' Roast lamb and gravy? Even now, inside the church, it's going on 27 degrees.

The pastor enters through a side door, stands on high in the pulpit, and when he sits, disappears altogether behind the lectern. He is quite young, late twenties perhaps, with short frizzy hair, a smooth, flat face and blackcurrant eyes. The service alternates between Niuean and English and most of the sermon is devoted to giving thanks in diverse directions. The pastor is assisted in his expressions of gratitude by a surprisingly adult Boys' and Girls' Brigade, who marched in at the beginning with banners and who frequently take up positions at the lower lecterns.

A collection is taken up during a hymn, and the stilt woman and I both put five dollars in the dish. The collection is promptly counted by a man at a table in the front of the church, who also writes figures in an exercise book and delivers the book to the pastor, who at the conclusion of the hymn gives thanks, 'For the offerings made today, which total twenty-six dollars and eighty cents.'

The hymns are sung in rollicking fashion to the accompaniment of a synthesiser played by a tall, slim, greying man with a small moustache who sits two pews in front of me. The singing lacks the volume and part-harmony of Cook Islands congregations, but is melodious enough to lull me into a very secular stupor.

There is a laid-back aspect to this service which is extremely relaxing. People shuffle and scratch, a dog strolls in the pastor's door and up the aisle without admonishment. The Boys' Brigade yawn, one young one goes to sleep and is woken by another passing around a packet of Cheeseballs. Babies in their grandmother's arms goo, gurgle and eventually fall asleep. My only discomfort is caused by the woman sitting immediately behind me, who has the worst case of halitosis I've ever smelt. Every time she holds a high note I'm engulfed by her toxic breath, and even by shuffling a metre to the right I can't escape the oral fallout. I should specify, I think, that a portion of my offering go towards a large packet of breath freshener for the lady parishioner behind me.

But by the time we amble out into the sunshine the air has cleared and I feel undeniably benevolent and reposeful, as if I've been meditating, which in a way I suppose I have.

The stilt woman walks off jerkily to baste her leg of lamb, a couple of elders shake my hand and thank me for coming, and that's it. There's another service after lunch, but I'll leave it to the locals. Church in the morning I can take, church in the afternoon seems excessive.

Sunday is high Victorian in its strictures: no shopping, no fishing, no working, no playing games. Swimming is just tolerated. As elsewhere in the Islands, the Mormons have poached parishioners from the traditional denominations and their besuited, beaming palagi missionaries can be seen cycling in pairs, doing God's work. But I also get the impression that the church's function is more social than spiritual, that the services, like the cricket games, are a chance for the community to get together, talk and enjoy themselves. And there's nothing wrong with that.

Later, browsing through a Seventh Day Adventist pamphlet, I see under a drawing of the Lord, a quote from Psalm 122, verse 1. 'I was gald when they said to me, Let us go into the house of the Lord.' I wasn't gald on my visit to his house, but after reading the pamphlet I do feel that the Lord on Niue, at least the Seventh Day Adventist version of Him, could do with the services of a proof reader.

Kuso Pavitti is a middle-aged Niuean whose family land is within the domain of Avatele village, at the southern end of the island. He has just completed building a bar, restaurant and surrounding bungalow units a couple of kilometres out of the village, to provide entertainment and accommodation for the tourists he hopes will now come to Niue in steady numbers.

He calls his restaurant Island Style. It is open-sided, sturdily constructed and spacious, with plastic tables and chairs to seat about fifty people. His opening night last Saturday saw the restaurant full and the palagi customers enthusiastic over the traditional Niuean food and dancing, all for just $20 a head. The menu includes the now-rare Pacific delicacy, the uga, or coconut crab.

Over a fruit juice, Kuso tells me he has put his faith in tourism by undertaking what has been at times a frustrating venture.

He points at the ceiling. 'See that big beam there? The laminated one? I had to have that to hold up the roof, it's so wide. But when the boat came with the framing and the roof iron, there was no beam.' He shakes his head. 'I can't build without the beam, so I have to wait until it comes on the next boat. Weeks later. But now I'm open, and it's okay.'

It's a brave venture, I can't help thinking as I drive away, a big investment by local standards. If the tourists come, it'll succeed, if they don't . . .

Later in the week I'm contacted by the local television station. The tourist people have heard there's a writer here and want me to appear on the local news programme, giving my impressions of the island. I've certainly formed some impressions, and I'm happy to have them recorded. They'll do the filming at eleven o'clock in the morning.

The headquarters of Niue Television is a long, barrack-like building near the hospital. Inside I meet the presenter. It's the man who played the synthesiser in church, Hima Douglas. He's affable, articulate, amusing. We loosen up, talk about what I've done since I've been on the island, what I've yet to do. Hima nods, satisfied with the way he wants the interview to go. He stands up.

'Are you happy to do the filming now?'

'Yes.'

'Fine. Let's go through to the studio then, shall we?'

I follow him, past a desk, through a door and outside on to the grass. Looking about for the studio building, all I can see is a camera set up on the grass, and two chairs under a coconut palm. Hima grins, gestures at the palm.

'Here it is then, our *outside* studio.' With the sun streaming down, and the purple Pacific in sight, we do it in one take.

Oz Vesefolu is a New Zealand-born Niuean who's returned to the island to live. Although he's done a bit of everything in his thirty years, work in New Zealand has dried up, and he's come back to Niue to see what opportunities there are now that the economy is being restructured.

Oz is small, genial, vibrant with enthusiasm. He tells me he's seen the need for a laundry on Niue, one with modern machinery which can deal with the washing of linen and towels that the hospital, the motels and, eventually the hotel will produce. He's got a friend in Rarotonga who did just that, and business is thriving. So, why not a laundry on Niue too?

Well, Rarotonga had over forty thousand tourists last year, a staggering number for an island with a population of nine thousand. Forty thousand tourists can stain an awful lot of sheets, providing the raw material for a very busy laundry, but Niue so far has had only a few hundred this year to soil the linen. All will depend on how many come from now on.

But Oz is enthusiastic and energetic, and he's spotted an opportunity, as you might say. I hope fervently that he succeeds with his enterprise, just as I hope that Niue itself succeeds. I'd happily stain a few sheets myself to help Oz's business.

The New Zealanders in the Niue Hotel are not only escaping the wretched winter, they're also husbanding their stricken currency by coming to a place where they know immediately what their dollar is worth, because Niue uses New Zealand money. And as usual, the holiday group is a farrago of the pleasant, the inoffensive and the obnoxious. And as usual too it is the obnoxious who, by their very obnoxiousness, dominate.

They are schoolteachers, physical education teachers, in their early twenties, from some small inland town like Taumarunui or Tokoroa. There are four of them, two men and two women, but they seem many more because they are very loud and very physical. They shout, at each other and to each other, around the hotel pool where they spend most of their time, in the lounge, in the dining room, on the dance floor, and they laugh, loudly and hysterically at each other's antics and each other's jokes.

Worst of the unruly quartet are a pair who may be a couple, although the thought of them coupling immediately brings to my mind an image of two mountain gorillas rutting in the rainforests of Rwanda.

He, Barry, is short, muscular and hairy. His long black hair hangs down the back of his thick neck, he has a curly black beard and a Neanderthal gait as he struts and cavorts around the pool.

She, Vicki, is short, muscular and fair, bow-legged, perhaps from weightlifting, with a freckled, punched-in face and a voice constantly amplified, probably from shouting during swimming and athletic sports. Vicki shows off constantly, walking on her hands, doing flips into the pool or climbing up the nearest vertical object, be it tree, wall or cliff, then hanging there with her arse sticking out like a baboon's. Worst of all, she has a voice like a braying mule.

'Barry! Hey Barry! Yer neck's gawn red! Awl red! Yer a red-neck, Barry! I always knew yer woz a red-neck, Barry! Look Russ, look at Barry's neck!'

This, on a minibus crammed with passengers. Every time we disembark to inspect a sight of natural wonder, the P.E. teachers jump from the vehicle, throw themselves about, yell at each other, and Vicki climbs up something. Then they shout again.

'Hey, Russ, how d'yuh say g'day in Nu-ay-an?'

'Fuck-a somethin . . . How d'yuh say it, Vuck?'

'Ut's fucka-loafer somethin'. What's the rest of it, Bev?'

'I told you before. It's fucka-loafer-la-hee-ah-too, dummy. Like in Maori y'say ki-a-aw-ra, here huh say fucka-loafer-la-hee-ah-too. Go on Russ, say ut to that old joker over there-a. Fucka-loafer-la-hee-ah-too.'

'Fucka . . . oh Jesus, I can't rememba the rest of ut . . . You say ut to 'im, Vuck.'

'Okay. Fucka-loafer-la-hee-ah-too. How are yuh?'

The old man looks up from his chair, nods, smiles politely at the posturing fool, while the rest of the Kiwis on the bus cringe with embarrassment.

The crassness and the exhibitionism of the P.E. teachers grows by the day. The neighing laugh and bandy, strutting gait of Vicki, Barry's red neck and dangling goatee, Bev's miniscule bikini stretched over her huge breasts, Russell's hairy, leering face, all pose a real threat to the motto of Niue. Discover Tranquillity. The thought of these ghastly people being role models for adolescents fills me with despair.

Then, just as I think I can take no more, that I will berate the lot of them no matter how large a scene it creates, the P.E. teachers disappear and take their boorish antics with them.

They disappear not because they have moved on, or because they fall down a chasm, although I devoutly wished this to happen, but because they go under water. Being very physical, very macho people, they have to take a scuba diving course, and because there is such a course to be taken on Niue, the P.E. teachers take it. They have to learn pages of notes about air pressure and safety procedures, they have to shoulder oxygen cylinders and stick apparatus in their mouths, and best of all, they have to submerge for hours on end. All of which has the blissful consequence of shutting up the P.E. teachers and getting them out of everyone else's way. The peace of the Rock returns.

One of the most appealing aspects of any island is that it draws eccentrics to it, people who have retreated from a large, densely populated land mass to a circumscribed world surrounded by sea, in the hope or belief that their habits will go beyond the forces of convention, and so remain intact. And to a large extent that is so. I have met or observed many people on islands whose behaviour and way of life would be subjected to ridicule or disdain on a mainland, but which is accepted philosophically by their fellow-islanders, perhaps because all islanders, however conventional their appearance, are individualists at heart.

I couldn't imagine, for instance, the Italian environmental sculptor I met on Upolu, practising his art in Milan, where he came from. Gino went from lagoon-side village to lagoon-side village, setting up trios of trimmed palm tree trunks per-pendicularly in the sand, aligning them perfectly east-west. What for? To use the force created by his sculpture to repair the hole in the ozone layer, naturally.

On Niue you don't have to look far to find the E-team. Every evening, for example, just out of Alofi, a pair of swim-suited Americans, a man and a woman, come down to a small bay, bearing a kind of harness. They slip into a large rock pool, secure one end of the harness to the shore and the other to themselves, and swim.

They swim and swim, steadily, diligently, one arm over, then the other, for an hour, and they stay precisely in the same spot. When this aquatic exercycling began, some time ago, the locals would gather at the top of the steps leading down to the water and watch in wonder. Some of the children giggled, which upset the Americans, but now they are just part of local life. Rumour has it that the swimmers-who-go-nowhere are former flower children and acid-droppers who left not only their hearts but many of their brain cells in San Francisco.

On Niue there is also the usual impermanent population of yachties, moving through the Pacific before the cyclone season begins. Their boats are moored in Alofi Bay, and on their visits ashore they add a cosmopolitan flavour to the island. While I'm here the little flotilla includes some nautical Sloane Rangers — *very* Public School — some Americans, some Germans, and Philippe and Heidi, from Switzerland.

Within days everyone knows Philippe and Heidi. He is about thirty-five, and very skinny, with an untidy beard, and red hair like a pot-scourer. He goes around the island in shorts and bare feet.

Heidi is about 1.32 metres, with blonde, Joan-of-Arc-style hair. She is about sixty. Philippe and Heidi are burnt dark brown by the Pacific sun.

Philippe grins and shouts to everyone on the island as he passes. 'Hellaw! How are you! Ees fine day! Yes! Good day for swee-ming, for snark-ling, ah, yes!' And always at his side, tiny, ageing Heidi beams a grin as wide as the horizon.

One morning on the wharf I see them loading a palm-frond basket of coconuts into their inflatable tender and call out greetings. Philippe grins dementedly, waves his arms around his head.

'Yes, yes, ees lovely day! Wonderful day! We get coco-nuts, see?'

Heidi nods, beams, points down at the laden basket.

'Where have you sailed from?' I ask.

Philippe flings his arms in a roughly northern direction.

'Med-dee-ter-ran-ean! West Af-ri-ca! West In-dies! Pun-a-mah! Tah-hi-tee! Rar-ro-tong-ga! And now . . .' He looks around confusedly, as if seeking a signpost. '. . . And now . . . we are . . . here!'

'It's a long trip you're on then.'

His eyes widen further, he leans back, shouts. 'Yes, yes, long long trip! Not over yet! Rest of world! New Zee-land! Aus-stral-lee-ah! Malay-zhee-ah! And . . . oth-ers . . . Very hard work! We go now, to boat, with coconuts! Ees lovely day, yes!'

And the odd couple push off in their inflatable, a boatful of nuts and nutters.

On a visit to friends in a new motel atop a cliff in Avaiki, I ask if their accommodation is satisfactory. 'Oh yes,' says Jane, 'it's lovely here.' Then she frowns. 'Apart from the Germans next door.'

There are three Germans in the next unit, she explains, two men and a woman, who make a lot of noise. Not raging parties or anything like that, but radio transmitting, most of the day and all of the night. They call Berlin, Munich, Hamburg on their powerful transmitter, and the sounds of transmission carry through the wall, especially in the still of night.

Jane adds that she saw one of the Germans pay one of the Niueans who is working on the building site adjacent to the hotel $5 to climb up the big coconut palm outside their unit, with an aerial. He stuck it on the top, then climbed down again. The Niuean man told Jane that the Germans chose this motel especially, because it was the only one with a very tall palm tree right outside the door.

At first I think Jane must be exaggerating about the radio noise, but when on my departure I pass their unit, sure enough they are at it, headphones on, frowning with concentration, twiddling dials, speaking German into microphones. They're young people, only in their early twenties. What on earth is going on here?

Back at my hotel, I mention this odd behaviour to a friend, David, who happens to be Jewish. He laughs, but there is a degree of unease in his mirth.

'Are you sure they're Germans?'

'Quite sure. They come from Bavaria.'

David's smile goes altogether. 'Bavaria. Hitler had his power base there, didn't he?' He glances around, with feigned anxiety. 'Could they be preparing for the new world order?'

It's all too much for me to leave unsatisfied, so I enquire further. Yes, most people have seen the Germans, but no one knows precisely why they're here. People assume that they're just tourists, not having seen their broadcasting equipment. I get nowhere with my enquiries until I ask Stafford Guest, expatriate Kiwi proprietor of Sails restaurant, down the road. He shrugs.

'The Germans? They're radio hams. Lots of them come here, the reception's so clear. No interference. And by sending their calling cards to Europe from such an obscure island, the cards become quite valuable.'

'Relax, David. They're just radio hams.'

David frowns, conspiratorially. 'Radio hams? The perfect cover.'

There are extravagant eccentrics and tiny eccentrics. There is a Niuean woman on the island who serves delicious Devonshire teas, scones and strawberry jam on the concrete deck of her house, among the tropical foliage. The local Crown Solicitor plays bass guitar in the Alofi rock band The Black Diamonds. Best of all, these people are unaware that they are eccentric, which adds to their appeal.

As the 737 ascends from Hanan Airport I stare down at Niue, lying pikelet-like in the early morning light, surrounded by the fathomless Pacific. The island looks unexceptional from up here, but I now know what secrets that apparently featureless coast-line conceals: chasms, caves, arches, coves, rock pools and freshwater springs. The jet banks and I glimpse the notch in the wavy coastline that is Avatele Bay, then a sweep of green, a white-spired church. The plane levels out on its course for Tonga, then there is nothing but blue and a few spun-wool clouds.

About once a decade Niue is blasted by a cyclone which vents its furies on the island's exposed coast, land, buildings and crops. After each cyclone the Niueans, like other Pacific island people in the cyclone zone, pick themselves up and start again.

Buildings are reconstructed, trees and plants grow back. But as I fly to the south-west I wonder, can Niue, a rocky, isolated island, survive the much more prolonged economic gales of the nineties?

Nobody can say, but what I do know is that no island deserves to more, not just because it is a unique natural area, but because of the people who have stayed on the Rock to help stem the human haemorrhage of emigration.

Niueans are not as musical as Tahitians, as demonstrative and fun-loving as the Cook Islanders, as assertive as the Samoans, or as class-ridden as the Tongans. My initial impression was that the Niueans are introverted, even dour. Their dancing and singing certainly lacks the flamboyance and sensuality of Eastern Polynesia. This is probably a consequence of life on their thin-soiled, plateau-like rock, where they have had to toil to survive. Niue is almost the ultimate level playing-field.

Yet the Niueans proved in time to be the most gentle, genial people I have met in the Pacific: kind, considerate, unassuming, versatile. They have quiet pride in their homeland and their culture, and they are determined to build a tourist industry based on it, to wean themselves away from an aid-based economy. All they need is a steady supply of visitors. Not an excessive number, or the motto, 'Discover Tranquillity', will become, ironically, obsolete.

Niueans say that people who visit the Rock always return. I know why.

Daughters for the
Return Home

JUST A FEW HUNDRED YARDS from the red brick, Edwardian building which is the heart of Auckland Girls' Grammar School, the northern, southern and western motorways converge. Here, at Auckland's spaghetti junction, the bitumen roars from the wheels of thousands of vehicles per day, while the school goes about its business as it has done for a hundred years.

If the Newton interchange is the city's most vital motorway junction, then Auckland Girls' Grammar is its cultural cross-roads. The school is a microcosm of the city, minus its males. It is not uncommon for a class to contain pupils whose families have their origins in a dozen or more different parts of Polynesia, Asia or Europe. While the number of Pakeha students has remained constant in the last twenty-five years, the proportion from Polynesian, Asian and other backgrounds has grown as the school's total roll has increased, making AGGS the only truly multi-cultural school in the city.

Each culture is encouraged to assert its heritage in as many ways as possible. The results are seen most spectacularly in song and dance at the Auckland Secondary Schools' Maori and Pacific Islands' Festival, in April, a brilliant cultural spectacle. In their planning, practices and performances these groups dispel every generalisation that is made about Pacific Islanders: they are competitive, ambitious and punctilious, satisfied only with the highest standards of song, dance and costuming.

The journey began with the question, many months ago, 'Sir, will you organise a trip for us to Raro?' I am responsible for the school's Cook Islands Club, which won its section of the festival, so I can hardly refuse.

The planning begins: itineraries are considered, airlines consulted, fund-raising commences.

By April we have enough money, and a final list of thirty-five. The party is suitably representative of the school: Cook Islanders, appropriately, comprise the largest group, but as well we have Tongans, Samoans, Niueans, Maori and Pakeha students whose ages range from thirteen to seventeen. The group is to leave in the last week of term, the last day of the low season on an air route which is always notoriously expensive, in the high season acutely so.

30 APRIL, 10 P.M.

It is a cool Saturday evening at the airport. The girls have opted to wear their winter uniforms — dark blue skirts and jerseys, blue and gold striped ties. It is a sensible decision: not only are they meticulous, they are also luminous in the throng of the departure hall, and easily gathered together.

At the weigh-in, relations press cartons of apples and other food upon us. Airline personnel eye the scales nervously. Makiroa, an AGGS Cook Islands Club leader, has brought an enormous chilly-bin which in itself exceeds the weight limit: it gets through without penalty by courtesy of the few of us who are short of the limit.

We pass through the departure lounge doors, through security and into relative tranquillity. Mele, a fifth former who travels to AGGS every day from Otara, asks to say a prayer, the first of many invocations we are to hear over the next twelve days. She prays for a safe journey, for protection, for happiness, expressing what we are all hoping for. We are called aboard the 767.

The big plane soars, banks and we gasp at the brilliance of Auckland by night from the air, spread like gems on a tray of black velvet, stretching to the limits of our vision. Then there is only darkness, and the tedium of flying by night.

RAROTONGA, 5 A.M.

It is a barbaric hour to arrive. Drugged with half-sleep, we climb unsteadily down into the thick hot air and across the concrete to the terminal.

We are engulfed by family, friends, flowers. Eis, the garlands of delicately-petalled, divinely-scented frangipani — called here tipani — are draped about our necks. Suddenly we see that the extended family is no myth. 'Kia orana. I'm Moana's aunty, and this is her cousin.' 'Kia orana, I'm Sherael's uncle, and this is her aunty.' 'You must be Graeme. I'm Petevai's aunty.' 'Kia orana.'

'Kia orana. Kia orana. Your bus is over there,' someone calls, although we had arranged no bus. 'Suitcases over there, on the other bus.'

Makiroa's chilly-bin is dragged away. Dawn is lightening the sky, we can see the silhouettes of sharp mountains in one direction, long-necked palm trees in another, and everywhere there is the warm air and the fragrance of the tipani. The first hurdle has been cleared. We are safely here.

The Atiu hostel was completed in 1982, built specifically to accommodate the people of the island of Atiu on their visits to Rarotonga, particularly for the week-long celebratory festival of Constitution Week every August. There are mattresses downstairs on the floor, two-person rooms around an upstairs gallery, a large communal kitchen.

Papa Simiona, a respected Rarotongan elder whose grand-daughters all passed through AGGS in recent years, welcomes us with a prayer and a speech, then we have the remainder of the day to settle in and recover from the fiendish flight. With alacrity and the resilience of youth, the girls quickly unpack and head for town, five minutes' walk away.

It is still Saturday here, and cars, vans and mopeds jam the one main street. The AGGS girls are distinctive in their special centennial T-shirts, ideal for this climate. Prior to our arrival the weather has been wet and windy, but today it is hot and still.

We shop for provisions at Avarua's only supermarket, where the prices are alarming. Cheese $14 a block, toilet rolls 90 cents each, bully beef $4 a tin, bread $2 a loaf, lettuces nearly $5 each. Yet the place is full. How can the local people afford these prices, when the average wage rate is about $4 an hour?

Back at the hostel we are introduced to our security team: a dozen Atiu lads of about seventeen who are to guard our premises against undesirables. They begin their unpaid duties at ten o'clock and leave at seven o'clock the next morning. They prove commendably conscientious, if somewhat raucous the first night. A word from Nga quietens them down.

Nga is in charge of the hostel. She is a strong, independent Atiuan woman employed as a public health advisor by the Internal Affairs Ministry. It is she who has put around the hostel walls a series of excellent posters produced by the South Pacific Commission exhorting the people of the region to 'Eat More Island Foods', 'Get Regular Exercise', 'Drink Less Alcohol'. When we get up in the early morning to prepare breakfast, amber cockroaches as big as house mice scuttle across the posters, antennae waving wildly.

SUNDAY
It is clear that we are all expected to attend church, and the obvious choice is the big Cook Islands Christian Church just behind the hostel.

We join a stream of white-clad women and besuited men all heading in one direction, and fifty metres away hear the strains of a welcoming hymn through the open, lancet windows.

Surrounded by a vast graveyard, the church is imposing, built of coral limestone a metre thick and painted blinding white. Inside, fans stir the muggy air to a breeze and the singing swells to the towering, tongue-and-groove ceiling. The pulpit is five metres high, and twin galleries accommodate boys to the left, girls to the right.

The service is in Maori and we understand little, but the hymns come regularly and the singing is magnificent.

As we leave there is another downpour, sending us scurrying for shelter under the ironwood trees.

With church over, nothing else happens. The people vanish, every shop is shut. Ideal conditions, at least, for swotting for exams.

The ball-and-chain of internal assessment has been dragged half-way across the Pacific with us: the sixth formers must complete their exams in Rarotonga. As they sit and write at the long table in the kitchen, chickens stroll in and peck at their feet and a mongrel dog pauses at the open door. A tropical downpour provides another diversion before the two hours are up and the girls are liberated again.

Youth With A Mission, known by some local disbelievers as 'Why-Wam', holds a Sunday night concert in neighbouring Constitution Park and the girls drift over. From the balcony of the hostel the rest of us hear the sounds of evangelical rock and the cries of 'Praise the Lord!' It all seems decidedly tacky compared with the dignity and tradition of the CICC service, and it continues for a couple of hours. Many of the girls stay, a few drift back. In reply to the question, 'Did you enjoy the concert?' one of them makes a face. 'Those Americans think they can come out here and convert the poor natives with their holy rock,' she says.

Through the black night, from among the palms, comes the twang of electronic music and the shouts of 'Jesus, Jesus, Jesus!'

Exham Wichman is proud of his role as the father of Rarotongan tourism. For many years he has been taking visitors around the island in his ancient buses, explaining its history, its agriculture, its customs. An easy-going, chain-smoking, non-drinker, Exham is the ideal person to introduce the girls to the finer points of Rarotonga. He has close relatives at the school, including Chantal Napa, the Cook Islands Club leader who has not been able to come on the trip. We have brought Exham and his wife Maria a box of food from Chantal's mum. He collects us in his yellow bus and we set off round the island.

First stop is the beautiful but deteriorating London Missionary Society building of Takamoa. Exham knows missionary history as well as any historian — one of his forebears was a missionary — and he brings vividly to life the deeds of Williams, Buzacott, Papeiha and the rest of them who in a few years in the nineteenth century instituted the most radical social and religious revolution in the history of the Pacific. And as the girls listen attentively to his stories, there is added poignancy to what he has to say. Back in Auckland, nearly all of them attend the various Island churches: they are the inheritors of the LMS dream of a Christian Pacific.

The girls help Maria with the dishes and the tour continues. We call at the Rarotongan, the resort hotel on the western side of the island. Its luxury is impressive, but there is something off-putting about the place. Perhaps it is too neat, too orderly, too stage-managed to be truly Polynesian. We look with a kind of contempt on the few pallid papa'a who lounge on the beach and around the pool. *We* are not like them, *we* are honorary locals. There is the story of the elderly Takapuna couple lying on their loungers beside the pool at the Rarotongan, sipping their pina coladas. The wife turns to the husband and says: 'Why do they leave *all this* for a run-down house in Grey Lynn?'

As we complete our drive around the island, Exham asks me if I have heard about the hole in the ozone layer. We discuss the implications of the rise in the sea level. Exham pulls on his cigarette, frowns, then lets out a huge cackle. 'Soon,' he shouts, 'I will have a beachfront property!'

We are to see a lot of Exham over the next ten days. His bus takes us to the beach, to an Island Night, to the airport for the Aitutaki flight. He is unfailingly cheerful, punctual and obliging, though it is clear that his business has been hit hard in recent times by the big hotels providing their own transport and tours. A new bus would cost him $69,000 — far too much. 'So,' he shrugs, 'in two years I retire. I leave Lady Irene [his ancient bus] in the garden and grow a bougainvillaea all over it.'

By the fourth day the girls are totally at home. They have had their photo in the *Cook Islands News* and have been on FM radio. In fact, there is a blossoming love affair between the AGGS girls and the island. They are a cheerful and attractive addition to Rarotonga's daily life. They smile and wave at the locals and spend freely in their shops; they hire bikes and cycle round the island; they take a boat to the beautiful motu at Muri and picnic beside the lagoon; they climb a track which leads up through the tropical rainforest to a basalt pillar three hundred metres above the sea, and exclaim at the magnificence of the view; they repay the security lads with a hastily organised but hugely enjoyable social at the hostel, with borrowed stereo gear and decorations of brilliantly hued leaves and flowers plucked from the luxuriant vegetation which surrounds them.

And always, there are the families; the parents, grandparents, aunties, uncles and cousins who call with gifts of coconuts, pawpaws, mandarins, oranges, and a constant stream of invitations for the girls to visit them at home.

Ani is a sixth former at AGGS. She has not seen her Rarotongan mother for eight years. Ani writes:

Before leaving for Rarotonga I had had letters from my mother and other relatives, stories from my young uncle who had recently arrived from there, and my own childhood memories to prepare me for the trip.

Even with all of these guides, hints and expectations, Rarotonga proved itself to be more than I had ever dreamed of. The hospitality of the people was incredible; friends were made easily, and life was never dull.

I have always been proud to be half Rarotongan, and I love the culture very much. Now I feel that my half should be three-quarters, and my trips to Rarotonga never-ending.

All the big hotels offer an Island Night; dinner and dancing, Island-style. It is just a question of consulting the locals and choosing which one gets the most recommendations. We decide on the Manuia Beach hotel, which features the Royal Polynesians.

It is a warm, still night. The hotel is right on the lagoon, and dressed in their best clothes, the girls stroll among the palms and gardens under the moonlit sky. There is an excellent meal of marinaded fish, chicken, chop suey, taro and sweet potato, with the girls seated at a long table in front of the small stage. At nine o'clock the dancing begins.

The Royal Polynesians provide an hour and a half of pulsating, explosive drumming and dancing. The vigour of the men, the allure of the hip-swinging women: this must be the most erotic — no, let's not mess about with words — the most joyously sexy dance on earth. To see this dance done properly is to at once understand a great deal of history: the real reason the *Bounty* sailors mutinied, the cause of the missionaries' strictures, the reason why so many European men have fallen in love with Polynesia and continue to make it their home.

Our girls are easily the most appreciative and enthusiastic section of a full audience. The final item is the traditional 'Round the World', when the dancers descend to the audience and select partners to bring back to the stage. Traditionally too, the guest dancers look ridiculous.

The foxy men choose five AGGS girls, and the staccato drums begin again. One pair at a time, they dance, and the men are stunned to see their partners give as good as they get. Teaching these girls to dance is a bit like teaching your grandmother to suck eggs.

After the third dance, flash-bulbs popping, the audience is applauding and the compere is calling for more. It is a stunner of an evening: with a disarming mixture of beauty, modesty and chutzpah, the AGGS girls have again stolen the show.

Sarah is a sixth former. She is Samoan, and had not been to the Cook Islands before. She writes:

This trip was more than a holiday, it was an experience and an awakening. I had never felt any particular calling to get involved in my culture. However, after the warmth and the love that I felt from the local people, and the obvious pride that they had in their culture and nation, I suddenly wanted to be part of the scene.

The thing that I appreciated, and feel the warmest thoughts for, is the people that I met and the hospitality I encountered from them. I like the Cook Islands, but I love the people.

A man with a mop of black hair calls into the hostel on a motorbike. He has two nieces in our party and he has heard that one of the teachers is a writer. He introduces himself to me. He is the poet Kauraka Kauraka, born in Rarotonga to Manihikian parents. We discuss Pacific literature and exchange books. His *Dreams of a Rainbow* is published in English and Maori and is a celebration of pre-Christian spirituality, a lyrical interweaving of the natural and the supernatural.

Kauraka and others like him represent an exciting development in the Pacific: the emerging expression of a truly indigenous literature. He inscribes his book and I bring it back for the school library. With his permission, I reproduce a poem from it here.

RAINBOW LAND
Your coloured hills dazzle me
Immaculate and innocent
Your sailing winds
Soothe my hot head
Your watery body
Cushions my flesh of stone
This rainbowed land
Scented with gardenias
A bowl of gold
In the vast continent of lights
Guarded by butterflies
And inhabited by spectral warriors

Exham has arranged for our last evening together on Rarotonga to be spent at his local church youth club, Betela, at Arorangi.

We arrive at four o'clock, and the situation looks unpromising. The hall is small, the weather showery, and most off-putting is the obvious presence of a gaggle of Why-Wams. They are, as usual, joyous, radiant, exasperating. A sallow-faced youth from Virginia pronounces the island as 'Rar-row-tong-ga' and a fat blonde from Milwaukee is determinedly jolly. But there are large numbers of young locals too, and fraternisation eventually breaks out.

The girls make up teams for volleyball. The gravelled court is so close to the main road that the occasional high ball clears the fence and almost knocks a passing rider off his moped. Betela cleans us up at volley, then as darkness comes we move inside the hall for drumming and dancing.

A sturdy, handsome man in his forties holds out his hand. 'Hey, remember me?' I do indeed. It is Daniel Apii, cultural group leader and distinguished tennis player. Back in 1982 he brought his cultural group to AGGS while on an Auckland tour, and they gave a superb lunchtime performance. Daniel comments, without a trace of resentment, 'Half of the people on that trip now live in Auckland.' His son Tiki, who was thirteen at the time, is now a leading tennis coach at the Rarotongan, and the Cook Islands' number one player.

Daniel's drummers explode into action, and the Why-Wams' happy little tunes are obliterated by the machine-gun-like sounds of their instruments. We dance and sing for an hour. The AGGS Cook Islands group performs their ute, Mele with her Walkman dangling round her neck. Then the food is brought in.

Umu kai chicken, fresh coconuts, pale green seaweed, in bunches like tiny grapes, chop suey, taro, fish in coconut sauce, banana fritters and cake. In twenty minutes we make no evident impression on the table. As is to happen so often on this trip, local hospitality overwhelms us, with no apparent effort to do so. We are made to feel appreciated, honoured, special.

English seems a faltering language in which to reply to Daniel's speech, but our $200 donation to the Betela travel fund is received with obvious delight. We leave smothered with love and a hundred Aere Ra's.

Two hundred and sixty kilometres north of Rarotonga is an island called Aitutaki, part coral atoll, part high island, with a lagoon 180 square kilometres in size. From the beginning, Aitutaki has been an integral part of our itinerary: there are thousands of people from the island in Auckland, and several girls in our party think of themselves as Aitutakian first, Cook Islanders second.

It takes us four flights by Air Rarotonga to convey us to the island. This domestic airline — begun by New Zealander Ewan

Smith — is both efficient and enterprising, now serving several of the outer islands. We take off in their Heron at ten o'clock, bank to the west, giving us a glimpse of the bush-covered peaks and pinnacles of Rarotonga's interior, then there is only ocean, white-flecked, immense.

The girls point to the left. A patch of turquoise, rimmed by motus, lassoed by a reef of brilliant white. The shimmering patch grows larger, the turquoise more vivid, the contrast between lagoon and blue-black ocean more intense. We descend over the line of palmed motus, the coral runway is under us. Aitutaki.

Again, the eis have it. We are festooned with tipani, crowned with pandanus. Amid swirls of coral dust, the billets are allocated. Girls come forward, kiss us, garland us again. A man in a safari suit and bare feet introduces himself. Piri Maao, the local headmaster. Relations embrace the girls. Makiroa's chilly-bin, which we have cursed from Auckland to Rarotonga, has at last come into its own, while Makiroa herself is garlanded like a Polynesian princess. In the tiny terminal building there are prayers, hymns, speeches. Again we have this feeling that we are the chosen few, special, singled out for love and attention. It is not so — all groups receive this treatment — but it is very easy to believe that it is.

There are seven villages on Aitutaki, each with its boundaries clearly marked. It falls to the village of Ureia to welcome us with prayers, speeches and banquet. The village leader explains: his community welcomes groups who come by air, the neighbouring village greets those who arrive by sea. Given the infrequency of shipping these days, it seems that Ureia too often draws the short straw, but if that is the case, it doesn't show. The eating over, we again disperse to our various parts of the island.

Aitutaki is as different to Rarotonga as Kawau is to Waiheke. Aitutaki is hot — nearly 28 degrees — tranquil, seemingly unpopulated, demonstrably hospitable. Along the streets, from the gardens, on the beaches, people wave, call, greet us with beaming smiles and calls of 'Kia orana!' In some way, they already know who we are and where we are from.

The church encompasses the lives of Aitutakians as emphatically as the reef encloses their island. The Seventh Day

Adventists are strong here, as well as the Cook Islands Christian Church, with Catholics, Mormons and Presbyterians making up the other third. There appear to be, mercifully, no Why-Wams. With the SDAs worshipping on Saturday and the others on Sunday, Aitutaki's weekend is doubly shut down.

We have missed the famous Friday night show at the Rapae Motel (a friend of mine was wrecked in a yacht here on the reef once, trying to get into port after darkness so he could make the Rapae's Island Night), so we must largely amuse ourselves until the double sabbath has passed. In the one street of the village, only the chickens move.

My sons and I are accommodated in one of the island's three guest-houses, Tiare Maori, run by Mama and Papa Tunui, whose two grandsons attend our host school, Araura College. Mama has gone to Rarotonga for the weekend, so Papa will be caring for us.

Papa Tunui is seventy, but looks ten years younger. As brown as coffee, he potters about his property in shorts, T-shirt and bare feet, preparing food, mending machinery, servicing his van, and when the midday sun grows too hot, sleeping under the tree in the back yard.

In World War II, when there were one thousand (mainly black) Americans stationed here building the airfield, Papa Tunui became a driver. Since then he has been warehouseman, ship's pilot, boat skipper and guest-house proprietor. He has been a leading cricketer, tennis and rugby player. He knows the legends of his island and is a pillar of the CICC. At night he nets flying fish from his boat, outside the reef. He is self-effacing, laconic, wise, respected.

As Papa drives us around Aitutaki and recounts the coming of the master navigator Ru and the subsequent peopling of the island, I realise with envy and admiration that this man, and his children's children, are the direct inheritors of a line and a land which goes back one thousand years.

Later, in a teacher's house, we watch a video of the recent Cook Islands Dancing Championships. The 'Papas' section features, along with several others, our Papa Tunui. He comes onto the stage resplendent in Aitutakian finery, makes a fiery speech of introduction, then performs a drum dance with the agility and vigour of a twenty-year-old. He is, the commentator tells us, the defending champion of the Cook Islands.

Sherael Makea is fourteen. She writes:

On our trip I was overwhelmed by the kindness of the many people we met. I myself am half Aitutakian, and while there I was amazed at how much family I had.

In the Islands I learnt that my name is very honoured, as the Makea family are all respected chiefs.

The Cook Islands mean so much to me and I'm proud to be part of them.

On an island not much bigger than Rangitoto, it's difficult not to keep running into people you know. When on Saturday night Papa takes us and various Mamas (the Mamas and the Papas must have gone down well here in the sixties) to Island Night at the deluxe Akitua Island resort, we come across many others of the school party and their billeters there.

Cyclone Sally wrecked the causeway joining the two islands, so visitors must haul themselves across the channel by a rope attached to a small barge. It's a pleasant, romantic way to arrive, and the resort looks stunning, emblazoned with coloured lights among the palms and lush shrubbery.

Another show, another 'Round the World' and again our girls are brought up onto the dance floor, and they dance even more beautifully than before. The audience is delighted, and afterwards a slightly wild-eyed manager bails me up, introduces himself. 'Look, I'd like you to bring all the girls over tomorrow. We'll give them lunch, take them on the lagoon. All on the house, they'll be a marvellous attraction . . .' It has not been a good year for Cook Islands tourism, obviously. The invitation is declined.

Strange, but I find myself looking forward to the CICC service. Papa drives us to church in his van.

The Arutanga church — Tiona Tapu — shares the white-washed walls, the towering pulpit and ceiling of its Avarua counterpart, but there are intriguing variations. A fretwork frieze, its patterns picked out in bright green and red, surrounds the interior, and a huge ship's anchor is bolted to the ceiling.

The minister welcomes 'the girls of Auckland Grammar' and delivers his sermon in English and Maori. Earlier in the morning he had rung Papa Tunui at home to check on several points of detail concerning the tale which is the basis of his sermon: a legend about a beautiful girl who lived in a hole in a rock in the lagoon. The singing, as always, is magnificent, and although there is much in the service we don't understand, it does not matter. There is a powerful dignity at work here, and it is perhaps idle to wonder why the Creator regularly brings down scourges such as Sally upon a people who devote so much of their time giving thanks to Him.

After the service I ask Papa Tunui about the significance of the anchor. 'As the Bible say,' he replies, 'cling fast to the rock.'

After only two days on Aitutaki, the serenity and apparent remoteness produce a feeling of almost total detachment. We see no television, read no newspapers, hear no radio. Our homes in Grey Lynn, Kingsland and Devonport are difficult to recall. The rest of the world's problems seem to have no relevance here. It is as though we have passed into a Pacific Elysium, beyond which nothing else exists. Can this be the beginning of what is known as 'Reef Stare', the process by which Europeans lose all interest in the world beyond the reef and are content to sit and stare at the horizon for years on end? And if we feel like this on an easily-reached island in the Southern Group, what must it be like on Penrhyn, one thousand kilometres further north?

And what confusion must the reverse process cause, when the person from Manihiki or Rakahanga is set down in Mangere, Manukau or Karangahape Road? The shock of this transition is difficult to imagine.

Araura College, Aitutaki's one secondary school, stands on a broad plateau above the main village of Arutanga. The school, which is co-educational, is a long line of joined classrooms beside an expanse of playing fields. To one side is a high-roofed, open-sided assembly shelter ('Prince Edward Hall').

Today is the first day of the second term, and the AGGS girls come to school at 8 a.m. with their billets. We stand with the assembly while the Cook Islands' flag is unfurled and saluted, and the national anthem is sung. This happens every Monday. We join some classes, explore the library, play cricket and volleyball against Araura pupils.

In spite of the obvious dedication of the staff (now almost totally local) and the instilled discipline and regimentation, a palpable lack of basic equipment and modern facilities must be an impediment. Teachers describe the difficulties in even obtaining exercise books, supplies of which have a habit of being diverted for political rather than educational motives. Their problems here make the grievances of New Zealand teachers seem petty.

Instead of a bell, at Araura they have the pu, a conch blown by a senior boy from the deck of the school library. It is an entirely appropriate, if slightly Goldingesque way to punctuate the day on a small Pacific island. It also leads to some curious comments, heard around the school. 'There goes the pu,', 'The pu's due any minute,' or 'I thought I heard the pu.' But the system works well, and leads me to wonder whether a pu could be an addition to the routine of Auckland Girls' Grammar.

The fourth former stood in the old hall, looked at her Swatch, checked its time against the school clock in front of the Honours Board. Three minutes to go. She turned and walked to the staircase, climbed purposefully to the belfry high above the old building, to where the pu, a gift from the people of the Tokelaus, lay waiting in its carved kauri cradle. The girl checked her Swatch once more. Exactly 12.20 p.m. Lunchtime at AGGS. She picked up the pu, put it to her lips and blew long and hard. No one heard a thing: the sound of the conch was totally drowned out by the traffic on the Hopetoun Street viaduct.

Ngametua, aged fifteen, approaches me in the grounds of Araura College. There is a boy with her, in school uniform. He looks vaguely familiar. 'This is my brother,' says Ngametua. He smiles shyly as he shakes my hand.

I ask Ngametua when she last saw him. 'When I was little,'

she replies. 'His name is Ngatokoroa.' Then she smiles delightedly. 'I've got another brother on Aitutaki too. I met him yesterday. Two brothers, Junior and Ngatokoroa.' Ngametua writes:

Aitutaki is special to me. I meet my aunty at the airport. She took me to her house to meet my two brothers. My Aunty Barbara took me around the island on the motorbike.

On Monday I went to school with my brother Ngatokoroa on the bus and I meet heaps of friends.

I didn't want to leave the island because I miss my two brothers and friends at school.

The staff and students of Araura ply us with food and friendship. We are taken on another tour of the island; through the several villages, through groves of eerily beautiful coconut trees, through forests of banana palms and plantations of arrowroot.

We alight at the small promontory which stands at the end of the perilously narrow Arutanga Passage, one of the few breaks in Aitutaki's reef. Embedded in the promontory is a big slab of basalt. Makea Joseph explains that it is the place where Ru stepped ashore one thousand years ago, an Aitutakian Plymouth Rock. Makea adds that local legend also has it that whoever stands on the rock must one day return to Aitutaki. The girls rush at the rock, crowd upon it.

When Ru came, he brought with him a group of unmarried, warrior maidens from whom the island was first populated. More than once, in the many speeches we hear, the similarities between Ru's expedition and our own are alluded to, with great hilarity.

Time after time too, in these speeches, we are admonished for having stayed too briefly. There has not been time, we are told, to properly explore the beautiful lagoon, to climb Maunga Ru, to visit Akaiami and the other motus.

So when I speak to the school assembly on our final morning on Aitutaki, I first apologise for my unRu-ly behaviour in having to take the girls away again from a place which they have all taken to their hearts. Nothing, I add, can adequately repay their kindness to us, but as a token we present them with a bundle of

New Zealand books for their library.

And I feel bound to add, looking at the rows of earnest faces arrayed below me, that these young people should not leave their beautiful home permanently. These islands have already been too much sapped by the loss of so many of their best and brightest young people to the putative pleasures of Auckland, Tokoroa or Wellington. 'Go to New Zealand for your higher education,' I suggest, 'then return and make your nation stronger with the knowledge you have gained.'

Makiroa is seventeen. English is her family's second language.

The warm welcome of the people in Aitutaki, greeting us with kisses and French Tipani, the beautiful smell in the air, on an island surrounded with angry waves, hitting against the reef.

We were billeted out to families, scattered around Aitutaki, learning the way they live their life. It's way different to the way our families live. Around five o'clock in the morning their families are up to pick and sweep the rubbish around the house.

The family I lived with had to find their food, such as fishing, plantation. They have to kill animals such as pigs to feed the family, but if they have enough money, bread can be bought.

I had a wonderful time there, the first I got there the first thing I heard was, 'Who's the chilly-bin?' (i.e. the fat person) but that didn't worry me. It seemed like we had stayed there for a long time because I was so attached to the family and the people.

There was pain and sorrow on the last day, nobody wanted to leave, we were all so close to the island . . .

By the time we reach the airport, emotions are running at floodtide level. We are all garlanded again, inundated with the pink and white tipani. Papa Tunui gives us a box of bananas. We embrace. It is as if we have known each other for a very long time.

'Next time, bring your missus,' he says, then he hugs the boys again.

Makiroa hauls her chilly-bin onto the scales. For the return home it has been filled with the seafood delicacy pa-ua, a clam-like fish.

In the small terminal there is a hymn, prayers, speeches, tears. I reply in a kind of 'Ich-bin-ein-Aitutakian' way, but words are not equal to expressing what we feel, for the sad fact is that there will never be another trip quite like this one.

Out on the runway, the plane's propellers send up clouds of coral dust, and the trade winds are blowing in from the east. We wave once more, the door is closed, and in seconds we are airborne, the palm-covered motus slipping away beneath us, the waters of the lagoon a shimmering expanse of pale blue.

For the last day and a half on Rarotonga, the girls are in the care of their families. It is a chance to shop, relax, and reflect.

The Cook Islands are not paradise, no Pacific island can be. Their resources are too few, economic realities too harsh, they are too vulnerable to market forces beyond their control. Too many of their people have voted with a one-way air ticket for the largely illusory good life in New Zealand or elsewhere. But the islands still possess something beyond price, beyond economics: a blend of peerless natural beauty and human warmth matched by few other places.

On our last night on the island, there is a sunset which for ten minutes turns the clouds above the lagoon to crimson. Then the flaring sky fades, darkness falls, and there is the susurration of the sea on the reef and the wind in the palms.

That night I read Julian Hillas's classic work, *A Paradise of Islands*, and I encounter this passage.

In the rushing urgency of the long line of surf the traveller hears a Lorelei song as old and seductive as life itself, a happiness blended with sorrow, as though these lovely, far-off places sensed that the coming of modern man contained the seeds of their own destruction. The illusion is always there, like the eternal murmur of the seas in the heart of a giant shell.

At the airport for our dawn departure we are herded, weary, melancholic, into the 767.

On the plane Melvina, who is fourteen, writes:

In the Cook Islands I enjoyed eating pineapples, coconuts, mangoes, pawpaws and heaps more. But best of all was seeing long-lost relations and friends. The worst part was meeting them, then leaving them. Kia kite. Melvina.

Melvina's grandfather is Prime Minister of the Cook Islands.

The muddy Manukau, whipped by a strong cold sou'westerly, appears beneath us. Glumly we await our baggage, our boxes of fruit. Some of the gift boxes are confiscated by the dour functionaries from Ag. and Fish. Our eis are pawed.

Outside, winter has come down on the city like a portcullis. In its size and coldness, Auckland seems to threaten. The traffic is appalling, the newspapers filled with gloom and hostility.

Back at school, the plane trees are grey and bare, and only a few leaves still cling to the ivy vine which climbs across the face of the old building. Our party re-assembles once more, to see slides of the trip, to exchange photos, laughter. We have shared a special, a unique experience. For the pupils there has been a return to the region of their forebears; for the papa'a teachers a new awareness of our students. We know them much better because we now know what their families left behind to come here. There are about fifteen thousand Cook Islanders living in Auckland.

This year, Auckland Girls' Grammar, whose roots reach out and touch every island in the South-West Pacific, will be one hundred years old. Next summer, as it begins its second century, some third former will write, as one of them usually does in response to the question: Impressions of AGGS. 'It's a lovely old building, but why did they put it so close to the motorway?'

Tahiti, Moorea

IT WAS THE VILEST OF Auckland winters: mean, cold rain, driving in from the south-west for over forty consecutive days. Forty days of struggling to keep warm and dry. Add to this wretched weather the equally endless bickering of politicians, a spate of slayings and bashings, and a visit to the tropical Pacific seemed an alluring prospect.

As Gilly took me down to the Devonport ferry on the first stage of my quest and escape, the evening sky over Auckland had cleared. A change in the weather at last? Not at all. By the time we were at the wharf the wind-driven rain was lashing the harbour and city again.

I ran through the squall for the ferry. On the *Kestrel*, passengers huddled in the corners like creatures bereft of hope.

There is another reason for this journey. For ten months I have been trying to complete a novel, set in the Islands. The novel is about a man who runs away from his personal and financial problems, seeking salvation in the Pacific. In the course of his travels there he encounters a variety of other people who are endeavouring to escape their pasts. But at the three-quarter mark the novel has dried up, and after brooding about it for months, I knew there was only one solution. To get the fiction current flowing again, to connect up the jumper leads, I would have to go back to where the novel is set, to see again the islands which inspired me in the first place. Somewhere in that enticing region there will be people who can resolve my central character's problems, and in so doing, help to resolve my own. I am that most desperate of people, an author in search of his own ending.

After a four-hour flight through the night, I'm warm and dry without having to try. It's early morning in Tahiti, and from my second-floor hotel window I can see the high, serrated profile of Moorea emerging from the mist above a pastel blue sea. Below me is the harbour, a boulevard whose lanes are separated by a line of flame trees, and along which late model European cars and Vespa scooters are moving at a swift clip.

To get orientated I decide to take a tour around Tahiti as soon as possible. At 9.30 in the morning a small bus driven by a powerfully built Polynesian man with a broad face and flattened features collects me from outside the hotel. The cause of these facial irregularities becomes clear when he tells me that he was a boxer for many years. His name is Emil and he is a member of the Cowan family, who are something of a legend both in Tahiti and her sister island, Rarotonga. In the delightful way of the Pacific, where relationships intersect unexpectedly, I discover that Emil's sister is married to a friend in Rarotonga, Ross Hunter. A Cook Islander himself, Emil is married to a Tahitian, and Papeete has been his home for over twenty years.

Also on the bus are a Japanese trio, a youngish couple and a round-faced, aged woman; an elderly but spry couple from Wellington; a pair of grey-faced, obese Americans who look like brother and sister; a very tall, good-looking man from Los Angeles with an elegant Japanese-American woman who looks just like Yoko Ono. This pair hold hands constantly, even when eating lunch. Yoko steadfastly ignores the trio from Japan, who have brought along their own interpreter, a slim young man who also ignores them. Each time the bus stops, the young Japanese lights up a cigarette and wanders away, then as soon as he gets back on, falls asleep. After a few stops Emil dispatches him to the rear of the vehicle, where he curls up contentedly and sleeps without interruption. I gratefully accept his seat at the front of the bus.

We pass out of Papeete and between two large housing compounds where what Emil calls 'the nuclear people' live. We climb a huge hill, descend to the sea, drive out to the end of a level promontory. Point Venus.

Here, on the western side of the point, in Matavai Bay, on 13 April 1769, James Cook and his crew dropped the *Endeavour*'s anchor. They were here to prepare for the observation of the transit of Venus across the face of the sun, several weeks later.

Today the point is a picnic area, covered with coconut palms and ironwood trees. There is a nineteenth-century lighthouse amid the trees, and a monument to the missionaries who came in Cook and Bligh's wakes. Today there is a group of Tahitian youths kicking a soccer ball about, and on the black sand of the bay French families lie baking in the mid-morning sun. Most of the women are bare-breasted. Silken water laps at the volcanic sand, the palms crane out over the water, and in the distance the green hills swell to a towering, cloud-capped cone split into numerous ravines. Even today Matavai Bay is an idyllic spot. How much more so it must have seemed to those scabrous eighteenth-century English sailors, liberated on its shores after weeks of imprisonment at sea.

I wander about under the ironwood trees. Few places in the Pacific are as historically significant as this. Cook, Banks and the others here set in motion events which were to culminate in Bligh's breadfruit expedition, the sailors' sojourn among the Tahitians, the mutiny, and all the movies that followed.

Driving around Tahiti is like moving around the face of a huge clock, with Papeete at eleven o'clock and Point Venus at the prick of noon. After the little hand passes two o'clock, Emil is driving us through a succession of tidy, lagoon-side villages surrounded by gardens, breadfruit trees, frangipani with blooms like coral heads and hedges of flaring yellow crotons. Each village contains a few shops, a school, a church.

Emil continues his droll, practised patter. 'Every Sunday most people in the village go to church to pray, pray, pray, for those who stay at home to drink, drink, drink.' He is intimately acquainted with the island's history, politics, botany. 'Those croton plants are used as a laxative for horses. Oh yes, and for embalming bodies.'

As with most Pacific islands, there are horror stories of hurricanes past, and comedies of post-cyclone reconstruction and malfeasance. What is apparent to me is that the French have given to Tahiti, for their own reasons, naturellement, an infrastructure which must be the best in the South Pacific: fine roads, schools, power supplies, a palatial town hall for each district.

We pass the place where Bougainville moored in April, 1768, then at four o'clock on the island dial come to where Tahiti-Nui (Big Tahiti) splits into Tahiti-Iti (Little Tahiti) like a dividing amoeba. Tahiti-Iti, like its big sibling, rears dramatically from the sea, rising to peaks and pinnacles which vanish into the cloud. We drive across the isthmus which joins the two islands, past the estuaries of wide, clear streams which pour down from the precipitous interior, until we reach the Paul Gauguin Museum, set among gardens on the banks of the Vaite River. Here the artist enjoyed one of his rare periods of contentment.

The museum is laid out as a walkway with displays depicting chronologically Gauguin's life and works. But there are none of his paintings here. No doubt they, like their creator, would deteriorate rapidly in the tropical climate. And the commentary signs on the artist's career are bland. There is no mention, for example, of his syphilitic paedophilia. The place is to be enjoyed for its provenance more than its contents.

People amble about distractedly, perhaps they too had expected to see original paintings. The Japanese, though, don't bother with the displays, they go straight for the souvenir stand. The man videos his wife and mother-in-law buying postcards of Gauguin's paintings.

Next to the museum is a vast garden started by an American professor who settled in Tahiti in 1919. A lover of tropical plants, he established many species here from all over the botanical world. Unfortunately he also imported pests such as the African tulip-tree, which has colonised the whole interior of Tahiti. It's lunchtime when we reach the gardens, and no one seems interested except me and the American brother and sister, who stagger off, drenched in sweat, down a footpath and into the vegetation. I walk through the gardens, but there are few blooms at this time of the year, so I return to the bus. We all wait there, motionless in the heat of the midday sun. Twenty minutes pass, there is no sign of the Americans.

'Shall I go and look for them?' I ask Emil.

'S'il vous plaît,' he says sardonically.

After a time I find them standing in the shade of a huge banyan tree, florid and panting, looking like an overgrown Hansel and Gretel.

As we leave the area we pass a large group of Tahitians — obviously an extended family — preparing a picnic on the grass under a mango tree beside the river. Emil pokes his head out of the window and waves regally.

'Bon appetit,' he calls to the group.

'Ia Orana,' they chorus back.

Our own lunch is taken at a roadside restaurant — Chez Mahaiatea — run by a man who looks French but comes from Texas. The place is Mataiea, a particularly beautiful stretch of coastline, a wide plain bounded on one side by vertical, bush-covered mountains which spill cataracts over their sides, and on the other by the wide, palm-lined lagoon. It was in this very village that Rupert Brooke lived in 1913, with Mamua, the Tahitian girl who straightened out his sexuality, which had been confused by years of public schooling. Here too, he wrote his best poetry. It's not hard to see why. Even a university English lecturer could write a publishable poem here.

As we lunch on poisson cru, salad and Hinano beer, it occurs to me that few other places have as many literary or artistic associations as these islands. Just to be here is helpful to a blocked novelist. As well as Gauguin and Brooke there passed this way Herman Melville, Jack London, Pierre Loti, Robert Louis Stevenson, H.E. Bates, Somerset Maugham, Nordhoff and Hall, Jacques Brel (who is buried next to Gauguin, on Hira Oa), James Michener, and latterly and scandalously, Marlon Brando.

Perhaps, I suggest to Emil, he could run artistic tours, incorporating visits to the luminaries' locations. Might go down well with les Américains. Emil looks thoughtful.

We have almost come full circle. The villages are just as lush and orderly, but now they are closer together, and on the roadside there are racks of metallic bonito hanging by their tails for sale. We pass a sign declaring boldly, 'Non à la bombe'. I point it out to Emil, who flicks an eyebrow.

'I thought you couldn't read French,' he mutters.

Then, perhaps to change the subject he points out a large house on the left.

'The Godfather's house,' he announces. The murky affairs of la famille Brando are Tahiti's real-life soap opera. The tabloids regularly carry front-page stories of Cheyenne Brando's trial, and gossip and rumour surround the actor and his comings and goings from Tetiaroa, the island he bought in the sixties.

We pass Faa'a Airport. Emil wakes up the Japanese guide, who trips off sleepily to his hotel. The Japanese trio disembark, then bow confusedly when I call 'Sayonara' to them. A few minutes later we are back at Papeete, at Boulevard Pomare. We pass the monument to Bougainville, and to General de Gaulle, ' . . . who brought nuclear testing to French Polynesia,' says Emil mischievously.

'We should blow it up,' one of the Kiwis suggests subversively.

Next day I wander about Papeete. It's a big, busy, sophisticated town by day. There are even traffic lights here — one of the few places in the Islands where I've seen them — and everywhere in the streets there are Vespa scooters.

I've long had a love affair with Vespas. Every day for fourteen years I rode one over the Auckland Harbour Bridge and back, until the scooter and I could no longer bear the strain. I loved the scooter's design, its dependability, its style. I still keep it under the house, like the mummified body of a much-loved pet.

Now that the Japanese have grabbed the market for the little, low-powered scooter, there are only a few ancient Vespas left in Auckland, kept running by a small number of aficionados on hard-to-find spare parts. But in Tahiti they're everywhere; I can't help staring at them, examining those parked on the pavements.

These Vespas are not the ancient ones of home, the relics of the sixties and seventies, although the physical resemblance between them and their ancestor is still discernible. These modern ones have evolved into gleaming, streamlined models, with the latest appurtenances such as indicators, lockers and digital dials. As with their forebears, they're still a beautiful piece of Italian design, lovely to look at, the perfect form of transport for an individual in a bustling, tropical town like Papeete.

The Tahitians obviously think so too. They zip along the boulevards on their Vespas, around the market, up the side streets. They carry produce and pillion passengers on them and park them carelessly outside the cafés and on the waterfront.

I covet every Vespa I see in Papeete. If I wasn't so apprehensive about driving on the wrong side of the street among people with frenzied, Gallic-style driving habits, I'd hire one and take a nostalgic ride. Instead, I keep on staring at every one I see. Vespa voyeurism.

As well as the Vespas, late-model Citroëns, and Peugeots clog the streets, and sleek overseas yachts are tethered to the town's doorstep, a little way along from the huge, majestic cruise yacht, *Windsong*.

Like Apia, Papeete is a very Chinese town. Les Chinois have been very successful here since they came as coolie labour, first to grow cotton in the 1860s, and later, sugar. Not only are they Tahiti's leading entrepreneurs (even the delicious 'French' bread is baked by a Chinese baker), they have also integrated with the Tahitians to a remarkable degree. In a café by the market I watch an elderly Chinese woman engaged in long, earnest conversation with a young Tahitian man. All in French.

Francis Wong-Yen, hotel manager and a third-generation Chinese-Tahitian, recounts for me his own family story. Francis is slender, looks twenty but is thirty-six. His shiny black hair is longish, he wears silver-rimmed glasses, and he gesticulates Gallically as he speaks. Yes, he agrees, the Chinese and the Tahitians have an excellent relationship. As for himself, he was educated locally, then at university in France and California. He throws out his hands. 'I am Chinese by philosophy, French in education, Polynesian in my way of life.' His excellent English gives him a fourth dimension.

The key to this integration seems to be intermarriage. Again, as in Samoa, the Chinese and the Polynesians have interbred enthusiastically, and with the French adding their blood to the melting pot, miscegenation has produced a race of startling beauty: almond-eyed women with skins like café au lait and long, black hair.

The cultural adaptation has not been all one way. At another café there is a very elegant young European woman in a short sundress. The length of her right leg and arm is adorned with the intricate beaded and lattice patterns of the traditional Tahitian tattoo.

The bars of Papeete are well positioned for the toper who want to sit under their awnings and watch the passing parade of beautiful people. I sit down at one bar and buy a Budweiser — 600 francs. Christ, that's about NZ $11! As I drink my Bud at $1.50 a mouthful, I notice one of the reasons for this price. Standing by the bar are groups of young men, out of uniform, but their gawky, unsophisticated manner and cropped hair give them the unmistakable stamp of les militaires. Later, at a Chinese-run alimentation, I buy five bottles of beer for the same price as I paid in the waterfront bar.

Apart from the bars there's not a lot of night life in downtown Papeete. In late afternoon the shutters come down, and the town quietly expires with the coming of the tropical night. But this afternoon someone presses a pamphlet upon me in the street. Two hours of free entertainment at The Vaima Shopping Plaza, central Papeete, every Friday night. I'm always skeptical of 'free' offers, but I report there at 7.30 all the same. After all, there's not a lot to lose.

The evening starts uncertainly, with Edith Piaf shrieking from somewhere inside the bamboo roof pavilion. Then there's an audio-visual presentation of Tahiti's black gold, les perles noires. This I can take or leave. To me black pearls just look like exorbitantly priced, deformed ball bearings. Then, at the other end of the plaza, the Tahitian dancers come on.

Now one way or another, I've seen a lot of Polynesian

dancing. At its best, it's stunning, at its worst, embarrassing. This show, without a doubt, is the best I have seen: vibrant, seductive, exuberant. The girls are gorgeous, the men powerful and athletic, the drumming dynamic. To watch the women's hips pulsate until they blur is to wonder why every sailor who called into Tahiti didn't jump ship or mutiny.

Then, as if that wasn't arousing enough, the dancers are followed by a fashion parade: six models displaying the latest tropical fashions on a perspex catwalk in front of a crowd which has now grown to hundreds. The girls are classic Tahitian: dark, vivacious, confident, stylishly striding the catwalk to the accompaniment of brassy south American music. These are the real black pearls of Tahiti, and the Vaima's Friday-night entertainment has got to be one of the best shows in town.

I stroll back along the waterfront boulevard to my hotel. The restaurants are full, the bars still busy. In one, a Chinese man and a Tahitian are engrossed in a chess game. I like the little cries of 'Bon soir Monsieur,' I like the warmth, I like the panache of Papeete, the beauty of Tahiti. But now I have to have an early night. I've got a ferry to catch in the morning. To Moorea.

High, serrated, and from this distance seemingly unpopulated, Moorea rises slowly from the sea. It's Sunday morning, and I'm sitting on the side deck of the ferry, savouring its easy heave, and the view sternward, of Tahiti. Looking back, Papeete seems remarkably Mediterranean with its mountainous background, the houses of the rich on the foothills, the waterfront boulevard, the yacht harbour, and high above, an enamel blue sky.

This is an early morning sailing. The hold is full of cars, the decks crowded with people, mainly French and Tahitian families. For them perhaps Moorea is the Waiheke of the Society Islands, a refuge from the urban pressures of Papeete, only an hour away.

Moorea grows larger, greener, its great serrations reaching into bright white clouds. In less than an hour we are docking at a small wharf, then streaming ashore. Le truck is there to meet the boat. Tahitians and tourists pile aboard the sturdy, bench-seated windowless bus. The locals greet each other by holding up one hand and clasping their friends' briefly, a Tahitian 'high-five'. The bus fills, pulls away. Now I'm again travelling clockwise around an island, except that this time a map shows me that Moorea is shaped more like a flint arrowhead, aimed at Tahiti.

We rumble along in le truck, up the left-hand side of the arrowhead, along the edge of the lagoon. No one speaks, it's too hot for words. To the right, hundreds of metres high, and clothed in dark green bush, are craggy basalt peaks. We pass through small, widely spaced villages, between groves of coconut palms and hedges of hibiscus whose blooms glow like hot coals. But all the time my eyes stray back to those impossibly steep, green mountains. They have an ethereal quality, like the New Zealand mountains painted in oil by Victorian artists, except that these are not vertically exaggerated.

Le truck drops me off outside the gates of my hotel. It's clean and comfortable, without being luxurious. There is a pool, a dining room with a wide verandah overlooking the beach and lagoon, and fares thatched with pandanus clustered around the main complex. The sun is so bright that the pool burns the eyes.

A useful rule when taking up residence in a tropical hotel is to spot the resort bore, then take all necessary steps to avoid him. This one is easy to pick. He's American, about fifty-five, with oily grey, slicked down hair. He's at the bar drinking white wine, and his voice brays around the building. He's Gavin, he introduces himself to everyone, and he insists on reading aloud the T-shirts of everyone who enters. 'Hard *Cock* Café — ha, ha, ha! Where the hell is Rome? Ha, ha, ha!' He nuzzles pubescent girls in a way that brings a wild expression to their fathers' faces, and he hurls out his hand to strangers, reads their T-shirts and slaps them on the back in a way which proclaims, 'Have a drink! Talk to me please! I'm desperate for a friend!'

I take a beer outside onto the verandah, which is almost out of earshot of Gavin's blunderbuss voice. Out in the lagoon there's a small motu covered in ironwood trees, and white sand beaches in both directions as far as I can see. I can also see outboard-propelled canoes filled with visitors, streaming towards the hotel. I've arrived at the right time. Today is the midday tamaaraa — the Tahitian feast — and cultural show.

The tamaaraa is taken at long tables around a central courtyard open to the sky. On the tables are plates of wild pork, taro, breadfruit, palusami, poe, poisson cru, pumpkin and salad, as well as a dangerously large number of carafes of French wine. I sit beside Everitt and Cecelia, an elderly couple from San Francisco, and opposite a pair of young, pale, priggish Christians from Hamilton who resist all attempts at conversation. Later, when the Tahitians ask them to dance they refuse, a highly offensive reaction in this part of the world. But the meal is magnificent, the dancing very good.

Later, glutted with food and wine, lying in the pool like a bloated sheep, I see Everitt walking past and ask him how he enjoyed the tamaaraa. He sighs, frowns, shakes his head mournfully.

'Well, the taro leaves in coconut cream were very strong. The taro itself, very dry. Where was the fried fish? No fried fish. That pork was not wild.' He grimaces. 'And we asked for an ocean-front fare. We have not got an ocean-front fare.' Everitt pauses, sighs again, stares up at the cloudless sky, and without a trace of irony but much feeling, pronounces, 'My God, this is a *divine* place, isn't it?'

Later that afternoon I see standing at the end of the pool a stocky, red-faced man with a drooping moustache, dressed in black and white uniform of a soccer umpire, complete with boots. It is a surreal sight, but when he waves to me I know who it must be.

'Michel Mahe?'

'Yes. Graeme?'

'Oui.'

'Hello.'

'Enchanté.'

Two years ago my daughter Rebecca spent several weeks with Michel and his family in their village of Atiha, improving her French and experiencing Tahitian life. One of my reasons for coming to Moorea is to meet the Mahes and to see where Rebecca had lived. We drive off in Michel's battered Peugeot. He is a teacher, a fisherman, a soccer umpire, a man of strongly held opinions. His English is good, if a little rusty. He hurtles the car round a bend.

'Last week, there . . .' he points to a shattered coconut palm beside the road '. . . there was an accident. A man drove through that tree.'

'Killed?'

'Yes. The man too.'

The Mahe house is a large, Swiss-style chalet, a design which somehow manages not to look incongruous in its lush, tropical setting at the foot of the mountains. Michel gestures towards two rectangular mounds of fresh earth, side by side on the front lawn.

'The dog,' he says sadly, then adds, much less so, 'And Paulette's mother.'

Paulette is Moorean, so much so that in 1973 she was judged Miss Moorea. Michel's father was French, his mother Tahitian. In the local parlance, he is a 'demi'. His father was killed at Dienbienphu. They have five children, three girls, two boys. As I meet them all, Becky's photos spring into life. Manuella, Tatiana, Eileen, Michel, Kevin. We eat, and drink; they practise their English and I practise my fractured French. It's a lot of fun. The family's conversation is mostly in French, but from time to time slips into Tahitian. The difference is dramatic: from the lilting, consonant-rich cadences of French, to the more abrupt, guttural, vowel sounds of Tahitian, unmistakably similar to Maori, but spoken much more rapidly.

After dinner Michel proudly shows me the family album of last year's trip to France, their first outside French Polynesia. In most of the photos Michel is grinning determinedly, but the others look strained. It must have been, I realise, the first time in their lives that they had ever felt cold.

After dinner we watch the news from Paris, then Michel drives me back to the hotel.

'Tomorrow afternoon,' he announces, 'I will take you fishing.'

I retire to my fare where I am lulled by the sound of the sea on the reef, and woken by the exotic noises of the night: the cry of a gecko in the thatch, the call of a strange bird in the mango tree, the curse of an intoxicated tourist as he walks into a wall.

In the morning I go for a walk. The nicest thing about

walking on Moorea is that around the perimeter it's all level, and there's always a bend in the road ahead. Now it's hot, still and dusty. I pass some men listlessly building a block wall that is clearly not straight, the sort of wall that I build. They look up and grin as I pass.

'Bonjour, Monsieur.'

'Bonjour, bonjour.'

I walk on, dripping sweat. I can see the sea to my left through the palms, to my right are the mountains. It is very hot, very dry, and totally tranquil. I come across a roadside shop, the front half of a house, with a counter and a blackboard advertising drinks. I sit down, order coconut milk from the little girl serving. The drink comes in its original, hirsute container, and sitting in a kind of giant egg-cup. There's a straw through a hole in the top, and it costs just over $3. The juice is wonderfully cold and fresh, and there's a lot of it in one nut.

Back on the road I pass a backpackers' motel, where you can get a self-contained bungalow by a white sand beach for NZ$60 a night, a restaurant where main courses are NZ$12, and a small, green, mobile roadside diner where they're NZ$9. I have a delicious ham and cheese omelette at the restaurant, then a little more walking brings me to something called Le Petit Village. This is an attractively set out shopping centre which includes a restaurant, tourist bureau, supermarket, pharmacy, black pearl boutique and ice cream parlour. It's pretty and pleasant, and the Club Med is just over the road, but now there's a dusty quietness hanging over everything. The road is deserted, the garage apparently untended. It's lunchtime and, as in France, the hour is sacred.

Back at the resort I'm sitting beside the pool thinking of nothing much except how pleasant it is to be sitting by a pool on a beautiful island under a tropical sky, when a little boy of about three totters up from the beach, stares at the pool thoughtfully, looks across at me, waves. He calls out something which I can't quite catch, but which sounds like, 'Monsieur, est-ce que je peux me baigner dans la piscine?'

I wave back at him, thinking, 'friendly little chap', then close my eyes against the glare. When I re-open them the child has gone. I peer into the pool. At the bottom is a semi-human shape, something like a water baby.

I jump in, grab him and haul him to the surface. He splutters, coughs, spits, yells in what linguists would call desperanto. But he's okay. Seconds later a thin woman in a bikini runs up the beach, snatches the child and reproaches him in a torrent of French. The only word I can understand is 'Les floaters! Les floaters!' Later I see him bobbing happily in the lagoon, his inflated plastic bands firmly around each arm.

Michel keeps his boat in the lagoon a few minutes' drive from the house. It is ply, flat-bottomed, powered by a large Johnson outboard which he controls with a bar tiller from a cockpit set into the closed-over bow. We pole the boat into deeper water, Michel fires the motor and now we are rocketing across the lagoon through a gap in the coral and into that magical sphere, the water beyond the reef. From out here Moorea is multiple Matterhorns of green, jagged peaks whose summits taper into the cloud. I can see now that the mountains are unclimbable.

The water is inky blue, scuffed into a light chop by a warm wind. Michel cruises hungrily. 'Za birrrds . . . za birrrds . . . ' he mutters. It is the simple formula of the ocean fisherman: where there are birds, there are fish. There is just one complicating factor in the equation — there are no birds.

We pause beside another boat. The Tahitian's body language says eloquently, 'No fish'. Michel's face turns crimson, he is enraged. He swings the bow west and we power out to sea, out of the lee of the island.

The swells heighten, begin to roll, the wind whips their crests into spindrift. I am hanging onto a bar just behind him as he zig-zags further and further away from land. Michel's is the silent fury of the fishless angler.

The swells grow higher, steeper, the wind stronger. When I look back, Moorea is now disconcertingly small. Where are we going, to Samoa? If I could, I would tell him, *ah, look Michel, I don't ah, mind that much about not getting a fish, and, ah, aren't we getting a bit far from land?* But the noise of the motor and the wind make verbal communication impossible.

Just as we are becoming terrifyingly small amid the increasing swells, Michel spins the boat about, heads Moorea-ward. But now we are into the wind, and the boat bangs down from the crests of the swells and slews across their faces. Michel scowls as he continues to scrutinise the sky. 'Za birrrds . . . za birrrds . . .' We slide and hurl our way across the water for twenty minutes; gradually the swells diminish. Then Michel shoves the throttle forward jubilantly.

'Birds!'

And there they are, big and small, wheeling, skimming the wave tops, diving in their feeding frenzy. And we are in the midst of them. Michel fires out a handline, on the end of which is a blue plastic squid lure. We troll the water, surrounded by za birrrds. Seconds later Michel yells out, 'Ay-yay-yay-yay!' He throttles back, hauls in the line hand over hand, flicks an iridescent bonito onto the boat. It is a beautiful fish, blue-black, streamlined. He clubs it insensible, removes the hook, tosses the line overboard and we are off again.

When we have three fish we spin around and head back for the reef, crashing across the waves. To starboard, a flying fish we have disturbed takes off like a wind-up model aeroplane and streaks over the water ahead. Astern, the sun has become an orange lozenge sliding down the throat of the sky.

We pass through the gap in the reef and into the glassy lagoon. Michel calls up Paulette on the ship-to-shore radio he has bought in Los Angeles, on the way back from France. 'Troits bonits!' he calls. And by the time we lift the motor and pole our way back carefully between the coral heads to the mooring, Paulette has the car waiting by the lagoon.

'Une bière?' Michel suggests.

'Certainement.'

It has been a marvellous afternoon, but a dry one.

We call in at the local village magasin for our beers. The shop sells everything from Hinano lager to children's toys. I am introduced to all the Tahitians as 'Rebecca's Papa'. Everyone remembers her, everyone is extraordinarily hospitable. When we leave, the proprietor presses upon me a bundle of dried vanilla pods, a valuable commodity. The pods are thin and dark brown, physically unimpressive. But they exude a fragrance which is divine and which still perfumes my pantry.

Time to move on. I must get to Moorea Airport, some thirty kilometres away. At the resort I ask a small Frenchman with the
brick-red face and feral eyes of the tropical alcoholic if there is
un truck. He gives a tight smile of satisfaction.

'There is no truck Monsieur.' His mouth emits the sweet, per-
vasive odour of stale wine.

'So how can I get to Moorea Airport?'

'Un taxi.'

'Combien?'

Another maddeningly satisfied smile.

'3,000 francs.'

About NZ$50. I walk back up the road to Le Petit Village, to
the Tourist Bureau. In the little office is a young Tahitian woman
of startling beauty. Her name is Katrine. She offers me an orange
drink and rolls her huge brown eyes at my taxi story.

'There ees le truck. But eet leaves from 'ere, not from your
'otel. At sev-een o'clock een za mor-neeng.'

'And it goes past the airport?'

'Oh yes.'

'And how much is le truck?'

'200 francs.'

A bit over NZ$3, to go halfway around the island.

Le truck is right on time in the morning. It grinds its way
around the northern coast, past the many resorts clustered
around the beaches and motus, stopping frequently to pick up
workers and shoppers.

In half an hour le truck is crammed with men, women,
infants. We continue to hug the coast, passing through the little
villages and around the twin indentations, Baie de Opunohu and
Baie de Cook, which reach deep into the island and afford
marvellous views of Moorea's inner peaks. We pass through the
only town of any size, Paopao, pass more resorts, then the road
straightens and le truck rumbles to a stop once more.

'Aeroport,' calls the driver.

On the short walk down the link road to the airport terminal,
I reflect on my time on Moorea and how this lovely island could

be worked into my novel. Certainly, a man running away might find haven here, could meet and take up with a local girl. A girl who works in the Tourist Bureau, perhaps.

Bora Bora, Huahine, Raiatea, Rangiroa

IF A PERSON HAS TO SPEND three hours waiting for a plane, he might as well spend them at Moorea Airport. It's clean, modern, and airy, it has tropical foliage growing not only around it but through it, and it has natty little shops, a tourist bureau, and a café.

I'm sitting at a table by a café relishing a roll and a fruit juice and making notes for my novel when I notice two men walk up to the counter. Both are European, one short and long-haired, dressed in what appears to be striped pyjamas; the other tall, much older, and wearing a short-sleeved, open-necked shirt and a blue baseball cap. They buy coffee, light cigarettes and lean against the counter. As I look more closely I realise that the tall, elderly man is someone I know. I walk over and greet him.

'Francis. Hello.'

Francis Cowan is *Homo pacifica* personified. He is part-Tahitian, part-French, part-Irish, part-Maori; he is a sailor, a navigator, boat-builder, anthropologist, patron of the arts. He lives on Moorea, and has voyaged to all parts of the Pacific, usually the hard way, by outrigger or traditional Tahitian canoe, retracing the voyages of the ancient Polynesians. One of his vessels — the *Hawaiki Nui* — was built entirely of traditional materials, and was sailed by Francis and his crew all the way from Tahiti to New Zealand, via Rarotonga, using only celestial navigation.

Now Francis tells me he is planning another voyage, using a New Zealand totara log for the vessel's hull. I have the impression as I listen to his plans for this latest expedition, that if someone was to suggest that the Polynesians had originated in Greenland and sailed to Easter Island via Tristan da Cunha, then Francis would select a couple of logs, lash them together, and powered only by a sail of woven snow grass, prove that it could have been so.

Now he is about to board the plane for Tahiti. There is a roar outside as it wings in. He picks up his bag and his boarding pass.

'Your short story book, the one you were writing when I met you in Rarotonga, is it finished?'

'Yes.' I take the one copy I'm carrying from my bag. He looks approvingly at the cover. 'It's not one I can spare, though Francis, I'm sorry.'

'I will get one in New Zealand when I get my tree.'

We shake hands and he is gone, a tall, elderly but limber figure. Francis is a novelist's dream, a real, larger-than-life character. Now I am left with his companion. He is German, a painter who Francis has taken into his home. Günter is stocky and affable, and speaks impeccable English. We agree that Francis is a remarkable man.

'And did you know,' says Günter, 'that his wife has just had another baby?' She is French, in her twenties. I didn't.

'Yes,' says the painter. 'Not bad for a man of nearly seventy, don't you think?'

I do think. Yes, Francis *must* go into my novel.

Günter departs, and half an hour later an Air Tahiti jet is carrying me north, touching down briefly on Huahine before ascending again, cruising for thirty minutes, then lining up the runway of Bora Bora.

Bora Bora's runway is one of World War II's more useful

relics. Built by the Americans on one of the motus which surround the main island, its only disadvantage is that it is physically detached from the high island which is Bora Bora itself. This necessitates a transfer by launch across the lagoon. But it's always pleasant to arrive by water, and in preparation for this short journey I claim my small pack and wander out onto the jetty on the lagoon side of the terminal building.

There is the same soporific atmosphere here as I felt on Moorea, a feeling that everyone is about to fall into a sleep of Rip Van Winkle intensity. Out on the wide lagoon there is no visible activity, and in the distance I can see a massive block of bush-covered basalt, like a huge, tilted tombstone, on the other side of the wide lagoon.

As I wait, immobilised by the heat, a ground hostess approaches and smiles winningly.

'Monsieur Lay?'

'Yes?'

'Le journaliste de Nouvelle Zélande?'

'Ah . . . yes . . .'

'You 'av private transport. Thees way, s'il vous plaît.'

The transport is a flat-bottomed, shovel-bowed plastic speedboat, powered by a large outboard operated by a hefty Tahitian man dressed only in shorts. In seconds we are rocketing across the lagoon, and the central island is growing larger by the second.

Spray rises from the speedboat's bows as we hurtle across the still water. I feel like James Bond, an unfamiliar sensation, and one for which I can forgive the hostess for calling me a journalist instead of a writer. We skim closer to the central island. Around the huge basalt slab which is Bora Bora's core are bush-clad hills and a fringing lowland covered in coconut palms. The only buildings in sight are rows of bungalows, a spectacularly sited resort, built up the steep slope of the foothills.

We round a corner of the island and the boatman eases back the throttle. Clustered around a wide bay are the resort hotels, their overwater bungalows stepping out neatly into the lagoon like flocks of brown wading birds. We glide up to the jetty of the Marara Hotel and I step ashore.

Now you don't have to be on Bora Bora long to realise that it's different. The difference is that there are very few New Zealanders or Australians here. There are Italians, and French, and Americans, and Japanese, which gives me the impression that I'm in the Caribbean, not the Pacific. And your vacationers here are the beautiful people. They are cosmopolitan, sophisticated. They move gracefully from pool to bar, from bar to dining table. Their clothes are chic, their accessories glitter. Even their jandals look like designer jandals. Those who have children with them have tiny, perfect children who wear tiny, perfect Reeboks, and who order soft cocktails from the bar like miniature lounge lizards.

The facilities match the clients. There is a vast, open-sided dining room and bar. From the distant ceiling of the cavernous, fare-style lounge hangs a shell chandelier as big and white as an heiress's wedding cake. Cane tables and chairs reach to the horizon, from the direction of which comes the distant drone of excursion launches and power boats.

After the languorous atmosphere of Moorea it's all a bit much. Time is short, too, and I need to see all of this island if it is to go into my novel. So, I decide to take another round-the-island tour.

It's cloudy, and very muggy as le truck pulls up to the forecourt of my hotel to collect me. I climb on board the solid old vehicle. On board are two fat American girls, a young German couple and two pairs of elderly English people. This truck is driven by a plump, middle-aged Tahitian woman in a yellow pareu and a garland of woven pandanus. As the vehicle pulls away from the hotel I lie back against the side of the bus and relax. Then the driver's amplified voice booms back from the cab.

'Thees hotel is Marara Hotel. I theenk thees man who comes from Marara Hotel can tell us what ees Marara een Eengleesh.'

After a prolonged ensuing silence, I realise that her question is directed at me. She says again, this time turning and looking at me insistently, 'Monsieur, I ask you, Marara, what does eet mean?'

Disconcerted by this unexpected cross-examination, I reply, firmly,

'Madame, I haven't the *faintest* idea . . . '

My answer is greeted with gales of laughter from my fellow-travellers, and a bewildered look from the driver.

She frowns at me as she explains, 'Eet means flying feesh. Marara means flying feesh.'

Flying-fish Hotel. Well, that's not a bad name, I suppose. And I lie back again, hoping that there will be no more questions.

The seal ends, the tropical foliage closes in, and the narrow road shadows the edge of the lagoon. To our left is a narrow strip of flat land covered in banana palms and taro plots, then the ground rises abruptly to scrub-covered hills and that gigantic chunk of basalt, the petrified core of an ancient volcano whose summit is covered with a cap of grey cloud.

There are few villages on this side of the island, just isolated houses and the occasional Chinese-run shop selling fruit, drink and crudely hewed carvings. We stop at one shop, allowing me time to have an impromptu game of soccer in the dust with a very thin, grinning Chinese boy of about six. We drive on for a few kilometres before the driver stops and calls into an untidy house surrounded by banana palms. She returns with a bunch of small, plump bananas which she hands to her passengers. They are slightly acidic but otherwise pleasant, and we pluck the fruit from the stalk steadily as le truck grinds on.

The road rises, and at the top of the rise le truck graunches to a halt. Below, beside the lagoon, is an area of flat land. Among the coconut palms and the long grass are a few flat, broken slabs of stone. It is a forlorn, neglected place, but Madame points to it proudly.

'For one thousand years that has been our most sacred marae. There, meetings were held, new leaders chosen.'

The passengers glance at it, then go back to their bananas. As le truck pulls away again one of the American girls tosses her banana peel over her shoulder and out the window behind her. It lands neatly on one of the marae stones.

A few minutes later we come upon one of the strangest sights I have ever seen, in the Pacific or anywhere else. Built up the side of a steep hill, above the road, is a resort hotel. There are dozens of detached fares, built in neat rows, and more bungalows built out over the water. A narrow-gauge, funicular railway runs up the hill between the fares, to help service the units.

I realise that it is the resort that caught my eye when I was being whisked across the water to my hotel. It is a spectacular development, and must have cost millions to build on such a difficult site. And not only is it empty now, it has never had a guest in the several years since it was completed. And it never will. This resort is falling to pieces, the rotting thatch showing gaping holes, the floors crumbling away. It looks as if the complex has been subjected to aerial bombardment during some ruinous civil war.

But it is not the war that has ruined this venture, just old-fashioned human avarice. Built on speculation, to be sold to an international hotel chain on completion, it did not find a buyer. The developer built it on a part of the island where the lagoon is shallow, where there is no beach, no shops and plenty of wind.

Buildings deteriorate fast in the tropics, and this complex has clearly passed the point of no return. The untenanted hotel will rot until it collapses. Now *there's* a scenario for my novel. The greedy, ambitious developer who . . . yes, this folly will have to be included.

We lumber on round the island, passing the yacht club, the occasional church and a few rusting World War II cannons. Across the wide lagoon are the outlying islands which surround Bora Bora. Checking the map to identify them, I see that one of them — Motu Tapu — has been named after a book of mine, and I warm to the Bora Borans for this gesture.

Just after we pass through Vaitape, the main town on the island, and shortly before we complete our circuit of Bora Bora, the sky turns graphite-grey, then comes down to meet us. In seconds the rain is hurling itself down, on the bus, on the road, on the sea, on the land, in a blinding deluge. We throw up le truck's perspex shutters and the vehicle blunders on as if driving through a waterfall.

One by one the other passengers are dropped off outside their resorts, to sprint for shelter across a road which has become a river. I grab a complimentary brolly from reception, run to my bungalow and watch the rainstorm from the shelter of my deck, through the cataract which pours from the pandanus roof. A great, tearing noise accompanies the rain, as if the sky is being ripped in two, and the lagoon is a mass of white water, the gouts of warm rain turning its surface to a million leaping stalagmites.

In twenty minutes the show is over. The sky lifts, leaving the lagoon like a sheet of grey silk in the fading afternoon light. It's a good way to get your rain, I think, and on this profound note I go back inside to shower and dress for dinner.

The big lounge is a great place to people-watch. As I sit and sip my Hinano and wait for my host to arrive I can hear snatches of French, German, Japanese and American as the beautiful people take their pre-dinner drinks.

Next to my table is a trio of Americans: two young men and an elderly woman. One of the men, who is good-looking in a very 'LA Law' sort of way, talks constantly, and I don't have to hear every word to know what the subject of his conversation is. Himself. He is, obviously, a braggart. But the other man fascinates me. He has cropped hair, a sallow complexion and a small moustache. His shirt is cheap and ill-fitting, he looks out of place. He fidgets in his chair, nods and smiles tightly, but makes no real effort to interrupt the handsome loudmouth. The thing about the short-haired man is that he looks just like a serial killer, and the woman, who is obviously his mother, looks like his accomplice. I watch the trio, fascinated by the fictional possibilities of the group, and finding myself hoping that the braggart will be the killer's first victim.

'Ah, Graeme, bon soir.'

'Oh, hello.'

It is my host, immaculate in a grey lightweight suit. He is Pierre, a Parisian of about fifty.

'How was your tour?'

'Excellent, thank you.'

'Good. Come over and meet my other guests.'

Other guests. Oh hell, I thought there would be only Monsieur le Directeur, his wife and myself. But no, there are to be no fewer than sixteen at our table, fifteen French speakers and me.

Naturellement, they are charming. Several couples, from Paris mainly, young, urbane, discerning. Some have young children, who dine with us. Two of the men have just started a private airline which they hope will steal trade from the big airlines and which will hurl jaded French people to far-flung pleasure spots around the globe, including, bien sûr, the island of Bora Bora.

These men press upon me business cards with embossed gold lettering, reverently, as if the cards are communion wafers, but they have the jumpy manner and slightly wild eyes of people who have gone well past the point of financial no return, who will almost certainly make, or lose, millions.

As we sit and drink our white wine from Alsace and consume a stupendous dinner of pork, raw fish, chicken, taro and salad, my fellow diners' conversations grow more rapid and more voluble. They gesticulate, they lean across the table, they wave their knives and forks dangerously, they roll their eyes ceiling-ward, gasp, interrupt each other and shake their heads.

I can catch only the occasional phrase — les poissons, les touristes, le jumbo jet — and by the time I have, my com-panions' conversation has passed on. I look helplessly from one expressive face to another, as if following a doubles tennis-match.

My host is a considerate man, however, who realises that my French is not up to it. When there is a rare lull in conversation he turns to me and explains patiently.

'Excuse me, but we are tokking about thees special cray-feesh that lives down a 'ole in za reef. A special cray-feesh, oo ees very 'ard to catch.'

Another frenetic conversation, accompanied by much flinging of hands, then, 'Now we are tokking about ees new air-line. Eet must go from Par-ree to Abi-jan, eet cannot go directly from Par-ree to Ha-iti.'

'Now we are tokking about building thees very, very deluxe 'otel. Eet weel 'ave een every room a fax, a photo-copier, a video, a personal com-put-ter . . .'

Wine has a reputation as a linguistic lubricant, but now it makes my head spin faster, so I just sit back and let the torrent of words wash over and around me. It is like the tropical downpour, I am engulfed, but fascinated by it. There will, after all, have to be *some* beautiful people in my novel, and they could, perhaps, start an airline.

While on Bora Bora I read a story written by Alex duPrel, a European writer who lives in the Society Islands. The story, which is said to be true, is about a Polynesian woman from Bora Bora called Madame Dorita. The narrator of the story goes to the woman's house to fix her washing machine, and while there sees a beautifully made chest which is filled with old but perfectly maintained hand-tools. Intrigued, the narrator asks about the chest, and Madame Dorita, who is in her fifties, tells him the story of how it came into her possession.

The chest belonged to an American, one of the several thousand soldiers stationed on Bora Bora for nearly four years during World War II. At the age of sixteen Madame Dorita fell in love with one of the Americans, a young man called Mike, and became pregnant by him. Shortly afterwards, the bombs were dropped on Hiroshima and Nagasaki, and the Americans pulled out of Polynesia and occupied Japan. Mike told the girl he had to leave, promised to return to get her and the baby, and gave her his tool chest to look after until his return. He showed her how to oil the tools and polish the chest, to keep them in perfect condition.

The girl followed his instructions faithfully, even when the French soldiers came to Bora Bora from Tahiti to loot the island of everything the Americans had left behind. To stop it falling into the hands of the French militia the young girl carried the chest into the mountains and hid it in one of the caves where her ancestors placed the bones of their dead. And every week she went there and oiled the tools of her American lover.

He never returned. Madame Dorita bore his daughter, then married a local man and had children by him, but she still believed, thirty-five years after he left, that one day Mike would return to her.

Touched by this tale, the narrator decides to trace the American while on a trip to the United States. He learns at the Department of Veterans' Administration that Mike married in

1951, had a family, and is now living in the small town of Rio Minas, in New Mexico. The narrator drives to Rio Minas to meet Mike Shay.

It is a small, dusty town that he finds himself in, a place hostile to outsiders and palpably illiberal in outlook. The narrator has no difficulty in finding Mike, but does not disclose the real purpose of his visit.

Mike Shay is a pillar of this small, ailing community, and is only too pleased to talk about 'his' war. When the conversation is steered towards Bora Bora, the American's reminiscences continue. For two hours he talks of the island, in great detail, but never once does he mention Madame Dorita. When at last the narrator raises the issue of fraternisation with the local women, the American becomes secretive, then confiding.

Yes, he had had local girls on Bora Bora, native women, as he calls them. He even had a Jap girl, later on in Nagoya. Mike, it becomes clear, is an old-fashioned Southern racist, who hardly ever gave his Polynesian lover a second thought.

The narrator concludes his story by saying that he never told anyone about his New Mexico trip, and that as far as he knows, Madame Dorita continues to shine Mike's tools and keep them in the big, beautiful chest. The story, called 'The Hope Chest', concludes with some interesting statistics. The four thousand four hundred Americans on Bora Bora during World War II fathered 132 children by local girls. Only one came back to get his 'wahine' and marry her.

When I leave Bora Bora I take the slow boat back to the airport. It's early morning, but the air is already pleasantly sultry. It's good to be on the move again, away from the rarefied air of the deluxe class. The beautiful people must just move from one hedonistic centre to another. After a while it could get boring.

I stare at the line of motus. Could anyone be bored on Bora Bora? Not really. After all, I didn't get bored, and I didn't do half the things that visitors here should do. I didn't feed a shark, I didn't climb a mountain, I didn't go on the glass-bottomed boat. But I still had an interesting time.

On the launch, people doze. It's hard work this vacationing.

Opposite me is a very attractive young American couple. Honeymooners, by the look of them. He, tall, black-haired and handsome, smokes nonchalantly while she, slender, blonde and beautiful, caresses his hair and winds her pale arms about his body like a climbing plant. Just as I think they will consummate their marriage on the boat seat, we arrive at the airport jetty and they disentwine themselves reluctantly.

As the plane soars over Bora Bora and heads east for Huahine, I stare down at the lagoon, the motus, the town of Vaitape and the three great mountains, Otemanu, Pahia and Hue. I'm not thinking about the beautiful people, the resort or my novel as I look down. I'm wondering in which mountain Madame Dorita hid the Hope Chest.

I am sitting with my new Tahitian friend Armand in the middle of the island of Topatii. Topatii must be the smallest island in all of the Leeward Islands of French Polynesia. It is no bigger than a tennis court, no higher than a wine bottle above sea level, and is covered with ironwood trees. Topatii lies in the middle of the largest passage in the reef of the high island of Huahine, surrounded by deep turbulent water streaming through the breach from the Pacific Ocean, driven by the hot, strong trade wind from the east. Armand and I have come out to the tiny motu in his outrigger to snorkel, but the wind is too strong, so we are sitting on the white sand under the ironwood trees, talking.

Armand is about twenty-five. He is solidly built but not fat. He has a mop of thick black hair, a silver ring through one earlobe and his wraparound sunglasses are shoved up on his forehead. Intricate tattoos adorn his wrists. He could come from Rotorua, or Kaitaia, he has such a Maori countenance, but he is a Huahinian, and a descendant, he assures me, of the island's most famous son, Omai, first Polynesian to be taken to England, in 1774. Armand speaks Tahitian, French and English with equal facility.

'Tell me something, ' he says, very serious all of a sudden. 'I have heard that in New Zealand you drive on the wrong side of the road. Is that true?'

'We drive on the left, yes.'

Armand frowns. He makes a highway in the coral sand with his hand, a median strip with his finger.

'You drive . . .' he makes an arrow on the left '. . . on *this* side?'

'Yes.'

'What about the car steering wheel? That is on the left too?'

'No, the steering wheel is on the right.'

'Ay-yay-yay! On the *right*?'

'Right.'

'*Why* do you drive on that side?'

'I suppose because we were settled by the British, and they drive on the left.'

'So you must change your gears with your *left* hand.'

'That's right.'

'And the cars have to be specially made like that?'

'Well, yes, but they're mostly made in Japan anyway, and the Japanese drive on the left too.'

'*They* do, too?'

'I'm afraid so. And the Australians. Everyone else drives on the same side as you though.'

Armand nods, seemingly satisfied. He gets up, brushes the sand from his blue pareu. 'Okay, we go and feed the eels now . . .'

Ten minutes later he guides the big outrigger into the still water of the Faie inlet. This notch in the side of Huahine is surrounded by hills covered in coconut palms at sea level and behind them, stepping up the steep sides, delicate, flat-topped acacia trees. Small clearings on the hillsides are planted with grey, spiky pineapples, looking, amid the luxuriant greenery, like sea urchins in a rock pool.

In minutes we are at the head of the ria, and Armand ties up at a jetty, beside a cluster of other pirogues. He picks up the bucket from the canoe and we get out. In the bucket is the blue-black, meaty head of a very large tuna.

Faie village is three minutes' walk away; one street of houses, a couple of stores, a new Adventist church. Large mango, breadfruit and citrus trees line the little street, and staring up above them I can see ramparts of rock hundreds of metres high, completely enfolding the village. The towering mountains are covered in dark green bush, and are so high that only a sliver of sky is visible.

Today is Sunday, but being Adventists, the people of the village carried out their devotions yesterday, so the shops are open. Children are playing marbles in the dusty street and men are playing bowls alongside them. They greet Armand enthusiastically in Tahitian, joke and laugh as he passes.

A small stream cuts across the village street, channelled by concrete walls about a metre high. Armand gets down into the conduit, just below the bridge. The stream water is very clear, and comes to just above his ankles. Its floor is covered with small round stones, and the roots of a very large tree grow down from the concrete wall and into the water.

I stand on the bank and watch Armand hold the tuna head under the water beside the tree roots and waft it gently to and fro. A couple of village men sit on top of the concrete wall on the other side, smoking and staring down at what they must have witnessed many times.

Within a minute, the first head appears, emerging tentatively from beneath the tree roots and the concrete wall. Then another appears, and a third, and a fourth, a row of waving heads. Now they are fully out, waving gently in the current, and there are a dozen of them.

They converge on the tuna, then the smaller eels are shoved aside by a couple of massive ones as thick as a thigh, who twist and turn and flop out of the water as they gorge on the pink meat.

Eeling was a popular pastime of mine when I was a boy. There was something mysterious and sinister about the creatures, and as I watch these ones feeding, the memories come pouring back. The Faie eels are not black like New Zealand eels, they are dappled, although their eyes are the same pale blue as the ones I hunted. There are so many of them tearing at the hapless head now that it resembles Medusa with the serpents streaming all around it. And there is a legendary aspect to these creatures, because to the villagers of Faie they are sacred, as one of their ancestors was once an eel himself. The people feed the eels the offcuts of the fish they catch in the lagoon, and never harm them.

Armand pops out the tuna's eyes, and the eels go into a frenzy. The largest, a monster a couple of metres long, pushes the rest away, swallows an eyeball, then slides backwards into his lair, his watchful head still protruding. I stare at Old Blue Eyes, thinking how easy it would be to spear him. Armand sees me staring and laughs.

'You want to hold him? He won't mind.' He scoops up another one and strokes it as if it is a cat. 'Like that, see?'

'Not today, thanks.'

Later we sit out in the sun in the street with a Tahitian shopkeeper and his wife, drinking Pepsi and eating warm butter cake flavoured with locally grown vanilla. The shopkeeper wears only a yellow pareu, and his big belly is brown and perfectly round. Armand talks to him for a few minutes in Tahitian, and the shopkeeper's eyes widen in disbelief. He looks at me incredulously and says, 'Aaaaaeeee . . .'

'What did you say?' I ask Armand. He swallows his cake.

'I told him that in your country cars go on the wrong side of the road.'

Honeymooners are in season in the South Pacific right now. They come from the USA, Germany, France, Switzerland and Italy, but mainly from Italy. Tahiti and its surrounding islands are very popular among young Italians, and they and the other honeymooners comprise most of the guests in this hotel I'm staying at on Huahine. The other group of guests are geriatric Europeans, so that all around me are either the young and beautiful or the elderly and decrepit, with no one of middle years except myself.

It's interesting to study the honeymooners. They are like a species from a David Attenborough documentary, carrying out their post-courtship rituals. They change their outfits several times a day, depending on whether they're Strolling Beside the Lagoon, or Sitting By the Pool, or Having Lunch or Having Dinner, and although they do a lot of touching and eye-gazing in public, you can tell that for some of them, things are not quite as idyllic as the pre-wedding publicity led them to believe it would be. The husbands look distracted, the wives anxious.

One couple captures everyone's attention, because they are physically so outstanding. He is tall and dark-haired, only about twenty-two, with a straight nose and clear green eyes. He walks about the hotel with the confidence and command of a young lawyer on the way up. She is tall and fair and her long blonde hair cascades over her shoulders. Her face is not as beautiful as his, but her figure compensates: she has the long, perfect legs and the erect carriage of the catwalk. From her deportment and stunning clothes she can be nothing else except a Californian model. I have named them Lance and Carol.

Lance and Carol have an overwater bungalow, connected to the rest of the resort by a wooden bridge. Many times a day Carol walks over the bridge, carrying a tray from the bar to the bungalow, bearing coffee, fruit juice, beer, cocktails. The recipient of all these fluids, Lance, emerges from the bungalow mainly for meals, dressed in his designer jeans, boat shoes and floral shirt, open to the navel to reveal his hairless chest and glittering gold chain. Carol hangs on his arm, and just as they pass the bar on their way to the big dining room, for the benefit of the other guests, she nuzzles his neck and slides her long fingers across his tight buttocks.

I thought I was the only one to notice all this until I met Mario and Gina. They are honeymooners too, from near the Toppling Tower of Pisa. Mario is small and athletic, Gina is tall and powerfully built. He is a telephone technician and a fine soccer player, she is a physiotherapist and top softballer. I met them when Armand took us around Huahine in his outrigger.

Gina, Amazonian in her bikini, swims a lot; he, swift and nimble, plays football on the beach with the Tahitian guys who work at the hotel. They all want Mario on their side; they call him Maradonna.

The difference between Carol and Lance and Mario and Gina is marked. The Italians are perfectly natural, they don't act out honeymoon roles, but you can tell they are a well-matched pair, they enjoy each other's company without being soppy about it. I think they've probably lived together for a time.

Mario and Gina and I are sitting at the bar talking rugby — the presence of David Campese, John Kirwan and others in Italy, plus the televised world cup, has made rugby very popular in that sport-crazy country — when Gina nudges Mario. 'Look, therra she goes again . . .'

It is Carol, striding through the hotel, bearing a tray on which is placed two gaudy cocktails with straws sticking out of the tall glasses. Other heads turn at the sight of her long legs, tiny skirt and golden hair. The eyes of two elderly Frenchmen sitting on the terrace grow bulbous as they track her progress. Carol walks majestically across the bridge, then disappears into their bungalow. Gina laughs.

'I theenk she does thees all day, working for heem.'

'It's what they call room service,' I suggest. 'It's usually the hotel that provides it, though.'

'I wonder . . .' says Mario, 'for how long she will do thees.'

'Never once have I seen heem take her anytheeng,' adds Gina. 'I theenk he ees very . . . uh . . .' she gropes for the word.

'Spoilt?'

'Sì, spoilt.'

They go off to see the eels fed, and I go off to borrow a bike to ride to Fare, Huahine's main town. Mario and Gina had seen 'Repas des Anguilles Sacrées' on the hotel noticeboard but hadn't known what it meant until I told them about it.

Cycling is the ideal way to enjoy a Pacific island. You go fast enough to cover the ground, but slow enough to be able to absorb its sights and scents. I pedal through Maeva village, past the store, church and volleyball court and along the narrow plain at the foot of the pyramid-shaped mountain, Maua Tapu.

The plain is a tangle of banana and coconut palms, bougainvillaea, frangipani, breadfruit trees and the smothering creeper, pohue. Every few hundred metres there is a house set among the foliage, and opposite every house is an outrigger tied up on the shore of the lagoon. It's hot, there is a soft head wind, but the going is easy. In forty minutes I'm in Fare.

Cook and Bligh knew this bay well. Sheltered by mountains, it affords deep anchorages and the littoral is flat and fertile. Here Cook left Omai, late in 1777, after building a substantial house filled with provisions, including arms and ammunition. In spite of his worldliness and material European possessions, Omai was of low birth, was not respected, and died not long afterwards.

Today Fare is an attractive waterfront town with many large trees in its main street and a long line of two-storeyed, Chinese-owned shops. Children plunge from the concrete jetty into the deep, translucent harbour water and trucks filled with plantation produce are backed up to the wharf. Crowds of Tahitian people of all ages sit about or lean against their vehicles. As I park my bike and stare out to sea, the reason for all this activity becomes clear: on the horizon, rapidly heading landward, is a small, orange cargo ship.

The *Taporo IV* plies the waters between Tahiti, Raiatea, Bora Bora and Huahine, carrying cargo and deck passengers. I watch her swing in against the wharf with surprising speed. Mooring lines are tossed ashore, and even before they're made secure, a gangway is down, passengers are descending and cranes are swinging into action.

All is organised chaos. A cargo door crashes down, a ramp is laid and a Renault tumbles onto the wharf and speeds away. A container is connected to cables and hoisted aboard. Jandaled Tahitian passengers clutching bags and rolled-up sleeping mats climb aboard, and in only twenty minutes *Taporo IV* is on her lumbering way.

Before the airlines came and connected up the islands in minutes not days, all travel must have been like this. As I pick up my bike and ride away from the wharf, I can't help feeling regret that the days of scheduled passenger transport by sea in the Pacific are all but over. It's hard to get romantic over a squat interisland plane called ATR42, however efficient it is.

My short flight to Raiatea leaves early. Before dawn I sit in the hotel lobby waiting for my transfer. There was a young, heavily pregnant Tahitian woman behind the desk in the lobby when I arrived, but she went outside a couple of minutes before and now I'm sitting alone in the semi-darkness, staring up at the high, woven pandanus ceiling of the lobby.

Suddenly a European man bursts in through the front door and looks about wildly. It is the American honeymooner, Lance, dressed only in shorts, chainless, shoeless. His hair is untidy, he is unshaven.

He sees me and demands 'You speak English?'

'Yes.'

'Is there anyone official here?'

'There was a woman here, but she went outside.'

At that moment, the woman reappears in the hotel entrance. Lance turns to her.

'Have you got medicine?'

She blinks, points to a closed door in the lobby.

'Medicine in there. But it is locked. Not open till seven.'

Lance simulates gestures of strangulation, stares about apoplectically, swallows to calm himself. Breathing deeply, he fixes the woman with his gaze and says, slowly but still breathlessly, 'I need toilet paper, lots and lots of toilet paper. And I need water. Lots and lots of clean water. Toilet paper and water, you understand?'

The woman frowns, nods nervously. 'In the toilet, there is paper.' She points across the lobby. 'In there. I will get you water from the kitchen.'

Lance nods. His usually handsome face is ashen, his hands are trembling. He sprints over to gather the toilet paper, the woman slips off in the direction of the kitchen. Outside, in the growing light, the hotel van draws up. I pick up my suitcase.

Often, for the rest of the day, I find myself thinking: *Toilet paper, lots of toilet paper, and water, lots of water*, and my mind boggles.

From the mountains or from a plane you see them most dramatically. Les passages, the great gaps in the island's encircling reef, dark, apparently fathomless water, sinews of current streaming through them, egress for millenia, for the seafaring Polynesians, nautical on-ramps to an ocean highway that was to lead them eventually to the outermost points of the Polynesian Triangle, to Aotearoa, the Hawaiian Islands and Easter Island.

This is Raiatea, sister island to lovely Huahine. Raiatea is joined at the waist to its Siamese twin island, Tahaa, by five kilometres of lagoon, and on a map of the big twins les passages are all named: Passe Te Avarua, Passe de Nao Nao, Passe Rautoanui. Everywhere on Raiatea there are echoes of New Zealand, place-names just a glottal stop or a consonant away from home. Raiatea's highest mountain is Toamaru (Tokomaru), the inlet which plunges deep into the eastern flank of the island is Faaroa (Whangaroa), the village near the most sacred marae is Opoa (Opua).

Compared with its more seductive neighbours, Bora Bora and Huahine, Raiatea doesn't look as used to tourists, and neither does this resort I'm staying in. It's about twelve kilometres from the main town Ururoa, on a low, flat promontory facing east, very exposed to the trade wind, which comes on hot and strong all day, making the pandanus thatch eaves rattle like sheep's dags. The rocky, rough shoreline is only metres from the door of my fare, and although some sort of concrete arrangement has been built there to impound the water at the edge of the lagoon, it resembles an old-fashioned sheep-dip, and I find it as uninviting.

My fare looks old, or appears to have been untenanted for some time. The cutlery's corroded, the louvres have seized up and the curtain over the sliding glass doors flaps in the wind like an unsheeted jib.

The whole resort has a forlorn air. The only other guests are two silent young Frenchmen who are something to do with tele-communications installation, but they move on after one night. My radio attracts only static, there's no television in the fare, and its unappealing outlook drives me at first to spend the evenings watching Tahitian television in the small office-cum-lounge at the front of the resort.

One night I see an interminable documentary on the life of Eva Braun, a woman who clearly needed counselling, and the second night I watch a French game show. Here, in the centre of the wonderful Pacific Ocean, on the legendary island of Hawaiki, I can't help watching an asinine game show.

Game shows must be one of the most banal inventions of the age. Even though this one's all in French I can recognise clearly the features common to American, British or New Zealand versions of the genre: the patronising host, the contrived bonhomie, the ritual humiliation of the guests, the audience's dopey hysteria, the greed behind it all. So why am I watching it?

Perhaps it's the Frenchness of it which makes it hard to tear myself away from this show, the volubility and gesticulating which accompany it. Quite an elderly woman is invited to mount and ride a mountain-bike around the stage. When she succeeds, albeit shakily, the audience is convulsed, and the host, a grinning Gallic loon of about fifty, goes into spasms, as if he's being electrocuted. I'm disappointed in the French, I thought they would be too sophisticated for such stupidity.

I retire to my dismal, windy fare and go to bed with Maud and Amber. Not local girls, but the Reeves women, mother and daughter, New Zealanders and early twentieth century Fabians and feminists. The book which recounts their remarkable lives is by Christchurch writer Ruth Fry. I read that Amber had an affair with H.G. Wells, and bore his child. Was there any woman in England at that time who *didn't* have an affair with H.G. Wells? When did the little old goat find the time to write all those books?

The resort is run by a Tahitian family, or at least the distaff side of it. The father, a tall, silent, weatherbeaten man with grey hair, is not much in evidence. He leaves after breakfast, on foot, to do I know not what, and doesn't return until sundown. His wahine is short and dumpy, and slopes around distractedly in pareu and jandals. Her English is about as good as my French, but we get by. Her distraction, I learn, derives from the fact that her son, aged fifteen, is in the local hospital with an intestinal ailment. A daughter, a fat, plain, slow girl of about fourteen, spends her entire morning sweeping listlessly with an island broom along the resort paths, past the empty fares, between the croton plants, around and through the dining area. I greet her a couple of times but she just stares at me, mouth agape. I think she is retarded.

Out of this domestic confusion and part-time stewardship, evening meals are somehow conjured for the family and me. They sit at a long table under the open-sided dining fare: aunts, uncles, half a dozen chattering children. I sit alone a little way away from them. All around us is shadowy blackness and the chitter of tropical insects. The shapeless daughter brings a bowl of salad, plonks it down in front of me.

'Aimez-vous la langouste?' she mutters.

'Ah oui, s'il vous plaît.'

She goes to the kitchen and returns with a plate on which lies one half of a small, split rock lobster and two bowls of sauce.

I eat lobster, or crayfish as they're called in New Zealand, whenever I get the chance, which is seldom because they're usually so wickedly expensive. When I was a boy in Taranaki the local fishermen caught and brought them to shore by the sackful. There were no observed limits on catches. Sometimes my father, having been presented with more crays than our family could comfortably consume, buried the surplus in the garden, because the decaying crustaceans were good for his cabbages. Later, in the seventies, the fishermen were puzzled by the fact that their catches had dwindled almost to nothing.

Cette langouste which lies before me looks extremely palatable, and even before the Tahitian family has finished crossing themselves and mumbling thanks to god, I'm excavating a great chunk of its white flesh from inside the curve of its tail. I pop it into my mouth and bite expectantly on the flesh. And as I do so the whole world dissolves in an implosion of pain.

I am dimly aware that the source of this shock wave of agony must be a tooth, but I can't determine its precise location, only that it is on the right side of my jaw, a section of me that seems to have been cauterised by a white-hot iron. Adding to this is the mental shock from the realisation that the pain has been detonated by such a seemingly innocuous food as lobster, and a fairly petite one at that. Lobster can be stringy, yes, and a little rubbery, as this one is, but it still seems incredible that one piece of it could have provoked a tooth to ache so suddenly and so hideously. Eyes closed against the pain, I roll the chunk of fish around in my mouth, snatch up my glass of red wine, swallow some, and put my hand to my brow. Slowly the waves of pain subside, rhythmically, like a seismograph measuring aftershocks, still jumping, but a fraction less each time. Then the tooth settles to a dull, steady ache. I wipe fluid from my eyes with the back of my hand.

From the other table Madame turns, beams, waves her fork.

'Ow ees your cray-feesh, Monsieur?'

I nod my head, screw up my face.

'C'est formidable, Madame.'

For the remainder of this trip, amid some of the best cuisine in the Pacific, I masticate only on the left, and upon my return to Auckland an abscessed upper molar is extracted by my dentist, in a minimum of time and with a maximum of expense.

Ururoa, French Polynesia's second largest town after Papeete, is a bustling little centre one block back from the harbour. It is a town where the region's ethnic delineations are most clear cut: French administration, Chinese business, Tahitian labour. Ururoa has a spectacular new Town Hall, a rather tired market and an almost new community centre called Kuomintang.

It took me about half an hour to see round Ururoa, and now I've been here for four hours. Then, as I stroll along the main street once more, I notice an unusually large number of pale, panting European couples, cameras and camera straps slung across their chests, trudging glumly along the pavements. Tourists, obviously, but why in Ururoa?

As I round a corner, pass a busy café and approach a waterfront bar called Le Quai des Pêcheurs, the reason for these visitors becomes clear. Moored at the wharf is *Windsong*.

Windsong is a 134 m., four-masted luxury yacht which cruises the waters of the Society Islands. It is entirely white and entirely modern; its sails, now tightly furled like folded umbrellas, are computer controlled. I take a seat at the Fisherman's Wharf bar and watch the ship prepare for departure.

The tourist couples heave themselves up the gangway like refugees rather than privileged visitors who are paying US$2,000 each for a week of this. There are shouts, mooring lines are hauled aboard, and *Windsong* draws away from the wharf, stern first. Then it begins to motor silently in the direction of Tahaa. Well clear of the wharf its cybernetic sails unfurl and catch the trade wind, but the vessel remains perfectly perpendicular, and it moves into the mist like a ghostly galleon.

As it does so I see an extended Tahitian family arrive at the fishing boat basin: a couple in their mid-twenties, three young children and an old lady holding a tiny baby swaddled in a woollen jump suit and hat.

The family, laden with shopping, scrambles down into a wooden, flat-bottomed square-bowed boat about four metres long. Carrier bags of groceries and fruit are passed down, and the father passes up a pink plastic baby-bath. The sleeping baby is placed in it and handed back into the boat. The old lady climbs down and crouches in the stern, beside the outboard.

When all seven are aboard the boat's gunwales are close to the waterline. The man, dressed in jeans cut off at the knees, casts off and hauls on the outboard starter rope.

He pulls four times before the motor coughs into life, emitting clouds of blue smoke as it fires. With perilously little freeboard the boat moves erratically across the harbour, its occupants huddled together, its emphysemic Evinrude spluttering. I sit on a seat under a mango tree and watch the family pass out of the harbour and into the choppy waters of the lagoon, which from this level seems to engulf them. Far ahead *Windsong*, stately, shimmering white, veers to starboard in the direction of the passage. *Windsong* is unreal and quickly forgotten, but for some time afterwards I can't help wondering, did the family make it?

The resort is too far from Ururoa to walk to in the tropical heat, les trucks are parked, immobile and empty on a section near the town centre, clearly going nowhere, taxis are not in evidence. So hoisting my bag over my shoulder, I do something I haven't done since my student days — hitch-hike.

Now, as then, I walk rather than just stand at the edge of the road. For about five years of my life this was my only means of long-distance travel. Now I walk slowly and what I hope appears purposeful and unthreatening, making vague elliptical orbits with my left hand, thumb up, whenever I hear a vehicle approaching.

I walk for twenty minutes, passing out of town and along the road that winds south around the coast, past the public works depot, a guest-house, and then, beyond the town limits, European-style houses, some of which bear notices proclaiming,

'Attention: Chien Méchant,' but which, thankfully, have no dogs in sight.

The road is flat, it's very hot, and the coast is unattractive, rocky, sedgy, the lagoon choppy. I round one promontory, then another. The road is good but the grass along the verges is rank. None of the vehicles — utes, cars, motorbikes — take the slightest notice of my imploring thumb.

After half an hour I sit down on a boulder, feeling sweaty and ill-tempered. I've walked too far to go back, but it's still several kilometres to the resort. Merde! Where is le truck? Why don't they run in the afternoons? Then, when it is clear that the bus is not coming I think *fuck le truck* and the coining of this tiny expletive provides slight relief from my transport difficulties.

A big blue ute comes into sight, and I hang out my thumb. It passes me, then stops. I run to greet it.

The driver is a scrawny, elderly Tahitian man, very brown and wrinkled. He has no English, and pours a torrent of French at me as I climb into the cab. I'm so grateful to be uplifted that I don't mind that he speaks so fast that I can't understand a word. Just to be transported is enough, and I gasp, 'Merci, merci Monsieur, il fait très, très chaud . . .'

The ute is big, high, new, shiny and comfortable, and the deliciously cool breeze sluiçes through the open window. The old man drives around one headland, slows, stops beside a bougainvillaea hedge, turns off the engine.

'Chez moi,' he announces flatly, and as I glumly open my door, climb down and prepare to shut it he commands crossly, 'Doucement, doucement . . .'

On the road again. The old man took me no more than a kilometre and a half. I walk until my shins ache and my mouth feels like sand. There's no shop anywhere to get a drink. Vehicles swish past me at irregular intervals but none stop, including a big white Peugeot driven by the Chinese emporium proprietor from whom I made extensive purchases in Ururoa earlier in the day and with whom I had a long, cordial conversation. He stares at me blandly from behind the wheel, must surely have remembered me, then turns away and drives on. Now I reproach myself. It was a dumb idea to hitch-hike. I could be sitting in the bar back at the wharf, sipping cold Hinano and reading *Maud and Amber*. Instead I'll be walking for at least another two hours and . . .

Behind me I hear the growl of a large engine. A klaxon honks. I turn and see . . . un truck! A great, green, ugly, beautiful truck. It approaches and I wave frantically. It slows, stops. I haul myself aboard and it draws away. There is only one other passenger, and she is lying on the other side bench seat, asleep. It is the retarded girl from the resort. Curious, I peer through the front window of the vehicle and into the cab. The driver turns and chucks his chin in greeting. It is the girl's father, the grey-haired man whose wife runs the resort. So *this* is what he does all day, he drives le truck. I too lie down and close my eyes. Le truck, le truck, c'est magnifique!

I'm now in the company of a sixty-year-old Raiatean called Johnny Brotherson, a Tahitian whose grandfather was Danish. Johnny is tall, strong, big-bellied, and an orator and storyteller. He has been chosen to represent Tahiti in the world storytelling championships in Louisville, Kentucky, an apt choice for a man who lives in the town of Ururoa, which means 'Long-lips'.

Johnny drives me around Faaroa inlet in his ute. He speaks very good English and puts great feeling into everything he says, but has the Gallic habit of ending all his statements with an interrogative grunt.

We drive along the northern shore of the long, lovely haven of Faaroa. 'From heere, Kupe left for the first of hees voyages to New Zealand, uh? He returned heere three times. The last time, he buried hees can-nu een the swamp somewhere at the top of the harbour, uh? Ev-ver since, people look for the can-nu, but they nev-ver find eet, uh?'

It seems an eccentric thing to do, I think, to bury a huge canoe, but I'm diverted from this conundrum by the beauty of Faaroa. Its headwaters are deep and still, it is enclosed by steep hills and its shores are thickly clad in stands of banana, breadfruit, mango and coconut palms, all covered with the rampant creeper pohue, which drapes itself across the trees like living camouflage cloth. We round the top of the ria, follow the other shore. The road is now unsealed and cratered, and Johnny slaloms this way and that, pointing from time to time.

'There ees coconut plantation. Van-eella, pine-apple. Up there, government plantation. Teak, mah-hogany, uh?'

We cross a tidal estuary, pass through the lonely looking village of Opoa. The road deteriorates further, the land-crabs scuttle aside on tip-toes as the ute approaches them. It's late afternoon now, and the light is dimming. We round another headland. Johnny pulls into the side of the road, looks to his left.

'Taputapuatea, uh?'

The marae is located on a tongue of flat land about a kilometre wide, a promontory covered with coarse grass and a stand of very tall, slender coconut palms.

As we approach the marae I can see through the palm trunks the waters of the lagoon, grey now in the late afternoon light. Out there, handily placed, is Passe de Ave Moa, one of the ocean on-ramps. Through the pass, first turn right, sail for four thousand kilometres and you get to the Bay of Plenty.

Taputapuatea marae consists of a large area of dark grey coral stones, hewn flat and laid straight onto the ground. On the lagoonward side of the square, larger slabs have been placed upright in a line, so that they resemble a row of high-backed chairs. In front of the row one stone slab stands upright, alone. The dirt between the flat stones is pocked with land-crab burrows.

Johnny is clearly in his element here; he talks ceaselessly, passionately, as if he is already at the Storytellers' Olympics. He talks of the old gods, of Taaroa, Tane, Oro and the others, of myths and traditions, of the coming of the new Christian deity and the seismic shift in Tahitian spiritual perceptions when this occurred.

He refers to the traditional gods in oddly Christian terms, talks of the canonisation of Taaroa, of the interdictions of the gods, of the communion between them and the priests, appearing to make no distinction between the pantheism of ancient Polynesia and the much later worship of the single deity. Perhaps this blurring of beliefs is significant, it occurs to me later.

We reach the single, upright slab, which stands like a black tombstone in the fading light. Johnny lays one big hand affectionately on it, as if patting a horse's rump.

'Here, victims were sacrificed to the gods, uh? Ther-ra necks wer-ra put against thees rock, ther-ra throats wer-ra cut open, uh? Victims must be strong, healthy, not wounded in battle, because our gods demand much blood, uh?'

Trying to ignore Johnny's persistent use of the present tense, I ask 'Did this happen often?'

'Many, many times. Thees stone has been here since the eleventh century.' He points to the ground. 'All under here, many, many bones, uh?'

I shuffle my feet, regard the dirt uneasily. Johnny bends down.

'Land-crabs always breeng bones up, uh?' He picks up a yellowed, concave bone the size of a 50 cent piece, hands it to me. 'Skull bone, uh?' I hold it just long enough to see the cranial seam, then drop it back down the hole. I want to run from this lonely, creepy place, the light is fading faster and the palm trees are assuming spectral shapes. But Johnny is just getting into his stride; there are hundreds of stone slabs at Taputapuatea, and he has a story for every one of them. Moving from one marae to another, I pause at a small, altar-like platform, on which stands a thick, carved phallus of stone, pointing skyward.

'This is an ancient fertility symbol, I suppose, Johnny?'

'Nah. A man from Hollywood put that there. They make a movie here last year.'

As we wander among the ancient stones, Johnny tells me of seers, exorcists, witchdoctors who still have thriving practices in these islands. It seems that Christianity does not have its grip upon the Tahitians the way it does on other Polynesian people, especially the Samoans and Cook Islanders. I've already noticed that churches are not ubiquitous here, and this may be because the old gods are still a presence, and the Black Arts still practised.

Johnny tells me of the local witchdoctor who sacrificed his own adolescent son to keep up his potency, and of the killing a couple of years ago of seven people on one of the Tuamotus, in an attempt to drive evil spirits from the atoll.

None of this calms my fevered imagination. I could tolerate all this in the morning maybe, but not now, not with darkness closing in. I feel like screaming, 'Enough! Enough!' Then at last, just as I'm ready to bolt from the place, Johnny turns abruptly and heads back towards the road.

'Time to get back now, uh?'

My skin is still creeping as we emerge from the palms. And as Johnny turns the ute around, a little way further up the rough road, I am astonished to see that right beside Taputapuatea there is a small hotel and restaurant. As we drive away I think to myself: there is nothing, but nothing, that would induce me to spend the night in that place, in the company of the countless spirits of the slain.

We drive back around the ria in darkness, and Johnny the storyteller is still talking. Through all the legends and tales, one thing shines through: for the Tahitians, Raiatea was not just the homeland, but the spiritual fount. For Johnny Brotherson it was more. The way he tells it, this island was the hub of the entire Pacific. He explains that after every ocean voyage, for example, the explorers had to return to Raiatea, because it was their lodestone for celestial navigation. And the names of other Polynesian island and landfalls — Savai'i, Haraiki, Avaiki, Hawaii — are all commemorations of this, the original Hawaiki.

All this is intensely interesting, but it also begs the question, *where did the first Raiateans come from?*

Johnny is unfazed.

'I know where from. Only two peoples in the Pacific put their dead in the trees, uh? Tahitians and North American Indians. So, the first Polynesians came from North America, uh? From there to Hawaii, from Hawaii to the Marquesas, from there to Raiatea.'

Now this is highly revisionist stuff, and I would privately dismiss it swiftly but for one compelling, clearly discernible fact. Johnny Brotherson, teacher, storyteller and oral historian, even in the half-light of the early evening, looks more like a Red Indian chief than anyone I've seen since *Dances With Wolves*.

Taputapuatea might be Raiatea's heartbeat of history, but as for all these islands, its modern marae is the airport. It's clean, efficient, convivial, informal. As I sit and wait to be plucked up and flown off, I'm entertained by a parade of people of all ages, all races, checking in, picking up, dropping in, collecting, delivering or just calling by on the off-chance they'll see a friend or relation.

It's like Saturday morning shopping in a country town: bags and parcels everywhere, people milling about, greeting each other in the elaborate French manner — the proffered cheek, the kiss, the turning of the other cheek, the handshake.

I like these small, sociable, security- and document-free airports, surrounded by tropical foliage and giving glimpses of lagoon and sea as well as runway through their big windows.

'Excusez-moi, Monsieur.'

I move aside for a tall, elderly, patrician Frenchman, pushing a luggage trolley. In the upper compartment of his trolley is an overnight bag, unzipped. From the bag peer a pair of coiffured, curly-haired, eager-eyed black poodles, each with a red bow round its neck.

Outside I hear a faint drone which rapidly intensifies, subsides for a few moments, then swells to a roar as reverse thrust is applied. The god of the air has arrived at the modern marae.

The world has gone flat. Flat and very blue. It's as if I'm on the edge of the earth. After the high Society Islands, I'm experiencing mountain withdrawal. There is land where I am sitting, but it's an atoll, a spit of coral sand about 120 metres across, eight kilometres long and no higher than a metre and a half above the level of the sea. The sea! I never fully appreciated the Pacific's enormity until now. The steps of my thatched bungalow are just a croissant's toss from the lagoon, and the lagoon of Rangiroa is the biggest in the South Pacific. I can't see the atolls on the other side of it, and to scan the perceptibly curving horizon from east to west takes several seconds. Everywhere there is blueness, the high, pale sky, the dark, apparently limitless lagoon.

Rangiroa, Island of the Long Sky, is one of the seventy-five islands which comprise the Tuamotus, seventy-five coral atolls strewn across the Pacific Basin like a galaxy. The best known is

Mururoa, far away over the horizon to the south-east; the biggest and most populated (one thousand people) is Rangiroa.

So low and numerous are the Tuamotus and so powerful are the swells which strike their reefs, that they presented a formidable obstacle to the first European sailing ships feeling their way across the uncharted Pacific. Negotiating this archipelago, particularly in darkness, must have been like sailing through a sea sown with deadly natural mines. Charles Darwin, on H.M.S. *Beagle*, 20 October 1835:

We passed through the Low or Dangerous Archipelago, and saw several of those most curious rings of coral land, just rising above the water's edge, which have been called Lagoon Islands. A long and brilliantly white beach is capped by a margin of green vegetation; and the strip, looking either way, rapidly narrows away in the distance and sinks beneath the horizon. From the masthead a wide expanse of smooth water can be seen within the ring. These low coral islands bear no proportion to the vast ocean out of which they abruptly rise; and it seems wonderful that such weak invaders are not overwhelmed by the all-powerful and never-tiring waves of the great sea, miscalled the Pacific.

Charles would have little difficulty finding or avoiding Rangiroa now. There's an airport, a telecommunications centre and a satellite dish. On my second day here I was handed a fax from the other side of the world, and on the excursions blackboard on the wall of my hotel the French manager has just chalked the notice, 'Finale Coupe des Coupes: Werner de Bremen 2 — Monaco 1', after watching the European Cup Winners' final on television last night. The global atoll has arrived.

There are still natural deprivations here, no streams, no rivers, no soil, no crops, no pigs, dogs or chickens, no timber trees; all the things you take for granted on the bountiful, well-watered high islands to the south-west. There are also no trucks, no banks and no nightclubs. None of the lean, dark Tuamotuans I've met speak English, and all seem to speak French rather than their indigenous language.

But the lagoon is a vast hamper of fish, the complete absence of industry and commerce has left the water perfectly pure, and because the atoll is aligned almost perfectly from west to east and the moon is considerably full, I can watch it rise to my left, a glowing lemon disc, while to my right the sun slips down and turns the sky rose. Sun and moon here are like two beautiful, perfectly balanced cosmic counter-weights regulating the earth and sea.

The trade wind has dropped away with the setting sun. Along to my left an elderly French couple are standing on the coral rocks at the lagoon edge tossing bread to the fish, who are leaping and splashing appreciatively at their feet. To the right, a thin, dark figure glides from the palms, clutching a fishing rod. He stands on the rocks and flicks out a line. It lands a few metres away, he reels it in, casts the lure out again, reels in. After the fourth cast his reel rachet bursts into song, the rod bends, jerks. I stroll along, sit on the sand and watch him reel the fish in and flick it onto the beach. He grins at me as he does so. He is about nineteen, dressed in a blue pareu. He has a small goatee and his hair is a tangle, a Rangiroan Rastafarian perhaps. The fish is very pretty: pink, with yellow eyes. As it flaps about and he disengages the treble hook from its mouth, I call up my French, point to the fish.

'Ah . . . cette pêche-là . . . comment s'appelle?'

He grins again, but does not reply.

I think hard. 'Ah . . . le poisson, quel nom a-t-il?'

He extracts the hook, smiles, but says nothing. My frustration level is rising. 'Ah . . . comment s'appelle, cette . . . this fish. Fish, fish!'

The fisherman smiles tolerantly, replies in perfect English:

'In our language we call it Taia. It has a French name, based on the Latin, but I can't remember it. Taia is what everyone calls it. It makes excellent eating.' He holds out the rod. 'Would you like a turn?'

When I left home I promised my elder son Matthew that I would bring him back a shark's jaw from the Tuamotus. For years he's been fascinated by sharks. He's got books on them, posters of them, he knows their species and their sub-species. This fascination may have begun with the Jaws movies, or the fact that he's a Pisces, but whatever the cause, he's obsessed with the sinister predators, and so I've said I'll get him a set of their teeth. This should be no great problem, because I've been told that the lagoon of Rangiroa is full of sharks.

But when I ask Monsieur le Directeur of my hotel where I can get a shark's jaw, he just shrugs.

'I don't know. In the village maybe. 'Ave a look . . .' He walks away, his mind clearly on other things, the next European soccer final perhaps.

I bike down the atoll to Avatoru village, a straggling, untidy, apparently deserted line of houses, shops and guest-houses. I am aware from a map that I am almost at the end of this island, and the village street looks as if it ought to culminate in a pretty market square, or a small boat harbour filled with outrigger canoes, where the shore will be lined with racks of drying fish, including sharks and sharks' jaws.

My expectations heady, I cycle round the bend, past a small church, and stop. The road has become a rutted track which terminates at a cracked concrete jetty. No market square, no outriggers, no shark cadavers.

I lay the bike down and walk to the edge of the jetty, the underside of which soughs as the current sucks and tosses the sea against it. The cleft in the island is very deep, the torrent pouring through it as clear as glass. In fact the water in the passage looks as solid as a glacier, as if I could step on it and stroll over to the next atoll about half a kilometre away.

After being mesmerised by this pure but fearsome sight for some minutes, I pick up my bike and ride back into Avatoru in search of the jaw of *Carcharodon carcharias*.

A cycle tour of the strung-out street reveals shophouses which sell French bread, cakes, canned softdrinks, bottled water, bottled air, tinned meat, filled and unfilled rolls, Cheeseballs, potato chips, jandals, fishing lures, outboard motors, video tapes, gaudy shirts, pareu, beer, disposable nappies: all the commodities needed for a comfortable life on an atoll. But there are no shark jaws. In fact there are no souvenirs whatsoever. It's as if Rangiroa never had a tourist in its entire history.

I bike away, jawless, joyless. Surely, on an atoll surrounded by a shark-filled sea, on the edge of a vast lagoon where the predators lurk, someone would be marketing their otherwise unwanted mandibles? Evidently not. I resolve to try the market when I get back to Papeete, but I'm nagged by the thought that I've never seen any there, either. Presents for Gilly and Rebecca are straightforward. After all, where there are French there is French perfume, and I've already got Ben his Gameboy computer game. But it's a feral memento that Matthew wants, and it seems he will be disappointed.

Le petit déjeuner, French bread, jam and coffee. Big cups of coffee. I like it, I can't take a big meal at breakfast time. I especially like the coffee, it's dark and strong and bitter. I have a second cup, then a third, relishing as I do so the sounds of animated, lyrical conversation which drift across from the other tables in the dining room.

'Ah oui, oui.' 'Alors!' 'Vraiment?' 'Bien sûr.' 'Bon appetit . . .'

Breakfast over, I walk back along the lagoon edge to my bungalow. I think I'll borrow a hotel bike and cycle to the end of the atoll. But as I unlock the front door, the world begins to sway. I am pinned to the bed as if by gravitational force. I will my head to rise but it refuses. The room is scrolling upwards like a television screen without vertical hold. Warm sweat streams from me, the only movement my body is capable of, and I am slimy as the eels of Huahine. My gut growls like bad plumbing. What is it? What is happening? Malaria? No, there's no surface water her for mosquitos to breed in. Fever? Ah . . . that's it, the dreaded dengue fever has got me. And there's no phone; I can't call Monsieur le Directeur to croak out my condition. I stare up at the rows of woven pandanus thatch, unable to comprehend anything but the direst thoughts.

A saying drifts into my crippled consciousness, *feed a cold and starve a fever*. Starve a fever? But I am hungry, and I must replace these seeping body fluids. There is a small piece of French bread and a bottle of mineral water on the shelf on the other side of the room. I stare at the loaf and the bottle but I am unable to haul myself even a centimetre closer to it. I push down on the bed with both hands, but I cannot rise. It's hopeless, the dengue has me in its power, I will die here, rot here on this atoll and no one will know. I must do something, tell someone, call out to the Italian honeymooners in the next bungalow. I struggle up onto my elbows for a second before they give way. I drop back, lose consciousness.

I open my eyes. I can hear the waves sloshing at the edge of the lagoon. It's very hot, but I've stopped sweating. I try to sit up, and succeed. My head has stopped spinning. I put both feet on the floor, stand up carefully. The room stays in one place. I walk across, pick up the bread and chew it. I drink some mineral water. It's warm, but good. I open the door, walk out into the sun. I am weak but no longer giddy. I must have been unconscious for two days. I look at my watch. It's one o'clock. I've been asleep for just four hours. As quickly as it came upon me, the fever has gone.

The flat, sealed road runs straight down the centre of the atoll, looking like a licorice strap. On either side is scrubby vegetation and stunted coconut palms. The bigger bushes, mostly burau and tohunu, are no more than spindly shrubs, with the occasional frangipani and the elegant spreading kahaia trees standing taller than the rest.

I'm cycling east, towards the other end of the atoll. On the black road the sun's early afternoon rays are scorching. I'm not forcing the pace, but in only minutes I'm drenched in sweat. And Rangiroa seems to have shut up for the day: there is not another vehicle in sight, not a car, truck or motorscooter. I pass the deserted airport terminal, the silent satellite station, a labourless building site. Of course, it is siesta time. Mad dogs and Kiwi bikers go out in the midday sun.

I pedal on, panting, sweltering. I cross culverts which straddle breaks in the atoll, dried-up watercourses where the trade wind blows through. But the breeze is as hot as a jet exhaust and offers no relief from the heat. The sun beats down on my bare shoulders. I gasp at the hot air. The road runs on, straight and apparently endless. And it's eerie seeing no other humans whatsoever.

I pass a sign on my right which points into a stand of tall coconut palms. 'Kia Ora Resort.' There is no sign of life there either. This atoll is an insular version of the *Marie Celeste*. I bike on, my legs moving slowly and more slowly. How much longer can this sodding atoll be?

Then, just as I'm ready to give up, the road curves to the right, the vegetation thins out and stops, and the Tiputa Passage lies before me. It looks as if the entire Pacific Ocean is pouring through a channel about one hundred metres across. The water is pale at the edges and cobalt blue in the centre, its surface turbulent, shredded with current. The passage looks as if it contains enough energy to heat and light Paris. On the seaward side of the opposite shore is a squat lighthouse, on the inner side I can see a few houses and a church spire protruding from the palms. Tiputa village must be over there in the trees, but how do I reach it?

I park the bike and pick my way across the coral rubble to the edge of the passage. Swim? It would be suicidal, the channel must be hundreds of feet deep and the current would be unforgiving. No Tiputa. I get back on the bike and ride on another kilometre, to where the road ends at a concrete jetty and a few houses. Then I turn around and begin my return journey, with a planned stopover at the Kia Ora Resort.

Nothing could be more different than the inner thigh of Rangiroa compared to its exposed seaward side. The lee of the atoll is pure brochureland, the lagoon like a huge pond, the sand like talcum, the palms tall and regal. Out on the lagoon a few yachts lie at anchor and the glass-bottomed boats are filled with Italian honeymooners peering at the fish. I lean my bike against the Kia Ora's bar, which is right on the edge of the luminous blue water.

The barman is fat and bare-chested, a Frenchman of about fifty with frizzy grey hair dragged back in a ponytail. He has a bushy, yellow-grey beard about a foot long, into which three frangipani flowers have been inserted. He puts me in mind of the character from the Edward Lear poem.

Two Owls and a Hen
Fours Larks and a Wren,
Have all built their
Nests in my beard.

Well, the avian details are all wrong, but the effect is the same. High on the wall behind him, above the liqueur bottles, is a set of shark's jaws the size of a basketball hoop. Jammed over its lower teeth is a gendarme's cap. It's an effectively sinister piece of symbolism, but when I ask the barman where the jaw came from, he just shrugs. 'Been there for years,' he says 'since before I came here.'

Resigned to never finding Matthew's jaw, I explain to the barman the delicate state of my stomach. He grunts understandingly, produces a sachet of Enos and empties it into a glass of mineral water.

'C'est bon pour la dyspepsie.'

It's effective. In seconds I can feel my stomach's gratitude.

'Merci. Merci beaucoup. This morning I had dengue fever.'

His eyes widen. 'Vraiment?'

'Either that or French coffee doesn't agree with me. But that Enos was good, thank you.'

He nods. 'That's okay, I fix a lot of my customers. I used to be a doctor.'

'Really?'

'Yes.' He chuckles. 'But I killed too many of my patients, so I became a barman. Now I do cure people. What would you like to drink now?'

As I pedal wearily back along the flat, spear-straight road, it's mid-afternoon, the siesta has passed, and there are a few signs of life. The occasional car and motorbike overtake me. But there is still an overpowering sense of loneliness about this place, and just to come across another human causes surprise. I am sure this feeling drives from the enormity of the sea which surrounds this sliver of land, this skimpy strip of coral sand and rubble near the centre of the largest ocean on earth. That and the vastness of the hot sky, when there are no landforms to obscure it. What land there is, what land I'm on, seems irrelevant, just a geographic afterthought. Rangiroa. *Long Sky*, indeed.

I'm very thirsty, but when I call in at the airport it's deserted, its café closed. The one plane a day has come and gone. Back out on the road again my pedalling slows to a treadmill pace, and I curse myself for not taking a canned drink away from the hotel bar. Then, just as I'm contemplating stopping and plunging into the bush to seek shade, I see on the left of the road a rough handpainted sign. Pizza, Coquillage, Boissons.

I dismount and lean the bike against a bush. The shop is tiny — just an open booth and a counter over a glass case crammed with shells — an extension of the front room of a small house built on the coral sand and surrounded by tropical scrub. A pizza hut, one might say.

There's no one in sight so I lean in over the counter and call hesitantly, 'Bonjour, bonjour . . .'

A man pads out from the rear of the house. He's short, stocky, and bulges in the middle, like a brown egg. He wears only black shorts, has olive skin, fair hair, blue eyes set wide apart and a flat nose. He is clearly a demi, but a demi-who?

I buy a can of cold Coke and we chat. Didier is affable, voluble. He speaks almost no English, but I manage to learn that his mother was from Martinique and his father was in the French navy. Hence his negroid features. His wife is Tuamotuan, and I glimpse her — a thin, dark figure — moving about in the rear of the house.

Didier does a bit of everything: runs this le snack, collects shells, goes fishing. When I explain that I'm here to write about Rangiroa he becomes very enthusiastic, presses upon me his card, on which is a fax number. He welcomes guests here. So, is this a guest-house? I ask. No, but camping is possible. Visitors can camp on his land for a few dollars a night. It's a great idea, possible the only way some people could afford to stay on Rangiroa.

'Do you like shells?' Didier asks.

'Yes, I do, I love shells.'

He rummages in the glass case under the counter, to get at a trident shell. As he does so my eyes follow his right hand, and my heart leaps. There, among the jumble of coquilles, is a shark jaw, large, yellow cartilage, wicked white teeth, wide open, like a gin trap.

'Ah . . . voilà!'

'Comment?'

'Là, là. La mâchoire du requin. The jaw . . .'

'You want to see it?'

'Please.'

He passes it over. It's not as big as the one in the hotel bar, but it's threatening enough. The original wearer of this set of dentures must have been two metres long at least. I touch the teeth, gingerly. Each tooth is a triangle of razor-sharp bone, and there are dozens of them, arranged in neat ranks, with two reserve platoons behind the front line, ready to move into the forward rank. The jaw is fresh enough to have dried bits of its previous owner still clinging to the cartilage, and it gapes, as if some shark dentist had just commanded the creature to say, 'Aaah.'

But seeing they are so rare, it must be very expensive.

I grit my own teeth, ask Didier, 'How much?'

He shrugs, pushes out his lower lip. 'One thousand francs.'

Ten US dollars. I can't believe it. Not only have I found one, I can afford to buy it.

'Marvellous. I'll take it.'

He wraps the jaw carefully in newspaper, and as he does so, I ask, 'Did you catch it?'

'Oui. There are many sharks in the lagoon. I spear, catch, kill.'

And as he hands over the parcel in exchange for the note, I notice that the third and fourth fingers of his left hand are missing.

On my last evening on Rangiroa I have a long talk with Sylvia Deloubes, who runs the hotel with her French husband. She is a Nouvelle-Hébridaise, a Bourao, daughter of a French father and a New Hebridean mother. Sylvia is about thirty, with an olive skin and soft brown eyes. She and her French husband lived in Vanuatu, but had to leave under Walter Lini's administration. They tried living in France but didn't like it ('The people were not nice to us'). New policies of a new government in Vanuatu mean that they might be able to return there. Life here on Rangiroa is pleasant enough, but rather lonely. And until the new college is finished, their daughter has to go to school in Papeete, and Sylvia misses her very much.

Sylvia is wistful, restless, apprehensive. She knows her home is the Pacific, not Europe, but doesn't know exactly where she and her family will fit in. They have a role here but she is not sure what it is. The suspension of nuclear tests is good, but will cause people to lose jobs. What will her daughter do? All Sylvia knows for certain is that her family's future is uncertain.

Sylvia seems to me to personify the colonial dilemma of the French in the Pacific in the nineties.

Tourism, I read somewhere the other day, is now the world's largest industry. If this is so, and judging by the number of planes I've seen landing and taking off on formerly remote islands of the Pacific, it must be, then there is still an irrational aspect to much of it. Not the travel itself, which is a very well-organised activity, but the prices charged for flying from one desirable place to another.

When I planned the trip I am currently on, which was for the purpose of unblocking my imagination drain in order to complete a Pacific novel, I knew that I had to go to the islands of French Polynesia, Rarotonga and Western Samoa, in that order. The cost of flying from Auckland to Tahiti, and from Tahiti to Rarotonga, I estimated would not be considerable. After all, flying from Tahiti to Rarotonga — sister islands as they are often called — takes only a couple of hours, being comparable in distance to going from Auckland to Dunedin. I had forgotten that flying from Auckland to Dunedin is one of the most expensive air routes in existence. So, it proved, was the cost of taking scheduled flights firstly from Auckland to Tahiti, and then to Rarotonga, and stopping off. This fare came to well over $2,000. For that, I pointed out indignantly to the airline, I could fly right around the world and back. They were apologetic, but unrepentant: the scheduled fare was the scheduled fare.

While pondering this problem, of how to fly from Auckland to Tahiti and on to Rarotonga without taking out another mortgage, I noticed in a Pacific holiday brochure that it was possible to purchase a package deal for Tahiti, which included return air fares *and* accommodation, for $1,200. In other words, to fly from Auckland to Tahiti and back to Auckland, and be accommodated in what looked in the brochure to be a perfectly acceptable hotel, would cost half of what it would to fly from Auckland to Tahiti and on to Rarotonga.

When I observed from the airline schedule that the flight back to Auckland from Tahiti went *via Rarotonga*, this idea became very appealing. What was to prevent me, I reasoned laterally, from buying the round ticket and jumping plane, so to speak, in Rarotonga? The plane would be on the ground for at least an hour. Plenty of time to disembark. Then it should be fairly simple to get another ticket to get me on a flight a week later, from Rarotonga to my next destination, Western Samoa, and from there back to Auckland.

So, at a travel agency in Auckland I bought the package holiday, which included accommodation and a return flight from Auckland to Tahiti, three thousand kilometres of which I would not use, for half the price of the scheduled fare. As I said, irrational, but I prided myself on having discovered a way to circumvent this lack of economic logic.

So, here I am, on le truck from Papeete to Faa'a Airport, Tahiti, with my suitcase and briefcase. It is just after midday on a Wednesday afternoon. The weather is hot and sunny, the briefcase contains precious notes for my novel, and le truck is sweeping me along the short stretch of motorway to the airport. As we reach the terminal I make yet another check of the traveller's Holy Trinity: passports, tickets, traveller's cheques. All present and in order, including the separate ticket for a flight from Rarotonga to Samoa and back to Auckland.

I am deliberately in plenty of time, too, for this critical connection. Only one flight a week goes from Tahiti to Rarotonga, and my teenage sons will be arriving there in forty-eight hours, from Auckland, depending on me to meet them at four o'clock in the morning. I carry my baggage across the street and into the terminal building, behind which I can see the tail of the big bird which in a couple of hours will whisk me off on the short trip to Rarotonga, the setting for a crucial section of my novel.

I walk jauntily over to the check-in counter — just as well to get the formalities over as soon as possible. I hand the Tahitian woman behind the counter my ticket and passport, and place my suitcase on the scales. No need to mention to her, I reason, that I will be disembarking early from the flight. The woman opens the ticket, scans it, taps her keyboard, then picks up a luggage label and slips it round my suitcase handle.

As she does so, I have a hot flush. On the label are the initials 'AKL'. *Auckland*. Aaaah . . . Of course, my suitcase will be consigned to Auckland, along with where its owner is supposed to be going, my supposed destination. Oh God, *my suitcase* . . . In it, as well as clothing, are items indispensable to an itinerant writer: books, notes, my portable electric typewriter, diarrhoea pills and a variety of other tropical nostrums. I reach out, grab the case back.

'No, no. This case is going to Rarotonga, not Auckland.'

The woman has a dark, flawless complexion and lustrous brown eyes. But there is little warmth in her expression, only confusion.

'But, Monsieur, you are going to Auckland. It is on your ticket.'

Caught, discovered, exposed. I am like a book whose cover has been torn off. And an absurd but probable scenario flashes into my mind. I am forced to fly back to Auckland to accompany my case. There I claim it, then wait through the night for a plane to fly back to Rarotonga, from where I have just come. And the cost will be crippling. Swiftly assessing my options, which in the circumstances doesn't take long, I know that the only thing I can do is come clean. After all, I haven't committed any offence, all I've done is try to save myself $1,000. Writers have to sell an improbably high number of books to make $1,000. The last royalty cheque I received was $11.25.

'Yes,' I reply carefully, 'the ticket *says* Auckland. But in fact I want to get off in Rarotonga.' I add on a dissembling note, 'I've had a change in my plans.'

The woman frowns, looks at the ticket again, hard. The intensity of the frown, and its persistence, worries me. It suggests that what I have done *is* a deeply serious offence, comparable with hijacking, aerial piracy or French nuclear testing. At last she looks up.

'So you have a teecket to Auck-land, but you don't want to go to Auck-land.'

'That's right. When I noticed that the place was going to Auckland via Rarotonga, I remembered that I need to go to Rarotonga, so I decided to get off there instead.'

At this demi-lie, the woman looks down at the ticket again, thrums her slender fingers on the counter, looks very thoughtful. Behind me, a queue has formed, and I can hear multilingual mutterings of discontent at the delay. Dammit, why didn't I think of the case? Why did I *bring* the case? If I'd just had hand baggage, I would have got away with it. Too late, too late. At last the woman looks up, and speaks some of the most ominous words I have heard.

'Will you step over there please? I will get my superior to talk to you about this.'

It is like waiting outside the headmaster's office. The queue that I was formerly at the head of moves forward. It consists of ordinary law-abiding travellers whose tickets are checked and approved without question. Their cases are placed on scales, labelled and moved away on the strip of black rubber which takes them to wherever cases go from there. Their boarding passes are issued and they move off calmly, but not before they have given me curious looks which imply, *Why is that man not acceptable? What has he done?* And over on the other side of the terminal a pair of khaki-clad gendarmes is eyeing me with disconcerting interest.

A tall woman in an airline uniform emerges from a door behind the counter, holding my contentious ticket. She is about forty, tall, thin, French. Her blonde hair is drawn back tightly. Not a headmaster, but conceivably a headmistress.

'Are you the man 'oo 'as the teecket to Auck-land, and you say you are stop-peeng in Raro-tong-ga?'

'That's right,' I reply coolly. 'My plans have changed. I must get off in Rarotonga. I don't want to go to Auckland now.'

Her eyes narrow.

'So why deedn't you change your ticket when you were in Papeete?'

'I didn't have time. I just got in from Rangiroa this morning.' I decide to go on the offensive. After all, is it my fault that airline fares are so absurd? I fix her with a gaze which I hope is as penetrating as hers. 'Look, I'm not breaking any law, I just need to get off the plane early, *and I need my suitcase with me.*'

She purses her mouth, exhales through her nostrils, examines the ticket, frowns, looks up again.

'And for 'ow long deed you want to go to Raro-tong-ga?'

'Eight days.'

'And *then* you go to Auck-land?'

'No, then I go to Samoa.'

Her frown intensifies. My heart begins to beat at an uncomfortable rate. She is still frowning as she asks me, 'Do you 'ave a teecket?'

'To Samoa?'

'Yes.'

'Oui. Oui, oui.'

'Show eet to me . . .'

I open my briefcase, fumble in it. The detritus of my journey falls out onto the airport floor: notes, pamphlets, receipts, a paperback, dried vanilla pods, unsent postcards. I scrabble around, locate the blue plastic folder, pass it over. The woman takes out the ticket and opens it with pronounced distaste, as if it is a soiled nappy. Then, without looking up, she asks, in a tone which suggest she is addressing a congenital liar,

'So, you *are* flying from Rarotonga to Apia. On the ninth of September.'

'Yes.'

'And you 'ave a val-lid passport?'

'Of course.'

I pass it over. She checks it, nods solemnly, closes the ticket, puts it back in the folder, passes it over and smiles, tightly.

'Very well, since you 'ave an onward teecket from Rarotonga, you can proceed.'

But I do not move from the check-in counter until I see the other woman place a label around my case's handles that bears the letters 'RARO' and watch the case glide off happily along the black rubber conveyor belt.

My mental health restored, boarding pass in my shirt pocket, I move off towards the departure lounge. I feel exhausted though, and my day's journey has barely begun. But there's no departure tax to pay here, so that's a bonus.

Just then I see a familiar, grinning face, moving in my direction. It is my good friend from Rarotonga, Brett Porter, who's been in Tahiti on business. We shake hands delightedly: he too will be on the flight to Rarotonga. Brett is accompanied by a tiny, aged Chinese man with a crumpled face, dressed in a grey, open-necked shirt and baggy trousers. Brett introduces me to the man, whose name is Harry Woo. I assume he is Brett's driver, or perhaps an itinerant vegetable seller from Faa'a. The Chinese man bids us goodbye, and shuffles off. Later Brett explains that Harry Woo is a Papeete businessman. 'Real estate, hotels. One of Tahiti's wealthiest men. A multi-millionaire.'

Sitting safely in the departure lounge, staring through the windows at the runway and the shimmers of heat above it, I reflect on the day, and on Tahiti. My mind is filled with more pleasant memories of the Society Islands.

Earlier today, sitting by the waterfront, staring up at the profile of those marvellous mountains, it wasn't hard to imagine the island as it was when Wallis, Cook and Bligh first saw it. The huge, glossy-fronded breadfruit trees are still here, and looking out across the water I could savour the line-graph profile of Moorea, and picture Somerset Maugham leaning over the deck rail of his ship as it arrived — and perhaps already calling plaintively, 'Garçon, garçon', and understand just why James Hall and Charles Nordhoff came here to write the *Bounty* story, and never went home.

An hour later, ascending from Faa'a Airport, staring down on the town, the lagoon, the soaring green mountains, the white ring of reef waves, I now know why, when old Pacific hands gather and their talk turns to favourite islands, a dreamy look comes over their faces. 'Tahiti, Tahiti . . .' they murmur, in voices which carry a hundred affectionate memories. It is a conversation which I too will enter.

Men Behind Bars

FOR A WRITER TO THINK OF the islands of the Pacific is
to think of their colonial pasts, of the days when ships, not
planes, carried people to them, when writers could lose
themselves in a shack by a coral strand, write by kerosene
lantern and send their manuscripts off in a bottle, and on
infrequent visits to the island's town, rub shoulders and possibly
other parts of their bodies with a variety of human flotsam.

The core location for this fantasy is usually a waterfront bar, a
dingy establishment with sagging floorboards where deeply
tanned men with bloodshot eyes and murky pasts sit on stools
and stare at the line of spirit bottles with stained labels,
dreaming of those they left behind or of tropical schemes that
came to nothing. The bar is run by an unfrocked priest who
lives in the back with a native woman by whom he has had a
succession of children, and he has a love affair with a
missionary's wife who cuts the throat of his mistress before
slitting her own wrists on the beach. Somerset Maugham and
James Michener have a lot to answer for.

Most of the bars have long gone, or have been spruced up so
much that the romance, along with the dust and tired floorboards, have disappeared. Quinn's Bar, in Papeete, has gone

completely, in the bars of Pago Pago the patrons stare only at the big video screens showing live gridiron from Baltimore, and on Bora Bora there's only a Club Med, a yacht club and lots of deluxe hotels.

While I'm sitting on a plane lamenting these trends, I'm also reading an H.E. Bates story set on the island of Moorea. It's about an Englishman who lives with an ugly Tahitian girl who loves him but whom he does not love, and who ultimately tries to kill him while out fishing in a canoe because the man has fallen in love with another, beautiful Tahitian girl.

After a terrible fight the ugly girl falls overboard and is mortally bitten by a shark. The story is called 'The Grapes of Paradise', a title perfectly in tune with its melodramatic flavour, and although it is improbable, it is entertainingly so because it conjures up the colonial era so well. It is also the story that is causing me to regret the passing of Quinn's, and other bars of the past, before I had the chance to know them. As I swallow cold lager at nine thousand metres and listen to Mozart on the headphones, I read, 'He sat in bars on the waterfront and watched dust blow out of potholes in the road outside and then blow back in again.'

I put the book down and set my brow against the perspex window. This is not a long flight, and the Pacific seems very close, a bright, deep, inviting blue. All that lies between me and the sea are a few drifts of vivid white clouds. My mind dwells on Maugham and Bates and Michener and all those writers who immortalised the old Pacific. Was it easier to write a novel in those days, when time moved at a schooner's pace, and a writer could live well on a dollar a day? Maybe, but the question is an academic one. This is the nineties, and I'm writing about the present. But in forty years or so, I console myself, this era too will seem as quaint and dated as the twenties and thirties now seem to us.

As I'm contemplating the ironies of history, the plane suddenly makes a perceptible shift in its trajectory, and through a gap in the clouds, I can see my next destination: a mauve triangle of island, veiled by cloud, surrounded by white reef waves. Rarotonga.

I nudge Brett, point excitedly out the window. He just flicks his eyebrows. After all, it's his home. But I'm transfixed already by the sight of the island, which is growing by the minute. This will be the first time I have landed on Rarotonga at a civilised, daylight hour, four o'clock. On the other occasions it's been four in the morning, a brutal time to travel, and a testimony to the consumer-hostile policy of airline flight schedulers. To land on Rarotonga in daylight, you usually have to come the long way round, via Tahiti. The seat belt sign flashes on, and the under-carriage hydraulics whine.

'How long since you were last in Raro?' asks Brett, snapping his belt together.

'Two years.'

'So you won't have been to Trader Jack's new bar.'

'They were building it when I was last there. What's it like?'

Brett grins. 'In about ten minutes I'll show you,' he says.

Trader Jack's Bar and Restaurant overlooks the lagoon by downtown Avarua, at the mouth of the Takuvaine Stream. It is the closest building to the sea, and it is new because the previous Trader Jack's was struck by the full force of Cyclone Sally, early in 1987. A generous measure of the Pacific Ocean poured through the front of the bar, and out the back, radically rearranging the decor. Jack has a photo album on the bar documenting the event. When things calmed down again, Jack decided, either boldly or foolishly, depending on what happens in the next few summers, to rebuild his bar on precisely the same site, working on the theory that lightning doesn't strike twice in the same spot.

Lightning no, cyclones . . . maybe. These demented tempests always come from the north, and although there's now a massive, and very ugly breakwater angled across the stream mouth, designed by a former prime minister to prevent another Sally from venting her wrath on Rarotonga, no one knows *exactly* what will happen when the next big one comes.

The breakwater is composed of huge boulders, heaped together, and as I lean on the railing of the bar deck which projects over the lagoon, it occurs to me that these same boulders, placed in this very strategic position, may well provide a future cyclone with a ready supply of ammunition to hurl at Trader Jack's, and other buildings of lesser importance like Government Departments and assorted international banks. Trader Jack's is like the lead skittle in a ten-pin bowling alley, and even if the alley is a few hundred kilometres wide, if another cyclone strikes Rarotonga, it'll be the first building to be struck.

But all that lies somewhere in the future. It's not the cyclone season now, the air is warm but not uncomfortably so, the beer is cold, the lagoon is still, and the late afternoon sky is turning a delicate shade of apricot.

Jack proudly shows me his restaurant, which leads off the bar. The speciality is fresh fish (a commodity in surprisingly short supply in post-colonial Polynesia), and there's an equally impressive wine list. Gone are the days when Avarua restaurants threw out red wine because it was too old. It's the bar itself that is the focus of Trader Jack's. It's a beauty, a big, U-shaped bar where you can sit and watch a living cliché or two: the sun rise over the mountains and the rusting hulk of the *Yankee*, wrecked on the reef in 1962, or set over the coconut palms which line Avarua's foreshore.

Although the bar is new, there's nothing synthetic about the memorabilia round the walls: harpoons, thirties' diving suits, photos of game fish and schooners and the men who sailed them. Jack himself is not the ex-priest of literary bar legend, but he is an unfrocked rugby league player. He's about 1.95 metres, with a chest like a wine barrel and the reach of a gibbon. And he has an unorthodox approach to his branch of the hospitality industry: he curses his customers, often and loudly. He argues, swears, verbally abuses, looks wild-eyed, until just when you think he will toss you into the lagoon he claps you on the shoulder, grins and says, 'This one's mine, what'll it be?' This is the standard treatment, whether the customer is an 18-stone Samoan sumo wrestler or a little old lady from Cincinatti. I had a vision as I watched Jack saying to an elderly American woman who was standing in the restaurant, looking confused, 'Come on you silly old sheila, for Christ's sake, take a bloody table and sit down . . .' of the same woman recounting her South Sea Island vacation, saying to her friends at the bridge club in Cincinatti, 'And in Raro-tong-ga we went to this bar where this big, big man — the owner, no less — told me to get my fucking ass into gear. We had such a *swell* time there . . .'

Then there are Jack's regulars, the locals for whom the bar is the confessional, the market-place, the psychiatrist's couch, Blind Date and the Personal Column, all in one. They are the contemporary equivalents of those exiles of old: the planters, the traders, the sailors, the charter boat operators, the lawyers, the retired ships' captains. Men like Don Silk, who for years skippered the inter-island traders which sailed, often under perilous conditions, to the islands of the northern Cooks; or Ross Hunter, who married Vara Cowan and started an engineering business here, fathering along the way what will undoubtedly become a dynasty; and Ewan Smith, a pilot who began a small airline which today interconnects the islands of the Southern Cooks. All have put down roots on this island, all are successors to the Pacific dream.

As I sit at the bar and eavesdrop, I realise that these are conversations which are distinctly Pacific. There is a salvage opportunity after a big yacht was wrecked on Puka Puka, there is a rumour of more black pearl dealings on Manihiki, the latest developments in the saga of the new hotel at Takitumu, the price of export runner beans, and the cost of freighting produce out of the tropics. Everyone has an opinion, everyone expresses it. It doesn't matter that everyone already knows what everyone else's opinion will be, and how everyone fits into this microcosmic plan. It's all part of living on an island, in this case an island only the size of Wellington harbour.

After I renew acquaintances with all these old Raro hands, Jack takes me aside. Proudly he shows me a large, neat pile of photocopied sheets. He has a new computer upstairs, he explains, and its menu can be taken literally. It can produce a menu. He waves the sheet at me.

'The new one I've just had printed. Designed it myself.' He is about to pass it over when his big face momentarily clouds. 'Actually I should've waited till you came. You're a writer, you could've checked the spelling for me. Not that there's anything wrong with my spelling,' he adds hastily.

He hands the menu to me for approval. I run my eye down the lists of entrées, main courses, desserts. It is indeed a fine piece of layout, with a striking typeface. It could grace the tables of Maxims. But . . . oh oh . . .

'Ah, Jack . . . how do you spell "Locally"? As in "Locally caught Marlin"?' The menu's 'Locally' has only one 'l'. Jack's face darkens.

'Shit . . . ' he says, through clenched teeth.

'And Parrot fish,' says a voice over my shoulder, 'It's got two "r's", Jack, not two "t's".' The speaker is Ross Hunter, the man who reads more books than anyone else on the island. Now a curious crowd has gathered around the newly published menu.

Lawyer Mike Mitchell peers at the list, asks with feigned bafflement, 'Chess board. Why would anyone want a *chess* board with their coffee, Jack?'

'Anyone for a game of *cheese* after dinner?' says Brett Porter, grinning.

Jack's brow has concertinaed, his face is thunderous. Cursing, he picks up the ream of freshly printed menus, takes them over to a bin, drops them into it and bounds back upstairs to his word processor. One up to his customers, who go back to the bar, chortling. But Jack will have his revenge, somehow, tomorrow, or the day after.

Some hours later, the phone on the bar rings. Pouring a Cooks Lager with one hand, Jack picks up the receiver.

'Trader Jack's. Yeah. Yeah? Really? Great. Yeah, fine. See yuh.'

He hangs up, beams around the bar.

'Guy on Ted's boat just landed a tuna. Big yellowfin. He's bringing it over after it's been weighed up at the club.'

The fish comes on the back of a small truck which pulls up alongside the bar. A crowd swarms out onto the deck to see. It's enormous, the biggest fish I've ever seen: very plump, with blue-black flanks and a mouth held open in a rictus of astonishment. Its fins are long and curving, like pale yellow scimitars. The man who caught it, an American, can't stop grinning.

Jack buys the fish from the boat operator (who owns it), and it's lugged around the back of the restaurant to be butchered into manageable portions for marinading. The catch puts everyone in the bar in a celebratory mood, as if we can all take credit in some way for placing the plastic lure inside the fish's mouth.

'Fresh fish on the menu here tomorrow,' announces Jack to the whole bar.

'How do you *spell* tuna, Jack?' someone calls out.

'Piss off, arsehole,' replies our host, reaching out a long arm and giving the speaker a playful wallop across the side of the head.

As I sit on the deck and sip my lager, and watch the sun slip down into the lagoon, turning the palms to delicate silhouettes, I think, yes, the hero of my Pacific novel will spend a lot of his time in Trader Jack's. So, in the interests of literary research, must I. The evening sky flares to a crimson hue, and holds its colour for several minutes. Since Mount Pinatubo erupted in the Philippines, the sunsets have been even more glorious all over the Pacific. God knows what it's doing to the atmosphere, but it's certainly pretty to watch. Then my attention turns to the mountains, which rise very Bali Hai-like, above the town. They are jagged, precipitous, irresistible, the sort of mountains a man in a novel might try to climb. Soon, I'm going to.

Life on an island whose economy is based on tourism has an odd aspect to it because at any given time a substantial slice of the population is in a state of transience. On Vava'u or Bora Bora or Rarotonga, for example, several times a week a loaded plane drops out of the sky and discharges a group of total strangers who for varying periods roam about the island's roads, villages and beaches. A few days later another plane drops in, uplifts the visitors and in hours they're somewhere completely different.

For many of the locals on Rarotonga, monitoring these arrivals and departures involves a degree of social and economic opportunism.

I am in Trader Jack's enjoying an evening beer when Jeremy Erskine-Cartwright, ex-minor English public schoolboy, former army officer, part-time pawpaw grower and guest-house proprietor rushes into the bar. He is clearly in a state of excitement, and his breath comes in snatches as he announces to the gathered drinkers,

'Slovenian Olympic ski team, came in on the nine o'clock flight. Been training in Queenstown. Here for four days. Eight gels, twelve chaps. *Terrifically attractive*, I hear.'

Even by Rarotongan standards, this information is unusual. Inured to Americans, blasé about the British, only mildly curious now about Scandinavians, Slovenia is something else again.

Mike Mitchell turns to me and says, 'Where the hell is Slovenia?'

I think back to what my Slovene friend Anton, whom I got to know at the Seaside Inn in Apia, told me about his piedmont homeland.

'It's in what used to be Yugoslavia. Next to Italy, I think.'

'Oh. So where's this team staying, Erskine?'

'Edgewater. I'll ring up and invite them to PJ's.' He reaches for the bar phone, taps the keys. 'Vaine? Now listen very, very carefully. I want you to call the Slovenian ski team and say that they are invited over to PJ's for a few drinks. By the Cook Islands ice hockey team. When? Now, Vaine, right now . . .'

While we wait for a reply, Jack draws a map of Europe on a paper serviette on the bar. At least he says it's Europe. It looks more like the forequarters of a prehistoric animal, although the leg of Italy is recognisable.

'So where's fucking Slovenia then?' Jack demands.

I scrawl an oval on the serviette, to the upper right of the beast's leg.

'There. Just underneath Austria.'

The bar phone rings and Erskine-Cartwright snatches it up. He listens, nods, puts the phone down, grins jubilantly.

'They'll be at PJ's in ten minutes.'

In a remarkably short time Jack's is evacuated, we're crammed into Mike's Nissan Laurel and heading off in an anti-clockwise direction, past Avatiu harbour, past the airport, around Black Rock and into Arorangi village.

PJ's is a small but hot late nightspot: bar, dining area, dance floor, three-man band. The music is loud, the lights dim as we enter, and sure enough, the Slovenes are there, some of them dancing already. And the rumour about their physical attributes is entirely correct: they are very attractive: snow-tanned, lean, athletic, with longish dark hair and fine-boned Slavic faces. There's just one problem. They're all men.

They're in their early to late twenties, dressed in designer jeans, Reeboks and T-shirts which are stretched tightly over their enlarged pectoral muscles. They are smiling broadly as they dance with the one female on the floor, a Kiwi girl of about thirty who's already proved herself a bit of a goer in her short time on the island.

Now she's leaping frenziedly in the centre of the circle of Slovenes, jumping like an aerobics instructor, smiling at each one in turn, clearly relishing her favoured position. Erskine-Cartwright introduces himself to another team member at the bar, asks where the women's team is. The Slovene smiles.

'They are very tired. They get off the plane, they go straight to bed.' He looks at the dancing Kiwi girl. 'But we doan go to bed. Yet.' He laughs in a knowing way, and Jack's team joins in, thinly. The news that the female Slovenes have gone to bed is in itself sobering information, but the subtext is equally dejecting: these men are so virile and athletic, so Baryshnikov-like, that the likelihood of their women being enticed away from their own kind in favour of a bunch of overweight, middle-aged inebriates is remote.

We have a round of drinks at the bar and glumly watch the dancers. Then, in the middle of a hot number, the Kiwi girl suddenly bursts from her Slavic circle and go-goes her way out the door and into the night. The skiers look momentarily disconcerted, then continue dancing with each other. 'Shirt-lifters, probably,' Mike mutters. The evening is clearly going nowhere, it's nearly midnight, so I finish my beer and decide to walk home to Mike's place, just up the road.

Outside, along the road a little way, I hear a groaning, see a crouching figure on the verge. As I approach the figure it gets up from the long grass. I see it is the Kiwi girl. She shakes her head vigorously, wipes her mouth, says to me matter-of-factly, 'That's better.' She gulps, shakes her head again. 'I just chucked.' She gasps. 'Okay now though.' She gasps again. 'Must get back to the Russian spunks.'

And out here on the roadside she starts dancing again, jerking, jumping, snapping her fingers, and in this agitated manner makes her way back into the nightclub.

Next day I'm lying on the sand at the end of the little motu of Oneroa, across the lagoon from Muri beach, reading. Between this motu and the rest is a broad, shallow channel of beautifully clear water. I look up and see two snorkel periscopes approaching, two flippered figures moving lazily through the water of the channel.

The snorkels come closer as the pair glide into the water a few metres from where I'm lying. One figure, then the other rises from the water. Both remove their masks and snorkels, wade ashore. I recognise the man as one of the Slovenes who was in PJ's last night. The woman with him I have not seen before, but she is clearly another of the Olympic team.

She stands before the water's edge, mask in hand, looking about her, and instantly I'm put in mind of that memorable scene from the first James Bond film, *Dr No*, where Ursula Andress emerges from the tropical sea, in Jamaica or wherever it was. This woman, who must be about twenty-five, has the same proud stance, the same tall, perfect, athletic body. Her hair too is blonde, and hangs in wet strands over her finely deported shoulders. But there's one startling difference. This statuesque woman is naked from the navel upwards, and her high, firm still-dripping breasts are two of the most striking natural features I've ever set eyes on in these islands.

Wading back across the lagoon from the island, I pass several more snorkelling Slovene women, none so handsome or strikingly clad as Ursula, but all strongly built and clearly relishing their tropical stopover.

Back on Muri beach I pass the whole Slovenian men's team, playing volleyball. Most of them are wearing only shorts, and their bodies are unbelievably muscular, shoulders as wide as doors, thighs like barrels, stomachs flat as planks. I never thought about it before, but all that slaloming and poling across mountainsides must be a powerful body-builder. Certainly these skiers are magnificent specimens, and I have to stop and watch them for a while.

They're good volleyballers too, just to top things off, fast, limber, with fine ball skills. As they serve or volley or spike they shout, laugh and call across the net. Their language sounds rather like Russian, and is spoken with passion, accompanied by much waving of their powerful arms.

Time to get back to Trader Jack's, to watch another sunset, to catch up on the latest bulletin of Rarotonga news. The Slovenians are already history here. After all, they'll be on a plane out soon, and gone forever. But there'll be others dropping out of the sky to take their place, to excite the expectations of the locals, tomorrow or the day after. A netball team from Barbados, perhaps, or a film crew from Rome, or a dance party from Tahiti. Nothing so permanent as the temporary, as the saying goes.

Because They're There

EVER SINCE I FIRST SAW THE high islands of Polynesia, I've wanted to climb them. Mountains anywhere are fine objects, I'm all for them, but I've never had that Hillary-like yearning to actually knock the buggers off until I saw the volcanic peaks of the Pacific. It's not just because they're volcanic, either. I've climbed a good way up Ruapehu, and Taranaki, and I've conquered Rangitoto several times. I've even walked up Vesuvius and peered into its hole. All these were satisfying experiences, but they were the result of curiosity, not obsession. My need to climb to the top of a high Pacific island has become a fixation, the kind which causes people to be forever restless until whatever they are obsessed about is satisfied. It is the way writers work: a book written is an obsession fulfilled, another literary slope scaled.

So what is it about the mountains of Polynesia that makes me yearn to stand on top of them? I can remember very clearly the first time I saw peaks like that. It was my first visit to Rarotonga. My plane had, as usual, arrived in the early hours of the morning, and after a brief sleep I emerged, panda-eyed, from my motel room in Matavera. I looked up at the island, and blinked in the tropical light. I rubbed my eyes, then rubbed them again.

It was still there: a clutch of twisted peaks, a sheer-sided massif, piercing the sky. What astonished me, along with the steepness of these peaks, was the greenness, a jungle-green which could only be jungle, clothing them like a greatcoat. No other mountains I'd seen had foliage which came right up to their summits, and no other mountains seemed so accessible. From their peaks to the sea was only a few kilometres, and I wanted to get from one to the other.

But to my surprise, few people shared my compulsion. Yes, they agreed, the mountains were beautiful, but let's just look at them, shall we? The best way to see them is from down here, by the lagoon, or out a plane window as we approach or leave. Vertical movement in the tropics is a very uncomfortable activity, so, anyone for snorkelling?

The local people shared this aversion, I found, but for different reasons. Traditionally the mountains were shunned as places of settlement, which was not to say that they weren't well known. The remains of prominent Tahitians were buried in the mountains. But for practical purposes it was only the lowland fringe which was densely settled. This demarcation remains throughout Polynesia. Moorea's mountains, for example, are so stunning they immediately put me in mind of that notable scene from *South Pacific*, when Bloody Mary points across the water to Bali Hai. I was only sixteen when I first saw what she was pointing at, but I never forgot it. An island with sheer walls and saw-tooth peaks, soaring from the sea. It seemed unreal, but James Michener knew Moorea and Bora Bora and most of the others, and I know now that there wasn't too much cinematic licence in that magical scene. But when I was on Moorea, and asked a man who had lived there all his life if he had climbed the mountains, he looked at me as if I had a touch of tropical fever.

'Climb za mountains? Why?'

'Because . . . because it would be good to stand on top of them.'

The Moorean waved his hand dismissively and gave me a sharp look.

'Eef I wan' to go up there,' he pointed to Mount Tohiea,

twelve hundred metres above us, '*I weel get zee 'eli-copter to take me.*'

But now the humour is really on me. For days I've been sitting on the deck outside Trader Jack's waterfront restaurant, mesmerised by the sight of Te Kou, a forest-covered bluff looming nearly six hundred metres above the town of Avarua. I observe from a map of Rarotonga that Te Kou is proxime accessit only to Te Manga, the island's ultimate peak, and that there is a track at the head of the Takuvaine Valley, right behind Avarua, which leads to Te Kou's base.

Today, Sunday, when there's little else to do except Praise The Lord, will be the day to make the ascent. My two teenage sons, Matthew and Ben, arrived in the early hours of this morning on a flight via Tonga and Western Samoa. Straight out of winter, the boys are very pale and jetlagged after their circuitous journey, but after a few hours' sleep they're keen too to be up and climbing. It remains for us to get a lift to the head of the valley from Arorangi, where we're staying with Mike Mitchell and his teenage son, Joshua. Joshua has climbed Te Kou once before, he tells us, so he will be our Sherpa Tensing. But Mike is unenthusiastic about the expedition. He'd rather spend the afternoon reading.

'Okay,' I say nonchalantly, 'but if you can't manage the climb yourself, can you take us up the valley in the car so we can?'

He gives me a steely glare.

'I'll come.'

Mountain climbing in the tropics, as far as clothing is concerned, is a simple affair. The less you have of it, the better. We wear sneakers, shorts, T-shirts and I have a small back-pack containing a large bottle of Coke, a towel and my camera.

The five of us cram into Mike's old Nissan Laurel and drive around the island, through the deserted, silent town and up the valley of the Takuvaine, into the broken heart of this ancient volcano. To our left we can see clearly the green peak of Ikurangi, 485 metres.

'I've climbed that one,' says Mike knowingly, but when I press him for details he is evasive.

The valley narrows. Here there are just a few isolated houses between plots of taro and bananas, spreading breadfruit trees and the occasional family of pigs and chickens. Then the foliage closes in and the road peters out. We leave the car and begin to follow the well-defined track.

We come to a series of terraced water gardens, small plots of taro enclosed by low bunds covered in trimmed grass. A brook of clear water flows down from one terrace to another, channelled cleverly so that it enters each plot from alternate sides, freshening the plants before passing on down, through the low, lawn-covered bunds to the next, stepped garden. Although the gardens are clearly the result of careful tending, today there is not a person in sight as we pass up and around the beautiful, irrigated allotments, sprouting their lines of taro leaves. The garden plots look like giant playing cards, like tens of hearts.

The track moves up and around the gardens, which are surrounded by dense thickets of palms and taller trees. The three boys have already moved well ahead of Mike and I, though we can hear them chattering excitedly in the trees like foraging primates. Then the water gardens stop, the valley narrows to a V shape, and the track moves back and forth across the steeply falling, boulder-strewn stream. There are pandanus, huge ferns and arums all around us, and the rich smell of humus floats up from the forest floor. The only wind is Mike's and my panting.

The track leaves the stream, and steepens appreciably, moving around the base of large trees whose twisted roots bind the soil. The boys have moved well ahead, but we can still hear their incessant chatter. Where do they get the energy to talk as well as climb? Then, as the track swings right, the foliage parts, and Mike and I stop. Now we can see clearly what we have taken on. 'Jesus,' I murmur, when my breath returns.

Te Kou is not a peak but a wall of rock, soaring sheer, still hundreds of metres above us. The wall is almost entirely forested, except for one large, scapula-shaped bare section. The crest of the mountain is gently curved, but dips abruptly at both ends before soaring again to the east and west, to rise again to other peaks. I get out the Coke and we each swallow some.

Then, clutching at the branch of a big miro for support, I say, 'How the hell do we get up there?'

Mike, chest heaving, mouth agape, stares up.

'I think there're ropes. There'll have to be.'

Now it's hand over hand, the twisted tree roots giving a good hand-hold but slowing our progress. Luckily the earth between the roots is dry, in wet conditions purchase would be nearly impossible. We move on up, heaving, grunting, panting. The back of Mike's blue T-shirt is dark with sweat, and his hair is soaked. He looks like I feel. After half an hour of this, the track steepens again, and we come upon the first of the ropes, linking the roots of two trees.

The ropes are knotted at intervals, and it's now a matter of hauling ourselves from knot to knot, hand over hand, while trying to keep our feet in contact with the nearly vertical slope. It's noticeably cooler now, and the vegetation is changing: the trees are more stunted, ferns are more common. It appears that we are in fact following a spur of Te Kou which is taking us more or less directly to the top. To our right, now far below, is a huge forested bowl, and riding its thermal currents with contemptuous ease is a white, long-tailed bird — a kakaia — which soars, glides and dips, barely moving its wings.

My chest is as tight as a knotted hawser, my hands are slippery with sweat, but I will not stop, particularly since Mike is ahead of me, grunting and panting but showing no inclination to give up. It's nearly all rope stuff now, and I can't look up for fear that the top might still seem too far away. There is no sign or sound of the boys. God, if I'd known it was going to be this hard I'd never have started. *Crap! You always wanted to. You could never be satisfied until you had. You had to find out, and you're not giving up now.* But how much further can it possibly be? The rope I'm hanging on is slack. I lose my footing and swing wildly to the left, thumping into a rock. I wait, get some breath back, let Mike get further ahead, go on. We're not really climbing now, just heaving ourselves from one protuberance to another. It's taken two hours to get this far, and just as I'm wondering whether I can possibly go on, I hear the boys exclaiming gleefully from somewhere above. I think I hear them shout that they're on top. Up ahead, Mike curses.

'The buggers, where the hell do they get the energy to shout?'

The foliage becomes stunted undergrowth, just low ferns and dry grasses, the track levels out, and we step out onto the top of Te Kou, over six hundred metres above the Pacific.

To the north is Avarua, framed by the slopes of Ikurangi and a lower bluff opposite it, to the east is the long, narrow ridge shaped like a dragon's back which rises eventually to Rarotonga's apex, Te Manga. Now I can see that Te Manga has three sides which meet at a notched peak, and that each of the sides is precipitous. Every slope below, in all directions, is covered with bush, and apart from the Lilliputian town in the distance, there is not a building, or a road, or a vehicle to be seen. What there is, besides the view, is a fierce, cool wind which is sweeping up from the bowl below us, chilling the sweat which streams all over my body. I look around for Mike, but he's not there. From a grove of ferns not far away, I hear the sound of vomiting. Where the hell does he get the energy to vomit?

The boys romp up, looking as if they've just strolled down to the corner dairy. Words like 'Awesome', 'Cool', 'Choice' and 'So excellent' are repeated several times, and I'm too fatigued to reproach them for their unoriginal adjectives. Mike and I sink to the ground, but when we do, the boys become indignant.

'No, no,' protests Joshua. 'There's another place over there that's higher. We can't stop here . . . come on . . .'

Groaning, our objections overruled, we get to our feet and stagger off again.

The summit of Te Kou is something you could never tell from viewing it from Trader Jack's: a broad saddle, thickly covered with head-high ferns. We plunge into the ferns — 'There's a track here somewhere,' calls Joshua unhelpfully — and beat our way from one side of the saddle to the other, fern fronds raking our faces. A few minutes later we reach a clearing and a small steel shed. On the top of the shed there's a stayed aerial which serves the island's FM radio transmitter. During the war the shed was a lookout for the home guard, a contingent of whom sat up here twenty-four hours a day, scanning the ocean for Japanese. They still do that on Rarotonga, but now they hope they *will* come.

This side of Te Kou affords an even more sensational view than the other. We look down on several radial valleys, the district of Titikaveka and the Rutaki Passage.

Joshua, a marine biology student, gives us a useful lesson. The passage, a clear breach in the reef, through which we can see a powerful current pouring seaward, has been created by the fresh water of one of the streams whose headwaters lie somewhere beneath our feet. The fresh water kills the coral, and the gap opens up, a very useful exit for canoes, even today.

'But it's dangerous,' Josh adds. 'Two tourists were swept out through the gap a while ago, and drowned.'

From up here we can see the winding gorge the fresh water has cut in the lagoon floor, down there you wouldn't see it until you fell in. Then I realise a very fundamental fact about coral islands, and why they have gaps in their reefs every now and then. It's because of the streams. You get a stream, it kills the coral, you have a gap. Simple. So simple I never realised it until I got up here. The curve of the island is clearly discernible too, from this height, and looking west we can see plantations, villages, patches of ginger earth, and lines of tiny coconut palms. Then there is a broad band of pale blue, mottled with coral heads, a strip of white foam, and the dark blue, wind-whipped ocean.

I'm suddenly put in mind of a Keats sonnet, and I declaim madly into the wind.

> *Then felt I like some watcher of the skies*
> *When a new planet swims into his ken;*
> *Or like stout Cortez when with eagle eyes*
> *He star'd at the Pacific — and all his men*
> *Looked at each other with a wild surmise —*
> *Silent, upon a peak in Darien.*

The boys look at me as if I'm right off the wall, but Mike laughs.

'We had to learn that off by heart at school too. I'm stout Cortez, of course. But wasn't Keats wrong? Wasn't it some other explorer?'

I think he's right, but I can't remember who it was.

For a few moments we look at each other in wild surmise,

then he says, 'Balboa. It was Balboa who saw the Pacific.'

'Right. An A1 for Literature, and History.'

And upon a peak in Rarotonga, we're silent again.

The boys pose for photographs on the edge of a cliff which drops 244 metres, we finish off the Coke, then begin our descent.

Usually, the great thing about climbing a mountain is that it's a good deal easier going down. Not so on a high volcanic island. The descent is just as hard, because of the steepness, and the ropes. Gravity works against us, dropping us just when we are least prepared for it. We don't get so breathless, but I can feel the strain on a whole different set of leg muscles as they absorb the impact of jumping from one outcrop to another. It's long slow work to get back down, but there, on the other side of the water gardens, we find a low waterfall that plunges into a wide, deep pool. Stripping to our knickers, we all cast ourselves into the cool, rejuvenating, mountain-pure water.

Driving back through the town, the second miracle of the day occurs. Mike notices that Jack's car is parked outside his bar and restaurant. 'I wonder . . .' he muses. We pull up outside the bar, and yes, Jack is there, 'doing his books', a euphemism for having a few friends around for drinks on a Sunday afternoon. We move agonisingly up the steps and into the bar.

It's like that old World War II movie, *Ice Cold in Alex*, where some pommie soldiers fantasised about having a cold beer when they reached the other side of the Sahara as they took an old truck across the desert. When I hold up the cold Cooks lager, rills of condensation begin to slide down the side of the glass.

'You look wacked,' says Jack. 'What the fuck've you been up to?'

Mike looks indifferent.

'Nothing much. Just took the boys up Te Kou and back.'

Out on the deck of the bar, I stare up at the mountains. Te Kou is high, wide, impassive. We were up there, right up there, just two hours ago. My gaze moves a few degrees left. But Te Kou isn't the highest, the highest is Te Manga. And there it is, Te Manga, pointed like a green arrow at the evening sky. One more mountain to climb.

Resting on Our Laurel

THERE'S AN OLD JOKE about the distance around Rarotonga. If you go clockwise, it's thirty-six kilometres, if you go anticlockwise on the same road, it's thirty-four kilometres. How come?

I haven't kept count of the number of times I've driven around Rarotonga, but it must be getting on for a century. I never get tired of going round it, clockwise or anticlockwise. As with all the high islands of Polynesia, there are the mountains on one side, the Pacific on the other, and the pulchritudinous tropical vegetation of the makatea — palms, pandanus, hibiscus, bougainvillaea, mangoes, flamboyants, breadfruit — in between. If for some odd reason you get sick of the coast road you can duck inland to the ara metua, the narrow prehistoric road, and have the pawpaws and hibiscus brush right up against your windscreen.

Matthew and Ben and I are fortunate in that we don't have to hire a car or mopeds; we have the use of Mike's large Nissan Laurel while he's at work in Avarua. The Laurel was one of a number imported especially for a Rarotonga conference of global significance some years back, to convey visiting dignitaries from their hotel to the conference centre. The fact that these two venues were in the same building did not escape the attention of some of the shrewder island operators, and as the low mileage limousines were put on the market post-conference at knocked down prices, they were snapped up. Mike's is the only one still rolling.

As I said, it's a large vehicle, comfortable, with an automatic gear box and a stereo unit that could service a karaoke evening. It's got a few dents in the roof from falling coconuts, and the windscreen wipers find it a challenge coping with a tropical downpour, but it saw Cyclone Sally out, and it knows the way back to Arorangi from Trader Jack's almost by itself. The only time it has let me down was two years ago, when I got a flat tyre at Matavera while driving anticlockwise around the island. When I went to the boot to get the spare and the jack out, there was a spare, but no wheel brace, and no jack. Luckily I was able to borrow both from a nearby house, we changed the wheel and were able to resume our journey.

Now it's our last day on Rarotonga. We've snorkelled at Muri one more time, walked around the motu of Oneroa and had a doughnut lunch under the toa trees. I'm driving the Laurel slowly, savouring the view of the gardens, and the reef waves which I glimpse through the coconut groves to my right. There's a Johnny Lee Hooker tape on the car stereo. I'm just thinking that I could quite happily keep driving around Rarotonga for the rest of my life, when the Laurel's big steering wheel begins to feel leaden, unresponsive. The car starts to veer left, obstinately, like a doctrinaire Marxist. I slow right down, only too aware of what the problem is. A flat tyre.

The car sags disconsolately in its front left corner. We get out and stare at it for a few moments, and as I look at the collapsed tyre I'm conscious of the fact that we're only a few metres from the spot where two years ago the same thing happened. I'm also thinking that it's probable that in the meantime Michael will not have added to the vehicle's equipment. Still, I go round to the boot and check. Yes, there is a spare which appears to be in- flated, but where the jack and the wheel brace should be, there's just a big hole. But I'm not overly concerned by this, because I also remember clearly that the last time this happened I borrowed the jack and a wheel brace from the house back there. Both fitted the Laurel, so . . .

The house is one of the most beautiful on the island, a low, colonial villa surrounded by a verandah, set among palm trees behind a hibiscus hedge. It's the sort of house that planters built last century, to accommodate their large families and servants, and to have pink gins on the verandah as the sun dips behind the mountains. As I walk up the drive I recall that the villa used to serve morning tea and coffee and sell locally made perfumes and coconut oil soap to tourists. But now there's an air of desertion about the property; no tourists, no people. The french doors on the verandah are shut. I knock on all the doors. No response. The owners have gone, jack, wheel brace and all. As I walk back onto the road, wondering what to do next, I think of the wisdom behind that saying about those who do not learn from history being doomed to repeat it.

I now feel a pang of concern, too. We have a plane to catch this afternoon and we're about as far from the airport as it's possible to get on the island. I look up and down the road. There's another house on the other side, and a third further along on this side. I try the house on the other side first. There is a man there mowing his lawn. As I approach he cuts the motor.

'Kia orana.'

'Kia orana.'

I explain the problem. He nods, goes to his vehicle. It is a natty little Suzuki van, a late model. When he extracts the jack I see that it is like a toy, a little piece of folded alloy which, though clearly capable of raising his own vehicle, would barely lift the Laurel's tape deck. And the wheel brace is about the size of a tin opener.

'I'm sorry,' says the man, as I shake my head.

There are two young, semi-naked children playing in the front yard of the other house, which is a low, rambling affair with numerous lean-tos attached to the main dwelling. Washing is spread out to dry on the hibiscus bushes. I ask the children if their parents are home and they point shyly to one of the additions. I call at the open door and a large dusky, bare-footed woman appears, a blue, patterned pareu wrapped tightly around her plump body.

'Ah, Kia orana. We have a problem with our car. A puncture. Do you have a jack we could borrow?'

The woman makes an apologetic face.

'Sorry. We got no car here. Only the bike.'

Back at the car, the boys are looking forlornly at the Laurel. I can read their thoughts. This is such an old large model, it's going to be hard, impossible maybe, to find a jack capable of lifting it. There's no garage for miles, no AA, we've tried all the houses in the area, already it's an hour since we stopped, and we're due at the airport to catch a flight to Apia. *Shit.*

A utility approaches slowly, with some people on the back, sitting atop a heap of taro. It sees us, slows further, pulls into the gravel at the side of the road just in front of the Laurel. Two men get out of the cab, and three young people jump down from the taro. One man is about twenty-five, tall, with a drumlin stomach, the other is about fifty, short and stocky. Both wear shorts, singlets and jandals, both are unshaven. There are two girls of about twelve and thirteen in cotton frocks, and a slim boy of about the same age. They are all bare-footed.

They cluster around the incapacitated wheel. The older man issues a series of rapid commands to the boy in Maori, and he goes to the ute, rummages in the front, comes back with an old-fashioned hydraulic jack with a short handle, and a wheel brace. The jack looks solid, but is only about the size of a tumbler. The men bend down, examine the underside of the car, scratch their whiskers. The problems are obvious: the car is leaning, there is gravel under it, there is no suitable jacking point. The older man tries the wheel brace for size on the nuts, grunts with satisfaction. It fits, but nothing much else does. Then the boy picks up the jack, goes around to the front of the Laurel and slips underneath it. Lying on his bare stomach, he pushes the jack under the front axle, fits the handle to it and begins to work it. We all bend down to watch. The pad rises slowly, reaches its fullest extent. Several inches short of the axle. The boy emerges, frowns. There is more rapid talk in Maori.

'Perhaps,' I suggest, 'we could build it up, put bits of wood underneath it . . . ?'

Matthew is dispatched to the lagoon, and returns with some lengths of driftwood. We use it to make a platform, the jack is placed on top, and the boy begins to pump the handle again.

The pad inches up, reaches the axle, begins to bite. The boy is lying on his back now, in the gravel, working in the tightly confined space between the underside of the big car and the road. As the rest of us peer at him, I see the car begin to rise. I also see the jack begin to tilt on the uneven ground. It takes only a modicum of imagination to visualise what the effect of two tonnes of falling Laurel on the body of a boy will be, but he ignores my cautionary calls, continuing to work the handle until the jack reaches its zenith. The car will rise no further.

The car is balanced on the jack and the mound of driftwood, and the suspension is raised. It looks so precarious that a tap on the bonnet might send the whole arrangement flying, but the Rarotongans seem to know exactly what they're doing and have taken control. The two girls, standing to one side, break into a bracket of melodious island songs.

The man with the large stomach does nothing, but watches every development intently, smoking constantly, occasionally commenting in machine-gun fast Maori. The older man watches the wheel closely, frowning with concentration. We papa'a stand back and watch, uselessly.

As the girls continue to sing and the boy slides out from under the engine, the older man fits the wheel brace and begins to unscrew the nuts. The car rocks as he applies pressure to each nut, but the balancing act holds. The four nuts are removed, and the man grasps the deflated tyre and hauls it off. I roll the spare forward and the man lines it up with the threads of the hub. It will not fit. The jack has not been able to raise the car high enough for the inflated tyre to clear the ground. The man stands back, exhaling loudly. The girls stop their song. We all stare at the cursed hub and the vehicle, which looks like a dog with its leg cocked permanently against a tree. Nobody speaks, but there is an air of frustration about our whole group.

The man with the big stomach squashes his cigarette in the

dust, comes forward, issues a command to the boy, who shoves the flat tyre under the axle, to act as a buffer. Then the man puts his hands under the front bumper. He is about to lift when the older man shouts at him, and points to the jack. It's obvious what he's saying, though we can't understand the words. If he lifts, and can't hold, then the car will fall off the jack, and the tyre under the axle won't stop the axle snapping. The man steps back, making a swift upward movement of his chin which says, 'Yeah, you're right I suppose.'

Then the boy suddenly pushes his way to the front, snatches up the wheel brace, and with the sharp end of it, which is designed for inserting under and flicking off hubcaps, begins to dig feverishly in the dirt. The older man nods in approval at the activity, and the boys and I look at each other and make encouraging faces. The reasoning is highly logical: if you can't raise the car, you lower the ground.

The boy stabs, hacks and scrapes at the dirt until he has made a trench. He widens it, then casts the tool aside. He picks up the spare wheel and lines it up against the hub threads. It slips on to the four threads with a few millimetres to spare. The boy stands up, panting, grinning, the older man picks up the nuts and begins to fit them, and the girls break into song again.

The nuts are tightened, the jack extracted, the dud wheel stowed. Overcome with gratitude, I shake the hands of the boy and the two men, take out a $10 dollar note and hand it to the older man. He pushes it aside.

'Yes, yes,' I insist. After all, we have taken an hour of their time. 'Please, it's the least we can do.' But he refuses to accept the note.

'Otherwise you might think we just help you for the money.'

They climb back into the ute and drive off, honking, waving, calling 'Aere ra, Aere ra . . .' We start up the Laurel and resume our journey. I am filled with admiration for the Rarotongans, for their resourcefulness, their generosity, their sense of humour. We move on around the island, clockwise, towards the airport.

Oh yes, why is it thirty-six kilometres this way, and only thirty-four the other? Well, you see, this way we're on the *outside* of the circle.

Western Samoa

DESCENDING INTO WESTERN SAMOA from the east provides an aerial lesson in volcanology. Two tiny conic islands — Nu'utele and Nu'ulua — each bitten on their northern side by the sea, appear first, swiftly followed by Upolu. The spine of Upolu is a series of contorted humps, mounds, ravines and craters, covered in dense, dark green rainforest.

As the plane drops lower, moving parallel with the island, we can see that one of the cones contains a beige crater lake. We glimpse the townscape of Apia, which feathers at the edges into the surrounding forest, then the volcanic tumescences are replaced by more level land covered with apparently endless chorus lines of coconut palms, a plantation said to be one of the biggest in the world. The jet banks, giving views of the huge, dark hump of Savai'i, and the two little islands of Manono and Apolima, popping up like eggcups in the strait between Savai'i and Upolu, before lining up the expanse of concrete which is Faleolo's runway, and landing from the west.

Emerging from the plane we gasp at the heat. It is nearly midday and the sun's rays beat down fiercely on the concrete. Out on the concourse, clutching our luggage, I search the line of dark faces and wave away importuning cab drivers. I have an informal arrangement that we will be met by a former student, Repeka LeLaulu, but she is nowhere in sight. Well, I think, having one last look for her, there was nothing definite, so we'll take the bus and stay at the Seaside Inn.

The Seaside Inn is located on the eastern side of Apia, near the wharves and about ten minutes' walk from the post office. I was first alerted to its merits by an American woman in Tonga, who said it was clean and cheap, and more intriguingly, 'that you meet some inner-resting people there'. This turned out to be the Pacific understatement of the decade: in the space of ten days within its humble confines I encountered the most bizarre, exotic, variegated, comic, tragic collection of people that it was possible to meet in one small building outside of a half-way house.

The building itself could most charitably be described as unpretentious. From the front it resembles an old, wooden, single-storeyed house.

It has a small porch on the right, above which a sign declares 'Seaside Inn — Tourist Accommodation'. Built into the left-hand side of the frontage is a small shop selling food and drinks and an office which deals in some mysterious way with shipping. Inside the building is a long anteroom which is dark and worn, linoleum-floored, with a few battered chairs, a bench which serves as reception desk, and a kitchen which the guests are free to use. Off this cavernous chamber are a number of bedrooms, some of which have bathrooms.

I stayed in a room which did not possess this facility. It was located at the rear of the hotel, and was about the size of a largish pantry, but there were large louvre windows, a comfortable bed, and the communal bathroom was just around the corner. I quickly learnt that the flow of water in the mornings was intermittent, and by the afternoons dried up altogether, so washing was best done early. There were a few other rooms out the back, detached from the main building and separated from it by a dusty drive. Dogs, cats and pigs frequented the premises, but their behaviour was often more civilised than that of some of the human creatures found within the walls.

So strange were many of the guests that I at one stage

contemplated writing a novel set entirely within the Seaside Inn. I half-swiped a title from Anne Tyler (*Dinner at the Homesick Restaurant*) and called it *Breakfast at the Seaside Inn*. This was based on the interesting fact that breakfast, served on the porch, included in the tariff, never varied. Toast and jam, half a paw-paw, sliced lengthways, with a segment of lime on top, and tea or coffee. I found it the perfect way to start the tropical day, not just because of the meal's ingredients, for between the hours of seven and nine the inmates would emerge from the building, sit themselves down at one of the round tables and take their breakfast.

There was a plant geneticist from Slovenia, a pair of lesbians from Stockholm, an environmental sculptor from Milan, a Hawaiian used-car salesman, a redundant telecommunicator from Sydney, a solo mother from Bavaria, an anthropologist from Vienna, a novelist from New York and a Swiss mountain climber. In the space of ten days the Swiss mountain climber went to Savai'i for the day and never returned, the geneticist had a fight with the novelist, the sculptor was attacked by his Italian ex-fiancée, one of the lesbians spent the night with the solo mother, provoking fury on the part of the other, the Hawaiian committed adultery with the cleaning girl and the telecommunicator screwed the transvestite who ran the food and drink shop. This was fact: imagine the fiction that could have been grafted onto that. I did.

Most interesting of the guests was the only one who never came to breakfast, the novelist called Dan. To Dan the Seaside Inn was home, he had been there for two years. He was about twenty-five, a short, pudgy man with thin dark hair and a wispy beard. Astonishingly, for someone who had spent some years in the tropics, his complexion was the colour of a candle.

Dan was a nocturnal person who never got up before noon. He smoked continuously and drank Vailima for the fifteen hours of the day that he was awake. If he ever ate, he did so alone. Having been at the Seaside Inn for so long, he was proprietorial about the place, as if he was the de facto manager. He knew the staff and their habits ('Saera lies', 'Mary-Anne steals') and half of Apia as well. One day he would drink at Aggie's, the next at the

Tusitala, and if I ever wanted to find him, it was merely a matter of trying one hostelry or the other. He had an inheritance, so money seemed no object to him.

Dan came from Manhattan, but he hated all Americans. By late afternoon he would be intoxicated and abusive, usually turning his invective on the nearest of his fellow countrymen, stretching their tolerance to its breaking strain. I would watch the American guests' faces as they moved swiftly in the face of Dan's taunts and jibes from a state of bemused tolerance ('Ha, good one Dan'), to concern ('Hey, hang on there, Buddy'), to resentment ('Say that again and I'll kick your ass in.'). Anton the Slovene, a big, usually amiable man, threw Dan off the porch one night because he called him a 'dumb commie ox'.

However, it's often said that the only person who's got any time for a writer is another writer, and it's usually true. I liked Dan and I appreciated what he was trying to do. We drank beer and talked books and politics and sex and had a lot of laughs. He had a good collection of Pacific anecdotes. Once he had had to fly from Samoa to Tonga on 4 July, crossing the dateline and 'losing the whole fucking holiday!' He told me he had been in James Baldwin's writing class, and that the novelist had expelled him from the group for contradicting his opinion. ('The slimy coon faggot.') I gave him a copy of my first novel, first warning him of its deficiencies, and he seemed appreciative. He never showed me anything that he had published — indeed I began to wonder if he had ever been published at all — but he told me that the novel he was working on was based on a man smuggling gold from Hong Kong to India, the gold being concealed in his rectum.

I hadn't corresponded with Dan since I was last in Samoa, but I had spoken with others who had either stayed or visited the Seaside Inn, and they had reported that he was still in residence. Recently a publisher friend, Robert Holding, had called in at my request and introduced himself to the American. On his return Robert gave me the surprising news that Dan had married Saera, and that they were living together at the Inn. I had written to Dan some weeks earlier, asking that he book a room for myself and the boys.

Matthew, Ben and I get out of the bus and the driver gets down the luggage. The place appears no different, the purple bougainvillaea sprawls over the porch, and the frangipani tree is covered in white blooms. A thin yellow dog is asleep in the dusty driveway beside the porch.

In the subfusc anteroom, I have to blink my eyes a few times to see anything. A thin, dark, unsmiling girl in lavalava and jandals flip-flops out of the kitchen and over to the desk. 'Talofa,' I say, and she mumbles something in reply. I tell her my name, and that there should be a room booked for us. Licking a finger, she flicks through an old, hardcovered exercise book on the counter, finds 8 September, frowns. The page is blank.

'Your name not here.'

'Well I wrote and asked Dan Rosen to book one for me. Is he still here?'

'Dan?'

'Yes.'

'He still here.'

'And have you got a room for three?'

She frowns, screws her face into a ball. My heartbeat speeds up. I don't want to drag all over Apia on a Sunday afternoon looking for accommodation. The sullen girl turns the book around, shoves it towards me.

'Room 12. You sign name.'

'Thank you. And will you tell Dan I'm here, please.'

She leans back, shrieks like a banshee towards the rear of the building.

'*Dan!*'

The first sign that something is awry is that Dan emerges not from his former room, which was large and had its own bathroom, but from the cupboard which was my former quarters. Why on earth is a man of his means in there?

'Howya doin'?'

He looks dopey, and I realise that I've woken him up, but in other respects he is unchanged. In a way he even looks younger, like a child prematurely hirsute. But he is still one of the most unhealthy looking humans I have ever seen. His face is waxen, his beard patchy, the eyes drooping and dull. His teeth are the colour of greenstone. He wears a crumpled blue shirt with its sleeves rolled up, shorts, and his feet are bare. As we shake hands I wonder if he even knows who I am.

'Did you get my letter?'

'Oh yeah.' His voice is the slow, pleasant drawl that I remember.

'And did you book us a room?'

'I did, yeah.'

'They hadn't written it in the book.'

'Jesus, didn't they? They are fucking hopeless.'

'It doesn't matter, they've got a room.'

I introduce him to the boys, who look at him curiously, then we go outside and sit on the porch at one of the tables. It being Sunday, the shop is closed, and I can't buy a beer, so I ask Dan if he's got any. Before, the kitchen fridge was always filled with his private bottle store of Vailima. He gives me a crooked look.

'I've got no Vailima.' He looks at me intently. 'You could buy some up the road though, at the Harbour Lights.'

'Oh, okay. I'll go and get some.'

As I get up to go, Dan leans forward.

'They have the large bottles. And ah . . . while yer there, could you score me a packet of Peter Jackson?'

A few minutes later, it's a bit like old times. We're sitting on the porch drinking cold Vailima, Dan is chain-smoking, a cat is asleep on the next table. But he is clearly not the same; he seems dispirited, melancholic even.

'I heard you got married, Dan.'

He gives a sardonic smile.

'Yeah, Saera, you remember her?'

'Of course.'

His smile turns bleak.

'She's gone back to her village. On Savai'i.'

'Oh. Is she coming back?'

He shrugs, drags hard on his cigarette. Time to change the subject.

'How's the writing going, Dan?' He looks uncomfortable. 'Wal, not so good. Can't get a fucking publisher. Don't think I can stay here much longer, either. Fact is, I've spent nearly all my inheritance. I have to go back to New York and do something to earn some money.' He pauses, chuckles aridly. 'Think I might go into hotel management.'

I top up his glass and he drinks gratefully, but I can tell that his fire is nearly out. He is a long way from his fictional counterpart, and I prefer the other version, his alter ego, who never ran out of zest or money, or had to scrounge cigarettes. I'm thinking, it was such a mistake to confuse the real Dan with the fictional anti-hero I created, whose fire was inextinguishable. How did I ever think the two were one? How did I ever confuse the model with the painting? I must never make that mistake again. But there are still some facts which I must tidy up in my mind. I ask him, 'How long have you been in the Seaside Inn, Dan?'

He smiles dopily. 'Nearly four years.' He finishes his beer, runs his tongue around his lips, looks at me supplicatingly. 'That was good. Could you go up the road and get another couple?'

'No, not just now. I'd better go and get unpacked. We're in Room 12 if you want to come over later.'

'Oh, sure.' He gets to his feet, the cigarette stuck to his lips, then stumbles back inside to our cupboard. I never saw him again.

Room 12 at the Seaside Inn is out the back, a small annex room like an old shed, containing three beds, a toilet and shower. There is gauze over the windows to exclude winged wildlife, linoleum on the floor and a clothesline right outside the door. Across the dusty drive is another, slightly larger shed currently accommodating several holidaying Hong Kong Chinese who, every time I see them, are playing cards.

I like Room 12, it's clean and reasonably quiet, and it doesn't much bother me that the shower is a bit of pipe protruding from a hole in the concrete wall. But Ben and Matthew aren't impressed: teenagers are creatures of comfort; they have to learn to like seedy hotels and their cranky inhabitants. Trying to cheer the boys up, I point out the room's virtues: the private toilet, the gauze over the windows, the fact that we're set back from the busy, harbourfront street. It doesn't work, the boys just maintain a steady silence which I recognise as unspoken reproach. After

Rarotonga, where we have lots of old friends, Apia is strange to them. Strange because there are strangers everywhere, and because it's hot. Very, very hot.

'Okay', I say after a suitable interval, 'you boys go and have a look at the harbour and I'll go and get some lemonade.'

Ben and Matthew wander over the road and begin scaling a big mango tree by the shore while I stroll down the street to a shop. At first it appears unattended, so I lean against the old wooden counter and wait, relishing the afternoon sun on my face and admiring the sturdy lines of the *Queen Salamasina*, the ferry which butts its way across the often ill-tempered stretch of sea to American Samoa and back. Then from behind me a voice booms out, very deep and husky.

'Can I help you?'

The voice has startled me, and I turn quickly to see a large Islander with a full, very dark face and the build of a front-row forward, glaring down at me. The voice booms again, slow and deep, like a record on the wrong speed.

'What would you like?'

She has long black hair hanging loose over her shoulders and a purple cloth tie wound tightly around her top-knot. Small chandeliers of mauve glass dangle from each of her ears, her eyelids are painted iridescent blue and lined heavily with mascara, and there is a smudge of crimson rouge on each of her cheeks and matching lipstick on her fleshy lips. Across her big round jaw is a shadow of black stubble.

I blink at the sight before my eyes descend slightly to the shopkeeper's white T-shirt, which strains to cope with her wide shoulders, beefy biceps and prominent bust. On the front of the T-shirt, thrust out boldly, are two huge, sloping, painted eyes. The lashes are long, black and lustrous, the lids painted with the same iridescent blue as the wearer's real lids, but the painted irises don't have the same fierce look as the shopkeeper's eyes.

'Three lemonades, please,' I say to her.

She turns to the fridge. She obviously doesn't remember me, but I well recall seeing her before, in a waterfront bar. Her name is Belinda, and she is in Samoan a fa'afafine, in English a transvestite.

Europeans visiting Polynesia for the first time often find the blatant transvestitism disconcerting. I certainly did. It was on the island of Aitutaki that I had been watching a tall, shapely, beautifully gowned and sequined woman dancing at a resort hotel. She was stunning, with long black hair and bare, slender arms. One of the family I was staying with saw my admiring stare and laughingly whispered in my ear, 'That's Marlene. But her real name is Joseph.'

I know of palagi men who have chatted up gorgeous Island girls in Apia or Avarua nightclubs, invited them back to their hotels, and at a certain point in the evening, discovered that their beautiful partners possess appendages in unexpected quarters. One chap I got to know at the Seaside Inn made such a discovery. When he told me about it I was taken aback. 'What on earth did you do?' I asked him. He shrugged. 'It gave me a shock at first, but once I got over that, I just carried on and made the best of the situation.' He was Australian.

The interesting thing about the fa'afafine, which translates literally as 'to act as a woman', is that other Pacific Island people find no shame or embarrassment in their presence. They are even quite proud of them. As one real Samoan woman remarked to me, as we watched a tall, beautifully groomed female gliding across the lounge bar of Aggie Grey's, 'That's Cindy. She's our most beautiful transvestite.'

She also explained how the fa'afafine come about. It seems that when a Polynesian family has a number of sons, and they want but do not get a daughter, they will dress the youngest boy in girl's clothes and treat him in other ways, too, exactly as they would had he really been a girl. Dressed as a girl, treated as a girl, he grows up to be a fa'afafine. They have been an accepted and even cherished part of Polynesian society for centuries. The mechanics of the fa'afafine relationships I have no knowledge of, and am reluctant to explore, but above the waist they certainly appear to lack none of the more orthodox female attributes.

I take the bottles of cold lemonade over to the boys, who look at them curiously before swigging.

'Why did you get bottles?' Ben asks.

'No cans here, *only* bottles in this country.'

And it's not that feeble, no-deposit, no-return glass either. Here the bottles are strong and durable. All softdrinks and beer in Western Samoa come in bottles and have a refundable cash value. Children collect bottles and sell them for a few cents each, just the way I used to when I was a boy. A drink-can-free society means there's less wastage, bottles aren't smashed, kids can earn a bit of cash, and a major source of litter — empty discarded cans — is removed. Recycling takes care of itself. It's an enlightened policy which other countries could well learn a lesson from.

We finish the drinks and I take the bottles back to the shop for the refund. Belinda is sitting on a stool smoking, her red mini-skirt riding up round her shapely thighs. The bottles are taken and the money refunded by Belinda's partner, a tall fa'afafine with teased, hennaed hair and a blue mumu patterned with yellow hibiscus. Her bangles jangle and a cloud of perfume envelops me as she hands the few sene over. Her long fingernails are painted a rich plum colour, and glitter has been carefully applied to each of her eyelids. But she hasn't shaved today either, and her pointed chin is covered in stubble.

'Thank you,' she says as she hands me the money, smiling and batting her long, synthetic lashes.

'My pleasure,' I reply.

I cross the road and collect the boys, who are still looking disconsolate. What else can I do to cheer them up? Then I remember that there is another diversion nearby. Palolo Deep.

Palolo Deep is about eight minutes' walk from the Seaside Inn, near Vaiala Beach, Apia's main swimming area. I discovered the Deep on my first visit to Western Samoa. Its attractions were buried among the costly tours and excursions on the blackboard in the foyer of Aggie Grey's hotel. The notice stated simply, Marine Reserve, Palolo Deep, snorkelling, 1 Tala.

We organise togs, towels, flippers and snorkels, and set off up the road. It's still very, very hot, and hardly anything moves. What I swear is the same porcine nuclear family who so amused me last time has somehow been spared the umu and is still snuffling around the wharf fence, and as we pass the small church at Vaiala we hear the divine sound of unaccompanied, part singing coming through the open door and windows and drifting into the afternoon air. A minute later, we are at Palolo Deep.

There is a short path through luxuriant vegetation to a gate and a small, thatched booth. In the booth is a blackboard stating tide times, a chart displaying the many species of lagoon fish, and the custodian of the deep, the man I remember from last time: a wiry chap of about fifty, with bushy sideboards, a thin dark face and a soft, shy smile.

I make myself and the boys known to him. He tells me that Cyclone Ofa was very destructive to Palolo, which was right in the cyclone's field of fire. The gardens which he had so laboriously cultivated over the little artificial promontory, which he had also built by hand, were all washed away. He shows us what he has done since: carried more sand to rebuild the tongue of land, planted more crotons and palms, built more of the little thatched shelters and benches on the point — all by hand. He smiles as he talks, there is not a hint of disappointment or self-pity at the wanton destruction of years of work, only pride in having started again, and achieving what he has achieved. 'And the coral,' he says smilingly, 'is growing back again.'

Out on the sandy promontory, I immediately notice a new landform which is Ofa's legacy, a huge, dune-like mound of yellow sand, far out in the lagoon, possibly the old Palolo headland, moved north several hundred metres. But the rest seems unchanged: a short wade out in the lagoon, the rickety wooden platform on its tall legs, for clothes or sun-bathing, and beside it, the big, round patch of smoky blue which is the Deep.

We wade out across the lagoon to where the bottom falls away, fit our masks and snorkels and launch ourselves into the deep, into another world.

We lie on the surface, suspended like aquanauts, staring down at the apparently fathomless pit. Below and around us are numberless fluorescent fish, seemingly suspended too, hanging like mobiles in the smoky-hued water. As we move forward, some glide away in their groups, other dart like swallows, more remain motionless, totally unafraid of each other or the human intruders. The boys point excitedly at the larger, solitary specimens, and Matthew dives to the bottom, to where the coral sprouts like thousands of tiny brown antlers, each tipped with mauve neon.

Swimming further out, we can see only a blue-grey haze far, far below, but the shoals of fish, probably expecting to be fed, keep coming at us. Yellows, greens, turquoises, stripes flashing and gleaming as they dart and turn in formation. Occasionally a solitary specimen comes gliding up from the deep: a dark green, long-nosed creature with one vertical chartreuse stripe on its flank, then a baby shark hovering less than a metre below the surface.

Leaving the boys to the fish, I return to the shallows and climb the wooden ladder to the platform. From there I can see that Palolo Deep extends right out across the lagoon, like a giant comma whose tail pierces the reef itself. What created this extraordinary landform? Is it the crater of a submarine volcano? Possibly. What is clear is that it is a unique and marvellous place of natural beauty, one of the finest attractions in the Pacific, and the patient custodian of it deserves an environmental medal for his work.

The boys return, gleeful, excited, exclaiming at what they have seen. On the edge of the pit, some Japanese people have brought out food, and as they crumble the bread into the water the shoals cluster about their feet, causing the visitors to give little yelps of excitement.

We wade back to the point, dodging the coral rocks, sea slugs and spiny urchins which litter the lagoon floor. Some local children are racing toy boats with leaf sails, shouting, splashing and exhorting their little vessels. On the little headland there is an open-air, fresh-water shower where we wash off, dry in the sun and watch the races. The boys are happy again.

Back at the Seaside Inn, the girl who signed me in calls me over.

'Message for you.' She hands me a piece of paper, torn from the register. On it is written, 'Sorry I didn't get to the airport, I was late. You can stay with us. Ring me tonight and I'll come round and collect you in the morning. Repeka.'

'What is it?' asks Matthew. I grin at him.

'Bad news, boys. We're moving out of Room 12 tomorrow.'

We sleep well, free from mosquitos and with only a couple of dog fights to intrude on our dreams. We rise at seven, pack our bags, and report to the front porch for the legendary breakfast at the Seaside Inn.

Alas, it is not now the stuff of legend. Instead of a crazed Italian sculptor, a pair of Scandinavian lesbians and a Slovenian geneticist there are the Hong Kong Chinese, who are still playing poker, a pleasant but uninspiring Canadian woman backpacker and two nice young trainee doctors from England who are both called Andy.

Andy and Andy have been working during their summer vacation in Tonga, and they have the striking combination of golden hair and amber skin. The breakfast menu is also an anticlimax: the pawpaw sliced lengthways with the wedge of lime on top has been struck off: we are given only toast and jam. As Dan said to me yesterday, 'Things aren't quite the same as they were.' When I ask Andy and Andy how they have found the place, they grin meaningfully at one another, and at the cross-looking waitress. 'Well,' says one Andy, 'put it this way — you've got to work pretty hard to get a laugh out of her.'

He summed it up all too well. And I remind myself again, as I collect up our bags in preparation for our departure from the Seaside Inn, of the important lesson that I have learnt on this trip. A novelist should think hard before returning to the base of his fictional territory. In his mind he has made it and its inhabitants into something it never was and could never be, except in the special domain of the imagination.

A car draws up in the dust in front of the hotel, a hand waves from the other side of the windscreen. It is Repeka, come to collect us.

Even in a nation of remarkable families, the LeLaulus are exceptional. Two of them are featured in that fascinating book, *The Samoans: A Global Family* — LeLei, who is a journalist with the United Nations in New York, and Laloifi, who spent many years working in the Middle East. Other family members live in the United States and New Zealand. Repeka is a former air hostess, an international netballer and now, a businesswoman in Apia.

I have often thought that one of the most gratifying of all experiences in a strange land is to meet up with someone you know, and this is confirmed by our meeting with Repeka. She is as affable and ebullient as ever, and it is very, very good to see her. But how, I ask as we get into her car, did you know where we were staying? She backs the Corolla out.

'I just went around the hotels and asked. There aren't that many palagis travelling with two teenage sons . . .'

The car is air-conditioned, deliciously so, and makes me appreciate just how hot Samoa is after the islands further south. The boys are even more grateful, lolling back on the rear seat and gasping their appreciation. They are even more pleased when we reach the LeLaulu family house, set back on a large section in the district of Fa'atoia. The house is palagi-style, but surrounded by frangipani trees in full bloom, towering mangoes, flaring bougainvillaeas and broad-fronded banana palms.

Laloifi has recently returned from Kuwait to live in her homeland, and she makes us very welcome. Like the rest of her family, she is versatile and energetic — a counsellor, an aerobics instructor and an accountant. On the bookcase in the lounge are photos of the sisters' father, receiving a special decoration from the New Zealand Governor-General.

We also meet the canine family members, two males and a female who has just had several puppies and who suckles them outside the front door. The dogs, like most Pacific dogs, have large teeth and lean and hungry looks and are astonishingly alert to any violation of the family territory. Anyone who sets a toenail inside the front gate sets off a cacophony of barking as the pack, their long tongues hanging out, lope towards the intruder. Although a single harsh bark invariably sets off every other dog in Fa'atoia, day and night, it must be very reassuring for Laloifi, who usually lives alone, to have the pack there. I'm impressed, and relieved, that after just one sniff they accept us, distinguishing very swiftly and efficiently between those who are acceptable on the property and those who aren't.

Although the house is modern — there is even American television, which comes from Pago Pago — we are still very much enclosed by fa'a Samoa. All around us are the traditional fales, raised, open-sided, with iron roofs hipped like conquistadores' helmets. Long lines of washed lavalavas hang like multi-hued bunting between the trees.

Repeka makes us lunch, then takes us to her shop in one of the back streets of Apia. The shop is small, and offers an unusual mixture of goods: toasters, radios, perfumes, soaps and children's clothing. Such a medley is not unusual in this part of the world, however, and Repeka is clearly relishing her work. Tonight she is leaving for Hawaii and mainland USA on a buying trip, so, what do we want to do? Would we like the car while we're here? One look at the jostling trucks, buses and cars in the crowded streets of Apia, their distinctive methods of movement and the unfamiliar right-hand side of the road driving, and I decide against transporting ourselves. Taxis will do — there're plenty of them and they're inexpensive for hiring around town. So, what do we want to do, apart from going back to Palolo Deep?

The world's most marketable tourist image is a tropical beach with white sand overhung by coconut palms, bordering a shimmering lagoon. A scantily clad, beautiful young woman in provocative pose is an optional extra to the scene. For people living in temperate climates this image takes on the dimension of fantasy in the winter months. Most of the Pacific Islands have at least one beach whose reality (subtracting the young woman) lives up to the brochure, some have more, some islands don't really have one at all. A large number of Pacific beaches are in fact black sand, or are enrubbled with coral, or covered in mangroves and mud, and their lagoons are shallow and sluggish.

However, the fantasy of the white-sand, blue-water beach is still lodged firmly in my mind, and even more so in the minds of Matthew and Ben, and the Samoan beach which has caught their attention in all the posters, which looks so like the ideal, is Lefaga. But Lefaga is miles away, on the south coast of Upolu. There are tours, but for three of us they would be inordinately expensive, so how on earth are we going to get there?

Repeka has a suggestion. 'I'll take you up to Ah Kam's Motel. Teina's there, and he's got a car.' I don't know who Teina is, and I've only glimpsed Ah Kam's Motel from the street, but in minutes we're back in the Corolla and zapping across Apia.

The motel is a modern, two-storeyed, L-shaped building in a back street. We pass through the entrance into a courtyard crammed with tropical plants and tables and chairs. There is a thatched bar on one side, an open-sided dining area on another, and the main building on the other two, creating a secluded, sheltered compound where guests can eat, drink, sit, read or watch videos. Behind the bar is a short, muscular man in his early thirties. He has a deep brown face with prominent cheek-bones, spiky black hair and the shape of his eyes clearly indicates his Asian forebear.* But Stan Ah Kam is Samoan to the core. Above his lavalava, surrounding his shapely torso, are the intricate tattoos which are the marks of manhood in these islands, and this motel has been built on land belonging to his family for generations. Repeka introduces us, and Stan flashes his bright white teeth. He indicates the tables and chairs in the dining area.

'Tea? Coffee? Beer? Coke?'

The boys and I take seats at a table covered with a tapa-patterned cloth and a spray of pink bougainvillaea. Repeka strides to the door of one of the ground-floor units, and thumps it, shouting in Samoan as she does so. Nothing happens, so she

---

* One of the more preposterous and inhumane edicts issued in 1916 by the very blimpish Colonel Robert Logan, New Zealand's first Administrator of Western Samoa, was Proclamation No. 42, which prohibited any sexual relationships between Samoans and the eight hundred or so indentured Chinese who Logan had not been able to repatriate. The edict included existing Samoan-Chinese relationships, ignoring the reality that the Samoans and Chinese cohabited harmoniously. Human nature prevailed, and today a great many Samoans can claim a Chinese forebear and often a Chinese surname. The integration of the Chinese and the Samoans has been highly successful. Added to this racial blend is the substantial German population element, giving Apia one of the most racially mixed peoples in the Pacific.

bangs and shouts again. A few minutes later, the door opens.

The occupant of the room is a short, very fat man of about thirty, with black, curly hair and a large moustache. His lower eyelids sag with sleep, and he clutches his yellow lavalava about his body. His feet are bare. He blinks, grins at Repeka, who points to the boys and I, then talks earnestly to him in Samoan. The man waddles over, barefoot, grinning, and introduces himself.

Teina is a representative of an international, US-owned security firm. He is based in Guam, but travels the Pacific constantly. His main bases are Honolulu, Auckland and Western Samoa, where his family live in a village, near Apia. He and Stan are old mates, he and Repeka are old mates. In fact it seems that Teina is one of those interesting chaps who is everyone's mate. But now he is bleary-eyed and seriously hungover after nightclubbing until four o'clock this morning. Certainly he will take us to Lefaga, but not today if you don't mind. He shakes his head vigorously, shudders, winces, recovers enough to focus on Stan, who is grinning at him from behind the Full Moon Bar.

'Hey, Stan, are you going up to your plantation today?'

Stan looks thoughtful. 'Yeah, could do.'

'What about taking Graeme and the boys up to the sliding rocks?'

'Okay. You guys like to see the sliding rocks?'

'Yeah, sure.' I've heard of the sliding rocks, but I've never been there. 'When would you be able to go?'

Stan looks at his watch. 'Now.'

Stan has a four-wheel drive utility with tyres that look as if they've come off a 747. It's a big, blue truck with gleaming chrome bumpers that he's imported from Hawaii. The boys, delighted at the 'awesome' transport, climb on the back, I pay for 20 tala worth of petrol at the gas station round the corner, and we head off out of Apia in a westerly direction.

A little way out of Apia, Stan turns off the main road and heads inland. The road climbs steadily, passing between plantations of pawpaw, taro and bananas where the plots of turned ground lie in rich brown heaps, and the vegetation almost smothers the open-sided fales. Away from the coast there is no wind, and the air is heavy with heat. The road narrows, steepens, there are verdant hills all around us. Stan turns off the road, along a bumpy track, draws up on a patch of rough grass. He points to a fale a little way off, surrounded by mango trees.

'Okay. Over there, you pay the lady three tala. Then go down the steps to the sliding rocks. I go up to my plantation to work for . . .' he shrugs '. . . a couple of hours. Then I come back and collect you guys.'

The steep path has been concreted, and a hand rail built along it. The path descends to a deep, narrow valley completely hemmed in by tall trees whose lower limbs are smothered with creepers. Incised into the solid rock bed of the valley is a stream which flows in four distinct stages to a long dark pool far below. Each stage is like a huge step hewn into the grey rock, and at the foot of each step is a dark green pool. Marking the path that the flowing water takes over the rocks is a light green, rubbery slime.

The first rock, up to our right, is about three metres high, the lowest is about a metre and a half, the middle step nearly five metres from top to bottom. The stream water accumulates in each pool, then flows down the rock, accumulates again, pours over the lip of the next and so on until the stream vanishes out of our sight in the distance below.

The boys plunge into the water of the highest pool. It is cool and fresh and deep, the perfect antidote to the superheated air in the high-sided valley. Then Matthew scrambles up the dry part of the solid rock, sits in the water on the lubricating slime and goes with the flow. He plunges into the pool, disappears, surfaces with a splutter. 'Cool!' Ben tries the short slide, holding himself at the top for a little longer than his older brother, then slipping forward, he plunges, surfaces, shakes his head.

'Choice!' They repeat the performance, then we move down to the next step, the highest of the sliding rocks.

It too has a cushion of green slime, a smooth groove created by millennia of stream wear, and a cascade of white water. But standing on the brink and looking over, it seems a *very* long way down to the wide pool at the bottom: like standing on the high platform of a diving tower. 'Hang on,' I warn and I climb down over the rocks to the pool. I scramble in and test the depth. As Stan has told us, it's several metres deep — no danger there. But looking up from the base of the narrow waterfall, the boys look very small as they peer over the precipice.

'Okay,' I call up to them, 'it's deep. Who's going first?'

Matthew sits on the brink, bracing himself with his hands. He's been a gymnast, a diver, he has a simian love of swinging and climbing, does not fear heights. Once when he was five he climbed to the very top of a Norfolk pine that was about eighty metres high, nearly inducing a heart condition in me.

'Here goes,' he calls, and he slides forward, plunges. It takes about four seconds for him to slide, plummet, plunge and surface. He comes up jubilant, beating the water.

'That was *so* excellent!' And he scrambles from the pool, gets into position, launches himself again. Slide, plummet, plunge, surface; slide, plummet, plunge, surface.

In the meantime, Ben and I watch with a mixture of admiration and envy. Ben is more circumspect with heights, and his father takes after him. There is no way in the world that I'm taking that plunge, but I have age as an excuse. Ben knows that he must do it, or suffer sibling humiliation.

'Come on, it's *so* good,' Matthew exhorts him. Ben sits at the top of the rock in his blue swim shorts, peers forward, backs off and sits up hastily. 'I can't go over there, it's way too high.'

'It's okay, it's okay,' replies Matthew. 'Just do it once, you'll see.' And to make his point he sits, shoves himself forward, vanishes. He plunges, surfaces, blows out water, stares up. 'See?' he calls from far, far below.

Well, it's all very well for him. Ben sits miserably, inches forward in the water, reaches the brink, stops, shakes his head.

'I can't do it, I can't do it.'

Trying to be tactful, I tell him, 'I think if you do it, old chap, you'll be pleased. And if you don't, you'll always wish you had.'

'I know that!' says Ben. 'But I still can't.'

Matthew scrambles up and sits beside him. 'I'll counsel him,' he says. 'Now what you have to do is realise that it's only water. It can't hurt you.'

'It's not the water, it's the height.'

'Well, try closing your eyes the first time.' Ben swallows.

'All right, I'll try.'

He grips the rock, inches forward until he's close to the point of no return. He gulps, holds himself rigid.

'I think I'm going to do it.'

'Good boy,' I reply. 'Now go for it.'

He takes a huge breath, pushes himself forward. Matthew and I rush to the edge, peer over. Ben shoots up out of the water, shakes his head like a dog, calls up ecstatically.

'Wow, that was *wicked*!'

Over the next hour we swim, slide, sunbathe, explore the upper and lower reaches of the steeply descending stream. It's an enchanting, primaeval place, the sliding rocks. There are no buildings or roads or vehicles in sight, just forest, rock and the invigorating waters of the mountain river. And when I think about the fact that the Samoans have been on this island for about three thousand years, it's not fanciful to suppose that they've been enjoying this natural hydroslide for most of that time. In other words, I muse, people have been sliding down these rocks since the days of Homer and the other ancient Greeks.

Just before noon Stan comes down the path with another man. He is dressed like Stan, in lavalava and jandals, but he is very large, with a corona of frizzy, black hair, a long, full face, and the shoulders and arms of a wrestler. Stan introduces him as Bill. We three men sit on the largest rock and enjoy the boys' antics as they continue to launch themselves into space and snorkel in the pools. I ask Bill about the sliding rocks. He has piercing brown eyes and a very intense stare. The area is called Papase'ea, and yes, he says, dragging on his cigarette, it's true that they have been used for thousands of years, by people of all ages.

'The girls, they especially like the sliding rocks,' he adds, looking at me meaningfully. 'They enjoy the sensation of the slide over the inside of their thighs.'

Bill tells me he's very interested in his country's history. He tells me that it was he who coined the title *Manu Samoa* for the fabulously successful World Cup rugby team. Gesticulating strongly with his big hands as he talks, he explains that manu in the sense that it was intended means 'spirit', or 'essence', although literally it translates as 'smell'.

'In the old days, when we were at war with the Tongans,' Bill goes on, 'and they sent a spy to a village, we could smell them, because the Tongans and the Samoans smell different.' He pauses, frowns. 'I don't mean this in an insulting way, you understand, and even some Samoans had to have the true meaning of *Manu Samoa* explained to them, but it was the right expression for our team. *Manu*'. He savours the word again, clearly proud of it, and the team.

As he does so, and I watch Bill and Stan squatting on the rock and appreciate their powerful physiques, their beefy arms and shoulders, and contrast this with their gentle courtesy towards the boys and I, I'm reminded of what a skinny American whom I met once in Tonga told me about the Samoans. This American, who taught English in Japan but who had been all over the Pacific, was once in a bar in Pago with three Samoan friends. An argument developed between himself and a crowd of American sailors, and one Samoan mate came to his defence, laying into the sailors, who outnumbered them four to one, knocking them in all directions. The little Yank shook his head in admiration. 'Those Samoans,' he drawled, 'once they're your mates, they're staunch, they'll do anything for you.'

And I think as I look at Stan and Bill, yes, if anyone ever started threatening me in a bar, it would be very comforting to have them around. And watching the Samoan rugby team piling into the opposition, tackling like men possessed, this thought is confirmed. They *are* possessed, by national pride and determination more ferocious than anywhere else in the Pacific. It was this fierce patriotism, combined with exceptional natural ball skills, that enabled them to take on the rest of the rugby world and nearly beat them. *Manu Samoa*, indeed.

We drive back down from the hills in Stan's Bigfoot ute, passing along back roads, through rampant vegetation studded with flowers, past the open fales containing prostrate, sleeping figures, back to Apia. As we drive through the crowded streets of town, many people grin and call out to Bill, who waves back. At every corner groups of men wave, shout and laugh, and Bill calls back in Samoan, precipitating more laughter. He is clearly a very well-known personality in Apia. As we park by Ah Kam's Motel and I climb down from the cab, I ask him, 'What do you do for a living, Bill?' He heaves himself across the seat.

'Drug squad. I'm an undercover cop.'

Inside the courtyard, Teina is now fully conscious and enjoying his first beer of the day. Over glasses of Coke, the boys enthuse to him about the sliding rocks and the pools of Papase'ea.

Before we leave, Teina says, 'Tomorrow, you guys come with me to Lefaga, all right?'

Lefaga, Lefaga, it has become like a password to the perfect beach. Walking through town we see the poster again, in an airline office window. White sand, craning palms, aquamarine sea. Lefaga, tomorrow!

Apia is a hot, rough, unkempt town, spread around a wide bay. Most of its buildings are old and wooden, and its eastern and western boundaries are marked by two modern, luxury hotels, Aggie Grey's and the Tusitala, which prop up the buildings in between like bookends. There are some new buildings in the town centre, but most date from colonial times. Once when I was here a film company was shooting a scene for a production set in the late nineteenth century, and using as a backdrop the wooden, government building. With the actors in their period costumes standing before it, the whole scene bore an impressive similarity to what Apia must really have been like a century before.

But now, as I walk around the streets, I can see signs of genuine decay, of dereliction even. The pavement flagstones are cracked or missing, there are holes filled with litter. The fire station is a lean-to which looks like a threat in itself to the appliances it houses. No doubt Cyclone Ofa contributed to all this, but it seems a shame that nobody is doing much about it. In its naturally attractive setting, Apia could be as pretty as Papeete, and a beautification programme would surely ease some of the unemployment, as well as attracting more tourists. When I broach this subject, most locals agree that something needs to be done, but short of blaming the government, nobody has any practical suggestions. Still, telling people how they ought to run their own country is about as easy as spending other people's money, and can be just as damaging, so I walk on towards where I remember there was a good restaurant.

At the backstreet corner I stop, stare at where Amigos was. The entire building has been razed: the block is covered with blackened timber and buckled sheets of corrugated iron. It looks like downtown Hiroshima after Enola Gay dropped her bundle. When later I ask a local what happened, he explains that a fire broke out in the restaurant, and when the fire brigade was called, the hoses couldn't be connected. By the time the airport appliance arrived, the entire block was beyond saving.

'Fire brigade service,' he muttered. 'Not a service, certainly not a brigade.'

Staring around at the two-storeyed, adjoining wooden buildings which make up such a large proportion of Apia's townscape, I think of what could happen if a fire breaks out there, and shudder at the prospect.

But when the boys are back at Palolo Deep, and I'm shopping for presents, I come across one decrepit building which should be preserved entirely as it is. It's old, ramshackle and inside, shadowy and dusty. It's Otto's, and it's the kind of waterfront bar that writers revelled in, in earlier times, the sort I thought had gone forever.

Otto's is up the Aggie end of town. It has a few wooden tables and chairs out the front, but it's the cavernous interior which is so appealing. It's dark and dingy and the floorboards sag. It's *just* the sort of bar where tanned men with bloodshot eyes and murky pasts sit on the stools and stare at the line of spirit bottles with stained labels. In fact as I buy a cold Vailima and look around me I see several palagi men who conform to this stereotype. They have florid faces, they drag deeply on cigarettes and when they laugh their laughter has the hard edge of desperation about it.

The bar is run by Otto's family, beautiful, serene afakase girls for whom nothing seems too much trouble. The only concession to fashion is a stereo system which plays loud music. Normally this is enough to drive me from a bar after one quick drink, but in Otto's even the music seems entirely appropriate, because it's the Jimmy Buffet variety, and his wistful lyrics match the decor perfectly.

In Otto's I meet and talk with a Kiwi journalist who's been deeply in love with Samoa for years (the feeling's evidently mutual, because he's been invited here to help judge the Miss South Pacific competition) and a small, gnome-like man in a pale blue, open-necked shirt, who gives me a long, loving exposition of *all* the bars of Apia. Waving his glass of lager like a wand, the gnome-man extols them all, tells me about the one where the transvestites go, the one where there's always a fight, the one where I can hear the best band. He is clearly a man with rich experience of the toping world.

'Are you in the bar trade yourself?' I ask my small, bright-eyed companion. His eyes widen with glee at the question, and he sets his empty glass down on Otto's bar for a refill.

'Good gracious no, my son. I'm Brother Dominic, I've been parish priest here for twenty-eight years.'

On the way back through town, in the Polynesian Airlines office window, we see that poster again. White sand, craning palms, azure sea. Lefaga. The perfect beach, and tomorrow Teina is taking us there in his car. Lefaga, tomorrow!

Next morning we take a taxi to Ah Kam's Motel. Our back-packs are crammed with beach excursion gear, including flippers, masks and snorkels. As we drive across town the boys are already restless with anticipation. Lefaga, here we come!

We enter the courtyard at the agreed time of nine o'clock, and sure enough, there is our friend Teina, sitting at one of the outside tables, wearing a black baseball cap, smoking. And as soon as I see him, I know something is wrong. His normally cheerful face is in a state of collapse. His eyes droop, his lower lip protrudes, his big jowls sag.

He looks up at us, sniffs miserably.

'Hi guys.'

'Talofa.'

Teina puts down his cigarette, looks at us with an expression of ineffable sorrow.

'I can't take you guys to Lefaga after all.'

'Oh. Why not?'

He screws out his cigarette in the shell ashtray, and his big body shudders like a blancmange. When he looks up again his eyes are those of a frightened little boy, and he speaks in nervous bursts.

'My grandfather. Found out I was back. I didn't tell him. Have to go to the village. This morning. And explain . . .'

'Oh . . .'

But I still can't quite believe it. A man in his thirties, born in Auckland, well-travelled, worldly, should still, on his return to Samoa, pay obeisance, make homage to his grandfather before he does anything else. Teina has not done so. Instead, he has been relaxing, seeing his friends, going out to clubs, like any sociable person would do. But in doing so he has violated fa'a Samoa, word has reached his village, and he is to be admonished for it.

I feel conflicting emotions at this moment: annoyance that our trip has been scuttled, bewilderment at the tyrannical hold that village rule still has over its sons and daughters, pity for our friend Teina, sympathy for Matthew and Ben, who are crestfallen. Teina looks up at us dismally.

'I'm really sorry about this, you guys.'

'That's okay,' I reply, insincerely, and when I look at the boys' disconsolate faces, I resolve that there is no way in the world that we will not get to Lefaga today. I sit down at Teina's table.

'Okay, now how else can we get there?'

Teina looks a little more relaxed, and I realise that part of his misery was caused by having to impart the bad news to us. He pulls at his moustache, thinks hard.

'Well, it's too late for Aggie's tour . . . The Tusitala might do one, though.'

He leans back, calls across in Samoan to the office. A woman comes out and they converse for a moment. Teina shakes his head. 'The Tusitala doesn't do a tour to Lefaga today.'

'What about a bus across the island?'

He shakes his head again. 'No, it would be too difficult getting back.'

I look at the boys, sitting glumly at another table, their backpacks at their feet. We've *got* to get there.

'A taxi?'

Teina scratches his unshaven chin, puts another question to the woman. She frowns, replies, then turns and goes back into the office and picks up the phone. Teina gets up, follows her. I hold my breath. Now what's happening?

Our friend returns, sits down again, explains carefully.

'Normally, a taxi to Lefaga and back is 100 tala, but she knows a man — her cousin — who might take you for 70 tala. How would that be?'

Seventy tala. About NZ$55. The boys are looking at me hopefully.

'That's okay, can you give him a ring right away?'

The woman comes back nodding, but I'm still a bit uncertain about putting ourselves into the hands of a stranger for a whole day, in an isolated area. I ask Teina if he knows the man, and he shakes his head.

About five minutes later a man in his early fifties comes through the courtyard entrance. He is wearing jeans with the bottoms rolled up, jandals and a pale blue shirt hanging out over his jeans. He has swept-back, greying hair and a full, round face, and one look at him dispels my fears. It is one of the most open, friendly faces I have ever seen on a stranger in a strange land. Teina exchanges a few words with him in Samoan, turns to me.

'This is Simi.' We shake hands.

'Talofa, Simi. You can take us to Lefaga and back. For 70 tala?'

'Yeah, that's okay. My car's out the front, when do you want to leave?'

There is a small shop at the front of Ah Kam's, and in five minutes I've bought soft drinks, bread, cheese and a tin of corned beef. In another two minutes we're heading west in Simi's worn but still spry Nissan.

The pocked road across this part of the island climbs through plantations of cocoa and banana, then past rough pasture land with an occasional giant banyan standing sentinel in the fields.

Looking back from the crest of Upolu we can see the wide coastal plain, a sweep of palm plantations, a misty sea and the dark sierra of Savai'i. Then we begin to descend the southern slope of the island, past dark, bare-chested, bare-footed men chopping weeds in the fields, past fales on their concrete pads, past villages and village churches of every known and some unknown denominations, until we join the main east-west road on the southern side.

Simi is genial company on the hour-long drive. Much of his conversation revolves around his car and how to keep it serviceable. The shock absorbers need replacing — something it is not difficult to detect as we zig-zag around one pothole after another — and it is not easy to get spares at a fair price, a perennial problem in the Pacific.

As we drive east I sense that Simi doesn't altogether know where we are. He peers about uncertainly, and at one stage stops and asks directions from a bent, barefoot grimalkin sitting by the side of the road.

I ask him casually, 'How long is it since you went to Lefaga, Simi?'

He looks around vaguely. 'I never been there.'

But he locates the turn-off to Lefaga a few kilometres further on, and we drive along a lumpy clay road for a few minutes, then into a village of exquisite prettiness called Salamumu, strung out along the lagoon edge. The fales of Salamumu are set among a level expanse of soft white sand, from which sprays of bougainvillaea, hibiscus and crotons sprout. The village fales are spread out and raised on substantial platforms of black volcanic rock. The bottom half of their supporting posts are painted brown, the top half white, and their woven wall mats are hitched up tightly under the iron eaves. Coconut palms tower all around them, and the backdrop to the village is a sea of pale blue so intense that it glitters in the late morning sunshine.

We drive through Salamumu, pay 4 tala to a girl who trips down from one of the fales, then on along a white sand track between tall stands of coconut palms. In three minutes we are at Lefaga Beach.

There is nothing we can do except gasp. The sky is clear

except for a scattering of cloud on the far horizon. The reef is close to the shore, and the inky open sea melts into the much paler water beside the beach. The beach itself is not large — no more than a small bay — but the sand is almost pure white, its powdery brightness counterpointed by the outcrops of black lava which extend into the water. There are small waves at the water's edge, which break and slide up the creamy, shelving sand. The beach would in itself make a memorable scene, but what renders Lefaga unforgettable is the manner in which the sand and water blend with the palms which adorn its shore.

They grow thickly from the coarse grass beside the beach and on the flat plain inland as far as we can see. The ones on the landward side of the track are close together, and grow almost straight, forming a thicket, but the closer they get to the water the more they incline towards it, until those which grow from the sand lean at 45 degrees, stretching far out over the water as if paying permanent homage to the sea. Their trunks are dappled grey, like elephants' trunks, and are crowned with fronds as delicate as ostrich plumes. The grass and beach are littered with their big, ginger-coloured nuts.

There are no buildings by the beach, and only one other vehicle. We park under the palms and the boys hurtle from the car, change and throw themselves into the sea. Simi sits on the grass on the edge of the beach and lights a cigarette.

'Nice place, eh?'

'Amazing, just amazing . . .'

We're not the only ones to think so. Here in 1952 they made the film *Return to Paradise*, starring Gary Cooper, and the name has stuck, with most of the tourists sub-titling Lefaga, 'Return to Paradise Beach'. I can imagine, too, as I stare around at this totally unsullied setting, what pressures the villagers of Salamumu must be under from developers to lease their land for a resort. It would be the most exquisite setting in the South Pacific, but I hope the Salamumuans go on resisting.

We swim, snorkel, pursue shoals of reef fish, eat our rough picnic lunch, swim again. Exploring the basalt promontory at the far end of the beach, I spot a posse of bonito cruising the silken waves, and in the far distance I can just see the shadow of

Savai'i, looming from the sea. The boys explore the bush, and pursue a family of pigs under the palms, creating an image which resembles something from *Lord of the Flies*. Matthew scuttles up a bowed palm trunk like a coconut crab, then straddles it, high out over the water.

In the early afternoon another couple of cars turn up, and a mini-bus full of tourists who eat their packed lunches under the palms, but the beach remains uncrowded, pristine. Immersing myself in the steeply shelving water is like wallowing in warm white wine.

We drive back to Apia along the eastern route, passing long lines of uniformed children just released from their classrooms, clutching their textbooks. I wonder how many of their families have left this sublimely beautiful coast for social and economic opportunities in Los Angeles, Honolulu or Auckland, and whether the mirage of civilisation has materialised for them. I think again of Teina, and the tyranny of the village, and how it would drive any free spirit away.

Simi tells me about a cousin who tried to start a business in Auckland, lost all his money, and had to come back penniless to his village. But he also tells me of his brother, who started a tow-bar business in Auckland, and who is 'making heaps of money' for the whole aiga.

'Whereabouts in Auckland is his business?' I ask him.

'Glenfield.'

I know his brother's business. Last year Simi's brother fitted a tow-bar to my car. The Pacific is a vast ocean, dotted with very small worlds.

Our last day in Western Samoa. We lunch once more at Skippy's, the cheap but decent little restaurant near the centre of Apia; I have an interview with the editor of the *Samoa Times*, a large, thorough, extremely patient man who somehow manages to produce his newspaper with the most rudimentary technology; we make a booking for the evening's fiafia at Aggie Grey's; the boys return to the house at Faatoia to watch American television, which captivates them, while I return to town to buy souvenirs and have a last beer at Otto's.

While shopping along the waterfront I come across a bookshop. Like most writers, I can never resist a bookshop, so I enter its spacious premises. Uh-uh, *it's one of those*, a Bible shop. I should have known.

But as I give the shelves a once-over in the hope of discovering some unexpected temporal title, I am startled to see an entire shelf of them. Dozens and dozens, but all dusty, all the same book. *Fergie*. No, not the Duchess of York, but the biography of Fergie McCormick, ancient All Black, penned by the equally ancient sportswriter, Alex Veysey, and published two decades ago. The spines of the identical volumes comprise a line which stretches from one side of the shop to the other. How did they get there? Why are they there? I am tempted to ask the girl behind the counter, who is reading a prayer book solemnly, but decide against it. She wouldn't know who Fergie McCormick was, she would have been born long after he hung up his boots. Anyway, some mysteries of the Pacific, like the building of the Easter Island statues, the identity of Hawaiki and the origin of the Fergie McCormick biographies, must remain forever unsolved.

I make a few purchases in a souvenir shop, then drop in to Otto's. Jimmy Buffet still wails from the stereo, the New Zealand journo does not seem to have moved from his bar stool since Tuesday, and I notice Brother Dominic's impish visage grinning at me from the other end of the bar. It wouldn't be hard to become a regular, or even a permanent, at Otto's, I think as I finish my Vailima.

Aggie Grey's is a world-renowned hotel. The big, newish, colonial frontage masks the more traditional buildings out the back, the rooms named after fading Hollywood legends (the Gary Cooper Fale, the Marlon Brando Fale), the covered walkway adorned with tropical plants, the swimming pool with the coconut palm growing from it. I've drunk here lots of times, used it as a rendezvous, but I've never eaten here, certainly never stayed here.

Laloifi parks the car in the basement and we walk up to the open-sided restaurant at the rear end of the building. Being a local, she knows the drill. This is a very popular evening in Apia, it pays to get here early and get a table at the front. We do both, and soon we're sitting at a table enjoying our drinks and watching the long room with its high, thatched roof fill up. I recognise a figure over by the bar. The New Zealand journo has switched drinking premises, but he is still sitting on a stool, still drinking Vailima, and I suspect, still telling the same stories.

The show begins with an exotic flavour: there is the un-expected presence of the Kings' College Choir, who sing to the swelling audience with the confidence and precision of chosen people. Then the Samoan Cultural performances get under way. After the brilliance of the Auckland Girls' Grammar Samoan group that I'm used to, only the very best looks good, and this is a polished show, although the performers are constrained by the smallness of their stage. But there's nothing gimcrack about their dancing, and the audience, a multi-national one, loves it. The items go on and on, until the show concludes with a fire-dancer who does his spectacular pyrotechnic stuff out in the dark, beside the pool.

The boys are ravenous by now, and their eyes keep straying to the heaps of food being set out on tables at the back of the building. Again, Laloifi proves invaluable. During the concluding act of the fire dance, she whispers, 'We'll go and get in line now. Otherwise we'll be last.'

Sure enough, employing these tactics, we're near the head of the queue when it starts to move forward like a human anaconda towards the feast. We're not quite far enough forward to head off a panzer-like formation of Germans who threaten to blitzkrieg the smorgasbord, but the quantity eventually proves too much even for them, and we come away with our plates laden.

The food is superb: impeccably prepared, sumptuously displayed, solicitously served by a team of handsome young Samoan men. Every Pacific dish is represented, from whole suckling pig to breadfruit, taro and marinaded fish. Matthew and Ben eat themselves to a standstill, and make no secret of their opinions.

'That,' says Ben, casting himself back in his chair, 'is one of the best meals I have *ever* had . . .'

Some hotels have a highly over-rated reputation, or having earned one, coast along on their past achievements. Aggie's has a reputation which she has earned, and she's doing her best to keep it.

Our last morning in Samoa. We say goodbye to the dogs, have a last game of rugby on the grass in front of the house, and savour the frangipani flowers one more time. Then we put our cases in Laloifi's car and head out of town, along the pretty coast road to Faleolo.

Along the way we see a game of kirikiti in full swing on a village green as picturesque as any in England, then minutes later Savai'i looms into view, out of the gin-and-tonic blue distance, and I immediately regret that there has not been enough time to show the boys that island. On the 'big island' is found fa'a Samoa in its purest form, villages of breathtaking beauty, and a lava field where you feel as though you're on Mars.

We round another bend, pass another church, and Savai'i grows larger still. It is the north-east coast that we can see, and I remember that on that coast there are natural pools in the rock, right beside the lagoon, where you can swim, or wash, or just lie in the softest water I have ever felt. Later, I realise, rereading Somerset Maugham's Samoa stories (three out of four of which end in melodramatic death), that he incorporated these very pools into his short story, 'Mackintosh'. Not that I blame Maugham, the pools deserve immortalising.

Savai'i, island of tradition. There I once met, at a hotel, a titled Samoan woman who turned out to be one of the sternest and most articulate defenders of pornography I have ever come across. In the same hotel I also met for the first time that strangest of all human species, the husband-and-wife anthropological team. This pair were German, in their mid-twenties, and they sat opposite me at dinner one night. He had a long, black, moustacheless beard, she had a round, pink face and blinked constantly. As we struck up conversation, I learned that they were writing a book on suicide in the Pacific.

Gerhardt and Ula were from Berlin, and they had the earnest, humourless manner of academics everywhere. It occurred to me as we spoke that a century earlier they would probably have been missionaries, in search of souls rather than suicides. When the talk turned to self-killing, Gerhardt became excited, voluble. The enthusiasm of the fanatic.

'In Fee-gee zay are mostly uss-ing guns vee haff found, in Papua New Guinea nearly always zay are hang-ging theirselves. Here in Samoa, vee are finding, zay are using veedkiller.'

'Yah,' put in his plump, blinking wife, 'so vee must ask ourselfss, vat iss der reason for zees differences?'

When I asked them how long they had been working on their research, wondering at the same time what the long-term effects of such a study would be on the couple's psyche, Ule replied, 'Alvays, vee are trafelling for our verk. Vee haff been on za run now for zhree years. Next vee go to Wanuatu.'

'Veedkiller there too, mainly, zay say,' Gerhardt put in thoughtfully.

Now we are passing the huge coconut plantation, while to our right is a wide sweep of blue bay. Laloifi points out another of the huge mounds of sand in the lagoon that were a legacy of Ofa. Little then did we dream that only weeks later another deranged harridan, this one named Val, would howl in from the north-west, blowing Savai'i and Upolu to pieces.

Faleolo. It's a big, unembellished, utilitarian building, already crowded when we arrive. We check in, pay our departure tax, then farewell Laloifi, finding it hard to thank her enough for her many kindnesses. We could not have wished for a finer hostess. Then we are on our own once more, wandering the big concrete hall, waiting for our call. I show the boys one of the slatted wooden benches there which I will not forget. I slept there once, waiting for a 3.00 a.m. flight to Rarotonga. When I woke up at about two o'clock in the morning, there was a bearded, barefoot Samoan man in a lavalava lying beside me. He woke up too, stretched, grinned. Grimy, half naked, unshaven, he looked like a cargo culter who had come straight from the bush to see the white man's big birds land and take off into the sky.

He grinned at me. 'Where you from?'

I told him.

'What you do?'

I told him I was a writer. He threw up his hands in delight.

'A New Zealand writer! I know New Zealand writing well! Maurice Shadbolt, Keri Hulme, Janet Frame, Maurice Gee! I read them all. I'm *very* pleased to meet you. What did you think of *The Carpathians?*'

I adore flying. I love the sense of expectation as I board a plane, knowing that in just a few hours I'll be somewhere else completely different. I love the sense of space, speed, and the beauty everywhere outside the window, whether it's cloud, sea or land. I love the feeling of contemplation flying induces, and I love the euphoria induced by in-flight liquor. Some of my most treasured memories are those from nine thousand metres.

Now, as we board the plane, I sense that the boys share my anticipation. The 727's engines are fizzing, the cabin crew bustle about purposefully. We take our seats, the three of us in a row, and the boys are tense with suppressed excitement. The passengers keep coming aboard, evidently this Polynesian Airlines flight will be full to the brim. The doors close, the crew mime their one-act safety play, and we are roaring, taxiing, hurtling into the air, then banking for one final look at the reef, palms and mountains of Upolu.

Unexpectedly, this flight proves to be something more special than most. I suddenly realise as we level out, that everywhere around me are people I know. There's an old varsity friend, John Chadwick and his wife Steve, a few seats further up. John, who's now a leading Maori lawyer, has been at a conference in Apia. Just back and across the aisle is a former student of mine, Luisa Kelemete. She's been in Pago, staying with her family. With Luisa is her elderly grandmother, who's coming to stay in New Zealand. The old lady speaks no English, but greets me graciously. Then as I stand to stretch my legs I notice, a little further back in the plane, Brother Marcel, from St Paul's School in Grey Lynn. He comes to Western Samoa every August with some of his New Zealand-born Samoan students, to do community work. This time they've been painting a mural on a school on Upolu. Marcel and I have a drink together, and swap stories from our trips. Up the front of the 727 I notice the Kiwi journalist, who's going home briefly to get up the necessary energy before returning to Samoa to judge the Miss Pacific Contest.

The beer and wine flow. It's an airborne party we have here, a very Pacific airborne party, cordial, relaxed, multi-ethnic, multi-enjoyable. I lie back in my seat, sip my beer, watch the clouds air-brush the plane as we speed south. We cross the International Dateline, and in an instant two o'clock Thursday turns to two o'clock Friday.

Somewhere over the Vava'u Group we are served an excellent meal. Matthew and Ben sit up and enjoy the fun. Matthew, who's doing a history project on the *Bounty* mutiny, spots the smoking island of Tofua, Bligh's first and last stop after he was set adrift by the *Bounty* mutineers. Ben scrutinises the airline magazine and commits to memory every technical detail of the Boeing 727 which is hurtling us all southward. Ben loves planes even more than he loves cars.

Not for the first time on this trip, I am overwhelmed with love for my sons. Their skins are now the colour of caramel, they are lean and fit and exuberant over what they have seen and done. To get to the Islands Matthew washed dishes at a restaurant, and Ben found and sold golf-balls. At times I have upbraided them for their insatiable appetites and their disorderly clothing arrangements, but they are my best mates and they are great travelling companions. I have relished their mixture of sardonic humour and youthful idealism and envied their zest and energy. Their enthusiasm for the natural world has been infectious. They have climbed a mountain, roamed a rainforest, dived to the depths of the lagoon. They have seen Robert Louis Stevenson's grave and slid down a waterfall. They have done things that I at their age only dreamed of.

'Another Vailima, Sir?'

'Oh, thank you, yes. And another couple of Cokes for the boys, please.'

The aerial party goes on all around me while I reflect on this my seventh trip into the tropical Pacific. I planned, and began this journey to gather material to finish a novel, a work of fiction. But as I wing home to New Zealand I realise that at some stage of this journey the real world of the Pacific took over my imagination. Just when my sensibilities shifted it is difficult to say. It may have been when I met the Mahe family on Moorea, or stood with the others near the top of Rarotonga, or when we swam among the fish at Palolo Deep. But although the exact moment is unclear, I know now that these islands and their inhabitants, their world and its realities, have for the time being pushed aside my fictional narrative.

Matthew points excitedly through the plane window. On the horizon is a wide, grey-blue smudge, spread like a bruise along a thigh, which must be Tongatapu. Two years ago, un-expectedly, I was strapped into a cockpit seat on this plane as it approached and landed at Tonga's airport, experiencing the incomparable thrill of watching the pilots get an ocean island's runway in their wide sights, line it up, descend and touch down with the grace of a glider.

The plane drops lower, the clouds thicken. Yes, in my mind the Pacific is no longer merely the stage and background, I will make the Islands and the characters who inhabit them the play itself. I will record rather than imagine. The novel, like all novels, will keep. There is another, more real story to tell of my journeys through Polynesia.